ANDREW WHEATCROFT

The Ottomans

VIKING

VIKING

Published by the Penguin Group
Penguin Books Ltd, 27 Wrights Lane, London w8 5tz, England
Penguin Books USA Inc., 375 Hudson Street, New York, New York 10014, USA
Penguin Books Australia Ltd, Ringwood, Victoria, Australia
Penguin Books Canada Ltd, 10 Alcorn Avenue, Toronto, Ontario, Canada m4v 3b2
Penguin Books (NZ) Ltd, 182–190 Wairau Road, Auckland 10, New Zealand

Penguin Books Ltd, Registered Offices: Harmondsworth, Middlesex, England

First published 1993
3 5 7 9 10 8 6 4 2

Typeset by Datix International Limited, Bungay, Suffolk
Set in 12/15 pt Monophoto Sabon
Printed in England by Clays Ltd, St Ives plc

A CIP catalogue record for this book is available from the British Library

ISBN 0–670–84412–8

For Janet, with love

Contents

List of Plates

Acknowledgements

Over the many years that I have been collecting material for this book, I have accumulated many debts of gratitude. I have been thankful that so many institutions have taken infinite trouble to gratify my curiosity, often in areas quite distant from their central areas of interest. However, given the mysterious logic by which libraries and archives are amassed, institutions have ended up holding some unlikely material; sometimes I must have been the only person who had asked to see it in a century or more. I can only list with deep thanks those institutions which have done more than duty required of them: I am grateful to the staff of the Archive of Oral Turkish Narrative, University of Texas Tech Library; Archivo del Alhambra; Archivo del Real Chancilleria, Granada; the Beinecke Library, Yale University; Beyazit Devlet Kütüphanesi, Istanbul; la Bibliothèque Nationale; the British Library; Edinburgh University Library; Espace Albert Kahn, Boulogne-Billancourt, France; the Humanities Research Center, University of Texas at Austin, Austin, Texas; Haus-, Hof-, und Staatsarchiv, Vienna; Heeresgeschictliches Museum, Vienna; the Henry Widener Library, Harvard University; the India Office Library, London; l'Institut du Monde Arabe, Paris; Kriegsarchiv, Vienna; the Library of Congress, Washington, DC; the Library of the University of California, Los Angeles; the Middle East Centre, St Anthony's College, Oxford; the National Archives, Washington, DC; the National Library of Scotland; the Research Centre for Islamic History,

Art, and Culture, Istanbul; the Semitic Museum, Harvard University; The London Library; the University Library, Cambridge; the University of Stirling Library; and the Victoria and Albert Museum, Department of Prints and Drawings.

I would also like to thank individually those who have provided intellectual challenge, criticism (usually constructive), hospitality or simply moral support. I have ruthlessly exploited anyone who could fetch and carry for me, or who would check information, translate or simply patiently explain things that either my ignorance or lack of linguistic skill has left blank in my mind. In some cases they have been waiting decades for this small return on their efforts. I simply list them alphabetically, because any other form of ranking would be invidious. To Dr Nur Altinyildiz, Don Jésus Bermudez Pareja, Salih Bey, John Brewer, Christian Cranmer, David Damant, Roy Douglas, Christopher Duffy, Hasan Duman, Gary and Miriam Edson, Roy Flukinger, Raja Fuziah, Dr Erich Gabriel, Carney Gavin, Gillian Grant, Professor Robert Hillenbrand, Peter Hopkins, Professor Ekmeleddin Ihsanoğlu, John Keegan, Sra A. Moreno, Rosemarie Morgan, Richard Pearce Moss, Abdul Rahman Musameh, Kaori O'Connor, Varol Özkoçak, Susanne Peters, Simon Schama, Victoria Smith, Carol Stapp, Jonathan Steinberg, Jelle Verheij, Barbara Walker, Warren H. Walker and M. K. Yilmaz, thank you.

I would also like to acknowledge, specifically, the help given to me by Charles Newton of the Prints and Drawings Department in the Victoria and Albert Museum. His expertise, covering a breathtaking range of visual material concerning the Islamic world, coupled with the resources of the Searight Collection in the Museum, made it possible to find the illustrations that I needed for the themes covered in the book remarkably quickly and efficiently.

I should never have followed up my interest in the Ottomans, and sustained it over so long a period, if it had not been for the initial encouragement of Vernon Parry, who listened to and commented on my ideas, and answered endless queries. His untimely death saddened his many friends and robbed the study of the Ottomans of one of its most supple and inquiring minds.

It is conventional for authors to thank their publishers – usually in terms of 'without whom this book would never have been written'. With Eleo Gordon this is literally true. Her capacity to pick up dispirited authors from the inevitable gloomy moments, dust them down and then gently (but not too gently) set them to work again is legendary. In my case, I recognize her professional energy and skills, but above all her sheer warmth of personality. I should also like to express my gratitude to Bob Davenport, whose careful reading of the text has rescued me from many errors and infelicities. Those that remain are the consequence either of my ignorance or of my stubbornness in refusing his proffered alterations.

Inevitably, however, my greatest debt is to Janet Wheatcroft, who has suffered the absences in Turkey and elsewhere, and the bombardment with the nth draft of some tedious passage, with good humour and above all endless forbearance. To dedicate the book to her is the very least I can do.

A Note on Editorial Practice

So much of Ottoman culture was bound up in its language that I have used a number of terms in the original Ottoman Turkish. Repeated uses are glossed within the Index, single uses where they occur in the text. Often the phraseology and consequently the concepts are hard to translate into English, or they occur in a number of forms. Thus the honorific opening to a proclamation of Abdul Hamid reads, 'Beneath the divine and benevolent symbol [his *tuğra* or seal] of the reigning sultan and under the iridescent seal of the great khan who protects the world'. This may seem simply verbose and meaningless to an English-speaking reader, but the subtlety of the language lay in this verbal painting. Ottoman Turkish mixed Turkish, classical Arabic and Persian, distorting each element to accommodate the linguistic peculiarities of the others within the framework of an Arabic script. Pronunciation is the least of the problems.

The language uses some letters and accents that are not found in English. For the purposes of this book, readers should note that *c* is pronounced like the *j* in *joint*; *ç* like the *ch* in *church*; *ö* like the *eu* in the French *seul*; *g* sounds like the *d* in *day* or the *eigh* in *neighbour*; *ş* is *sh* as in *shut*; *ü* is pronounced like the German *u* with an umlaut; *ı* is perhaps the most complex of all Turkish sounds – the most practical approximation is that given by Carter V. Findley: 'spread the lips as if to say "*easy*" but say "*cushion*" instead; the result will be the Turkish "*kısın*", "in winter"; Americans will recognize in it the sound of the first vowel of "*Missouri*" as pronounced by a native of that state.'

Where, however, there is a widely used English form, such that to use the Ottoman version would seem pedantic or perverse, I have used it – so 'pasha' rather than '*paşa*' – but I accept that this is, at best, an inconsistent consistency. In the same spirit, for the sake of clarity I have used English plural forms rather than the correct Turkish forms. While personal names occur in the forms in which they are normally used, I have decided to use the names of the sultans with a -*d* rather than a -*t* ending, and have presented their names in a way that makes them easier for an English-speaking reader.

A good short guide to Turkish is *Colloquial Turkish*, by Yusef Mardin (Routledge & Kegan Paul, 1961).

SULTANS OF THE HOUSE OF OSMAN
AFTER THE CAPTURE OF CONSTANTINOPLE

Mehmed II, 'the Conqueror'   1444–46, 1451–81
Beyazid II   1481–1512
Selim I   1512–20
Suleiman I, 'the Lawgiver'   1520–66
Selim II   1566–74
Murad III   1574–95
Mehmed III   1595–1603
Ahmed I   1603–17
Mustafa I   1617–18; 1622–23
Osman II   1618–22
Murad IV   1623–40
Ibrahim   1640–48
Mehmed IV   1648–87
Suleiman II   1687–91
Ahmed II   1691–95
Mustafa II   1695–1703
Ahmed III   1703–30
Mahmud I   1730–54
Osman III   1754–57
Mustafa III   1757–74
Abdul Hamid I   1774–89
Selim III   1789–1807
Mustafa IV   1807–08
Mahmud II   1808–39
Abdul Meçid   1839–61
Abdul Aziz   1861–76
Murad V   1876
Abdul Hamid II   1876–1909
Mehmed V   1909–18
Mehmed VI   1918–22

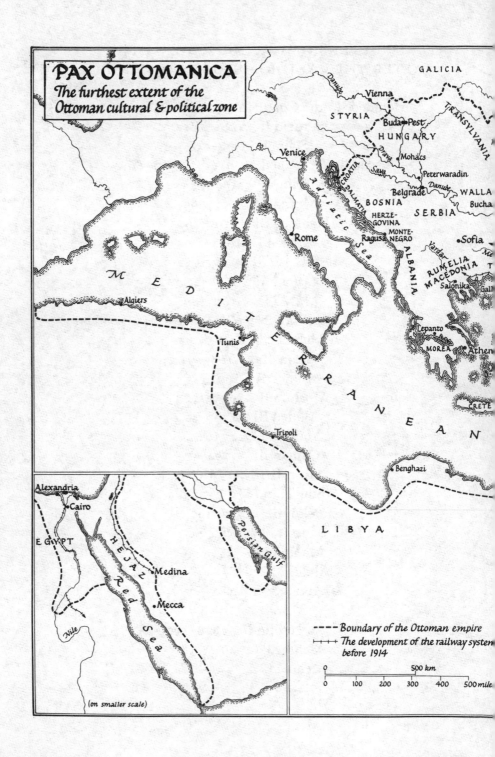

PAX OTTOMANICA
The furthest extent of the Ottoman cultural & political zone

GALICIA

Vienna

STYRIA

TRANSYLVANIA

Buda • Pest

HUNGARY

Po

Venice

Drava • Mohács

Sava

Peterwaradin

CROATIA

Belgrade

Danube

WALLA

Bucha

DALMATIA

BOSNIA

SERBIA

HERZE-
GOVINA

Ragusa

MONTE-
NEGRO

Rome

Sofia

Vardar

Me

ALBANIA

RUMELIA

MACEDONIA

T

Salonika

Gall

Adriatic Sea

M E D I T E

Algiers

Lepanto

MOREA

Athen

•Tunis

R R A N E A N

CRETE

Tripoli

Benghazi

L I B Y A

Alexandria

•Cairo

E G Y P T

Persian Gulf

HEJAZ

Red Sea

Nile

•Medina

•Mecca

Nile

(on smaller scale)

- - - - Boundary of the Ottoman empire

+ + + The development of the railway system before 1914

0			500 km
0	100	200	300	400	500 mile

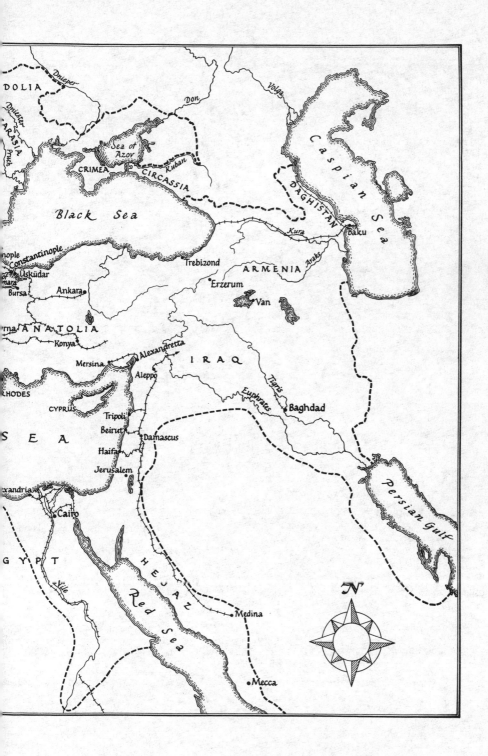

Preface

This is not a general history of the Ottoman empire; that has been thoroughly provided by Lord Kinross and Alan Palmer, whose books are listed in the bibliography. I have not (thankfully) had the task of presenting the intricacies of diplomacy, the tangles of international and Ottoman politics or very much on the economic situation of the Ottoman empire. Rather this book is about the idea of the Ottomans, and how, in the West, it became woefully separated from the reality. It would perhaps be possible to write a similar kind of book viewing the Ottoman misapprehension of the West, continuing the lines developed in Bernard Lewis's *The Muslim Discovery of Europe*.

I have also tried to avoid the overused drawings, watercolours and paintings of processions, ceremonies and public events from the sixteenth to eighteenth centuries which dominate most books on the Ottomans. This is not because such things are not important, but because they distort the image of the nineteenth-century Ottoman world. The nineteenth-century Western travellers did, however, expect to find the exotica depicted by the Orientalist artists, which is why some of these feature in these pages. I have also used cartoons and popular images, because they too reveal inclinations and prejudices. And in a sense I have followed the preoccupations of Westerners rather than the concerns of the Ottomans themselves. This is not from any feeling of superiority of the West over the East: in part it is the problem of the sources, indicated in the introduction; but also, by not being a Turk, I approach from a distance (the 'double veil') both of time and culture. But I come to the subject with that sense of wonder and admiration best expressed by Urquhart, which is outlined in the conclusion.

Since I completed work on this book, I have become aware that two very different additions need to be made to it. The first concerns a book. I received Billie Melman's *Women's Orients: English Women and the Middle East* too late to do much more than skim through it, add a note to my references and list it in the bibliography. Since then I have had time to read it more carefully, and would like to suggest that anyone interested in the ideas underlying Chapter 7 of this book would probably find her Part 2 as rewarding as I have done. She views the issues from a different perspective, and analyses a great many sources: the result is a book of genuine importance.

The second concerns the rebirth of genocide in Europe. When I wrote in the Conclusion that '*there is no closure: that the relationship between the Ottoman and Europe, between the Turk and the West is constantly changing and reforming*' it was impossible to believe that the ancient, visceral Balkan hatreds would resurface as they have done in Bosnia; or to imagine that the families of Turkish *Gastarbeiter* would be burned to death by neo-Nazis in a quiet, traditional German town like Solingen. Set against such horrors, the central plea of this book – the acceptance of human differences – seems a woefully inadequate response, but it is the only one that I can make. To suggest, as some are now doing, that what happened under Ottoman rule a century or more ago somehow 'justifies' current barbarities is a travesty of history.

Introduction

The Ottoman empire, straddling the long land route between Asia Minor and Europe, belonged wholeheartedly to neither. To Europeans, it manifested all the negative qualities they associated with the Orient: exoticism, sexual licence, cruelty and deceit. To its immediate neighbours to the east and south, the Ottomans also represented an alien force that set its central power and control against local ambitions and desires, aiming to establish a *Pax Ottomanica* to replace the earlier authority of Rome (a historical link that the Ottoman rulers made for themselves). From their arrival in Constantinople, which is the starting-point of this book, the Ottomans presented a Janus face, one to the East and another to the West.[1] My main concern is with this remarkable ambiguity, which coloured Western understanding for almost as many centuries as the empire existed, and, indeed, continues to do so through to the present day.

Who were the Ottomans? The scrupulously correct answer is: the many members of the family of Osman, and their numerous descendants. A more practical response is to count all those who participated in the running of the empire: a ruling class of officials, soldiers and administrators. But over the centuries, and certainly by the nineteenth century, being Ottoman became an attitude of mind, demonstrated by style of life – by dress, language and social customs. Just as Rome's empire became a way of life, forming the attitudes and relationships between Britons or Egyptians who would never see the

Eternal City, so too 'an Ottoman' became more a cultural than a political or, certainly, a racial statement.

This central fact, of Ottoman 'cosmopolitanism', produced a violent aversion among Turkish nationalists, who established the Republic of Turkey from the shards of the old empire. In their hands, over fifty years, the old Ottoman culture has withered; only now, almost three-quarters of a century after the effective political end of the empire, does republican Turkey look more respectfully (and sometimes longingly) at its antecedents.

But governmental fiat does not destroy the inner, psychological world. The Ottoman attitudes have persisted since the 1920s, almost unalloyed. Former Ottomans learned new habits of speech, called themselves Turks, abandoned the fez and the stambouline frock-coat for the fedora and the lounge suit; but in their hearts and homes they remained Ottoman. At the heart of their resistance to change was a paradox – supple rigidity.

For centuries, Ottomans presented a face of changelessness,

to the extent that it is hard to say whether a painting is of an eighteenth- or a sixteenth-century scene. Yet change they did, in response to governmental edicts even harsher than those issued by the ardent republicans of the 1920s – but on the surface, not within; impassive in the face of outward force, amenable to authority, but, equally, unyielding at every point.

These are the qualities which have carried through into modern Turkey, and are, I suggest, ineradicably Ottoman. And in understanding the underlying realities of Ottoman rule over almost five centuries, mentality is often more important than the passing shadows of political events. But understanding is perhaps an impossible task, for Ottomans are opaque, especially when a bright light is trained upon them. That opacity was all-pervasive. There are no inquisition records, dutifully recording the truth about heretics and dangerous deviants from the social norm, which have made it possible to shine a light into the secret lives of Europeans. Nor are there many confessional letters or diaries, documents which an Ottoman would only construct – or, one might equally say, fabricate – as evidence if he feared that he was about to be caught between the grindstones of the sultan's justice.

Even more silent are those who lived in the other world of the Ottomans, women behind the veil, beyond the gates of the harem, not just in the palaces, but in humble houses: *haremlik* and *selamlık*, female and male, two opposites barely conjoined.

Yet the evidence is there in profusion, if not perhaps the evidence that an historian trained in the Western, European, tradition would find adequate. But then, even in the areas where there is solid and acceptable documentation, the value of that knowledge is circumscribed. The value of the written text in the Ottoman world was both greater and less than in a European society. In a culture where the printing-press arrived almost three centuries after it took root in Europe, a society where the written text was first a sacred act, sharing the same visual qualities and character as the Holy Koran itself, and second a work of calligraphic art, written texts had a particular meaning. To find a parallel in European society, we need to go back before the spread of printing, to a point where a document, by the mere act of its existence, by the fact of being written down at all, acquired a validity quite separate from its content. Like the many fragments of the True Cross, whether a document was true or false mattered less than that it existed, and it was venerated for its antiquity, its beauty or its skill of composition. In the Ottoman empire, even beyond the invention of printing, a document was imbued with meaning quite regardless of its content.

In this area of the written word lies a central focus[2] of misunderstanding between East and West, and a suggestion of the approach adopted in this book. Time and again in the eighteenth- and nineteenth-century travel literature of the Ottoman empire Westerners stress the need for visually impressive documentation. What the document says, they suggest, is less important than its appearance. At worst, brandish any authoritative-looking paper and your path will be smoothed; at best, see if you can persuade a local pasha to append his signature. This lack of concern with content made no sense in Western eyes.

In part, of course, this is an issue of literacy, and these Western writers mock the 'unlettered Turk' for his ignorance. But in doing so they miss the hidden essence of a document for an Ottoman. It was not easy to obtain written authorizations, and often this was possible only by means of persuasion, deals or bribery. Appearance reflects the importance of their content, as may be seen from the elaboration of an edict from the sultan, and for an official to inscribe his signature upon a document was to commit himself irrevocably, and even fatally: many met the strangler as a result of an unwisely applied *tuğra*. Thus, for the Westerner the substance of the document was its content; for the Ottoman it was the document itself, as a carefully coded statement of power and authority.

Sometimes we can glimpse this careful reading of the subtexts of power in Europe, both in literature and in the historical record. Gogol's play *The Government Inspector* satirized the officials in a small town in tsarist Russia who assumed that some unlikely looking fellow was in reality the long awaited (and feared) government inspector. This fiction was transmuted into reality in the kaiser's Germany, where in the little town of Kopenik near Berlin, just before the First World War, an unemployed man convinced everyone that he was an army captain. In the Ottoman world the significance of such seeming gullibility would have been immediately understood. Did not sultans disguise themselves and move in secret among their people? Be careful, therefore, with a stranger, lest he (or even she, as Gertrude Bell discovered in Iraq) possesses secret power. Survival in the convoluted, complicated, always dangerous, world of the Ottomans required hermeneutic skills of a high order. Read the runes badly, and death or disaster followed close behind, for you and for your family.

To write of the Ottomans, therefore, every scrap of evidence needs to be examined not merely with a questing eye for detail, but archaeologically, looking at its context and its wider meanings. Such a task is immensely laborious, and this book sets out an approach rather than a conclusive answer. And, in response to a justifiable demand, *Quo warranto* – by what right do I, an alien, ill-equipped linguistically, attempt such a task – I can only answer, language alone is not the key, and, moreover, we are all aliens in the world of the Ottomans. A new style of historical interpretation is needed, and, as the government of Turkey begins to open the astonishing, complex riches of its archives to general examination, perhaps it is time to think how best to undertake the endless task of comprehending the Ottomans.

My mental subtitle for this book – 'dissolving images' – is

not simply some convenient verbal play, but suggests both the problem and the approach I have taken. The original certainties with which I began this book have dissolved as I came to realize that my original image of the Ottomans simply did not bear up under the weight of the evidence. That process has continued, and is continuing: each accretion of knowledge, produced by the small but highly productive group of scholars who have now been mining the Ottoman archives for the last three decades, subtly reshapes the image. In particular, working at two extremities of the subject both in place and time, in the Spanish archives of the seventeenth century dealing with the problems of the state's Islamic (Morisco) population, and in the archives dealing with the Arabian Gulf in the nineteenth, has provided an unusual external perspective on the Ottomans.

This book is not so much about the Ottomans as about the *image* of the Ottomans, and how that image has dissolved and reformed over four centuries. I could add that it is still dissolving and reforming, for the relationship of modern Turkey to western Europe is still trapped in the travails of nineteenth-century attitudes. The central question is: how can we use the large number of views of the Ottomans, seen from within, topographically speaking, but usually at a great distance in terms of sympathy and psychology? One approach is simply to marginalize all such material and rely only on primary and secondary Ottoman sources. But, as I have suggested earlier, these cannot provide all the answers. Indeed the external viewpoint can be more acute and interrogative; Richard Ford's indefatigable investigation of early-nineteenth-century Spain is a classic case.[3] In the case of the Ottoman empire, very few Osmanli officials travelled any more than they had to, and when they did so it was in the manner of a progress with a retinue. Few would roam, as did some of the foreign visitors, in distant regions and inhospitable circumstances. Indeed, much of the suspicion of foreigners grew from an incomprehension as to why they should wish to go to desolate parts of the country. Espionage could be the only answer, and the officials responded accordingly. There is a unique value to these foreign eyewitness accounts.

But with what eyes did these witnesses see? The only answer can be: through lenses of an Orientalist tint. Their accounts move from observation to bilious prejudice and back again: European visitors in the nineteenth century could simultaneously be both accurate, truthful observers and biased commentators. Where observation ends and comment begins is often hard to disentangle, but Edward Said, in *Orientalism*,[4] has provided the elements from which such an interpretation can begin. It is an exercise, which, difficult enough with texts, becomes infinitely more complex if, as I have tried to do, one extends it to the decryption of visual documents.

Specifically, I suggest that by the late nineteenth century, after seventy-five years of ever-closer contact, the Ottomans were stereotyped by the West under two attitudes. The first is as 'the Lustful Turk', which is the title of a widely circulated pornographic novel first published in 1828 and which remained popular throughout the nineteenth century. It stands for the prurient imagination which invested the Ottomans with such vices as enabled Westerners to dismiss them as worthless. The second stereotype is of 'the Terrible Turk' – a story of perverted valour, or how, in an evil society, even virtuous qualities are demeaned. Thus, the Turk can be courageous and honourable, but at heart he is a beast, which outweighs all else. The linkage between sex and brutality, the open 'floodgates of lust' and the dire 'refinements of cruelty', was made explicit by Gladstone.[5]

These attributes can be found in almost all the Western texts and images concerned with the Ottomans, and might simply condemn these sources as worthless. I suggest that it is possible to sift the texts, and to remove the grosser distortions, leaving (no doubt) subtle and invisible corruption but not so much as to negate the value of their testimony. With the images, where the power of persuasion is so much more allusive, I have tried to make contact with the textual framework from which they emerged. This is no easy matter, and the interpenetration of image and text is still an uncertain art, which we are slowly learning.

CHAPTER I

The World's Last Day

THE FALL OF THE BYZANTINE EMPIRE

Well before dawn the guardian monks of the church of St Theodosia began a centuries-old ritual. Billowing incense from a censer gave the air in the narrow chamber a heady and intoxicating sweetness as they processed slowly into the sanctuary. There the monks lifted a small gold casket from its resting-place and began a low chant as they turned and moved slowly towards the high altar, along a narrow path left through the great throng crowding the body of the church. In the galleries, women pushed to the rails to get a better view of the scene beneath; for them, Theodosia, by her life and the manner of her martyrdom, had a special significance. The monks set the casket on a low dais before the altar so that its contents were visible to all. They comprised a skull and small pile of bones tossed carelessly, it seemed, into a precious vessel created for some more worthy object. But these were what the vast congregation had come to see: the mortal remains of the martyred Theodosia were the most potent relics in all Constantinople.

Theodosia had given her life to protect the Christian traditions of the city. In 729, when the hated iconoclast Emperor Leo the Isaurian had given orders that the icon of Christ set above the great Bronze Gate to the imperial palace should be destroyed, Theodosia had led the women of the city to attack the soldiers carrying out his orders. The officer removing the holy image was killed by the enraged women, and Theodosia was taken prisoner. She was dragged to the Forum and killed

I

with a ram's horn which was thrust vigorously through her neck. It was a slow, painful and intentionally degrading death, and one with deep symbolic significance. However, if the iconoclasts' intention was to humiliate Theodosia the attempt went awry. The anonymous author of the saint's life wrote, 'The ram's horn in killing thee, O Theodosia, appeared to thee a new Horn of Amalthea.' To his readers the inference would have been clear. Amalthea was the nurse of the Greek god Zeus; for reasons not stated by the legend, but which may readily be imagined, she had assumed the shape of a goat. When her horn was accidentally broken, nectar and ichor, the drink which sustained the gods and the bloodlike fluid which flowed in their veins, poured from its jagged end. In the same way, the hagiographer suggested, the death of Theodosia nourished the life of her city.[1]

Theodosia quickly became a symbol of sacrifice and martyred womanhood. She had given her life in defence of the city against ungodly men, and her adherents (mostly among the poorer people of the city) grew rapidly in number. Her church, only a few yards from the Golden Horn, the city's incomparable harbour, became a centre of pilgrimage. Miracles of healing were attributed to her, and Theodosia's mortal remains soon became an object of veneration and the focus of pilgrimage from distant lands. Many miracles were attributed to their mystical power. After a particularly spectacular cure in 1306, when a deaf mute was restored to vociferous health, the emperor Andronicus II and his entire court came to the shrine and spent the whole night before the saint's bones in prayer and thanksgiving. Thereafter, Theodosia was honoured by the rich and poor alike. The ritual presentation of the relics was repeated as many as four times in a week, and in the words of one pilgrim, Stephen of Novgorod,

those were days of high festival. All the approaches to the church were packed with men and women eager to witness the wonders performed. Patients representing almost every complaint to which the human flesh is heir filled the court. Gifts of oil and money poured into the treasury; the church was ablaze with lighted tapers; the prayers were long, the chanting was loud. Meanwhile, the sufferers were borne one after another to the holy relics, and whoever was sick, was healed.

The saint's martyrdom was remembered each year on 29 May, and her day provided an occasion for general celebration throughout the city. By 29 May the long cold winter was finally at an end. Spring was in full flower. The people of the city could now pay tribute to their saint with the bounty of nature. Garlands of roses swathed the four great columns which soared up into the dome of her church, transforming them into the pillars of a huge verdant arbour. Wild flowers cascaded over the rails of the galleries. By the morning of 28 May the church on the shores of the Golden Horn would be transformed into a temple of Flora. On the eve of the saint's day, choirs of boys and monks began singing at sunset, continuing into the night and through the feast-day itself. The air within the church became intoxicating as the odour of incense from thurifers passing back and forth along the nave mingled with the scent of myriad flowers. It was a time of joy.

The brimming sounds and smells spilled out through the open doors of the church into the streets. The swelling chant of the liturgy could even be heard faintly on the far shore of the Golden Horn. All who heard, within the church and without, were joined in rejoicing for the life of Theodosia. The people came to her in time of trouble: she was their saint, who would always protect them in the hour of need. In 1453, their need was great indeed. That very day saw the capture of the city by storm. By the evening, the church was empty of worshippers, and stripped of its costly furnishings, icons and jewelled treasures. The city and everything within its walls had become the spoils of war. And the saint's bones, venerated for seven centuries, had been emptied from their golden casket into the mud outside her church and were fought over by ravenous dogs.

The cross of Christ had been the emblem of Constantinople for seventeen generations. The first Christian emperor of Rome, Constantine, had settled his capital in the old Greek city of Byzantium on the shores of the Bosporus, and on 11 May 330 had dedicated 'The New Rome which is Constantinople' to the Holy Trinity and to the Mother of God. The new city owed little to the old Rome and much to Greece, for the empire was Roman only by its political genealogy, which traced a lineage back to the Caesars. It was a Greek empire, gathering in all the residues of Hellenism in Asia Minor. For almost 700 years, this Greek empire had ruled as far south as Lebanon and the headwaters of the great rivers, Tigris and Euphrates. The Greek (Byzantine) armies had withstood the advance of Arabs from the south and the first Turkic nomads from the east. The power of the Byzantines had been checked at the battle of Manzikert in 1071, when the nomad Turkish warriors overcame the heavily armoured horsemen of Constantinople and took the emperor Romanus IV prisoner. But the most devastating blow had come from fellow Christians. In 1204, the Christian armies of the Fourth Crusade had turned on their Byzantine hosts and looted the city. The provinces which had formed the bulk of the old empire broke away from the Latin kingdom of Constantinople established by the crusaders, leaving only a rump state to be ruled from the great city. In 1261, the Greek kingdom had been restored by the Paleologues, one of the leading families of Constantinople, but the old empire could not be reclaimed.

The empire had been eaten away piecemeal. Turkish warriors whose ancestors had defeated Romanus IV at Manzikert filled the space left by the Byzantines. Who were these wild borderers whose name increasingly dominated the pages of the chroniclers? The name 'Turk' comes from the language spoken by many nomadic peoples of Central Asia, an idiom which could be understood from China to the frontiers of Europe. These Turks provided mercenary troops for many Eastern rulers: even the Byzantines used them. They were fearsome soldiers, with the mobility and speed that made the nomad tribes so deadly in war, but they also possessed an innate discipline and order. The Turks had come from the empty arid plains of central Asia to conquer the richer lands of Anatolia. In their turn they were overwhelmed by fresh surges of nomads – first the Mongols in the thirteenth century, and then the Tartars in the fifteenth. But these hordes came and went, while the Turkish tribes rooted themselves in Asia Minor. They displaced the earlier inhabitants, and abandoned their earlier nomadic way of life. The Turks built towns and cities, and hacked fields and orchards out of the harsh landscape of Anatolia. While sultanates and emirates fell to the waves of invaders, the Turks remained in control of the towns and villages. They banded together into groups of border warriors (*gazis*), and lived by raiding each other or the remaining Byzantine lands to the north. One of the most successful of these border tribes was the Osmanli or Ottoman clan, named after its founder Osman. From the time that Osman captured the ancient city of Bursa in north-western Anatolia in 1326 (after a ten-year siege), these Turks were a powerful and immovable force on the edge of Christendom. Twenty years later, under Osman's son Orhan, the Ottomans crossed the narrow sea into Europe. In 1361, the Ottomans captured Adrianapole (Edirne), the second city of the Byzantine empire after Constantinople, and made it their new capital.

The steady progress of the Ottomans was halted – temporarily – by an invasion from the east. The Tartars led by the terrible Tamerlane (Timur) – half Turk, half Mongol –

trounced the Ottoman Turks in battle at Ankara in 1402. Ottoman invincibility proved mythical when Timur captured their sultan Beyazid I and carried this proud Turk around in a cage (some sources say a litter) for all to see his humiliation. But the all-conquering horde soon returned to the east, leaderless after the death of Timur in 1405, and the Ottomans revived.

The Tartar conquest provided only the briefest respite for the beleaguered Byzantines: the Ottoman advance continued remorselessly. By 1453, all that was left of the once huge Byzantine domain was the city of Constantinople itself, a Christian enclave in a terrain ruled by Muslim Turks. If the young emperor Constantine XI Dragases, the ninety-fifth ruler to sit on the throne of Constantine, had looked out from the walls of his city in May 1453, he would have seen only enemies, encroaching on every side.

Yet the Turks had already tried and failed to capture the city. In 1422 a Turkish army had besieged Constantinople, but all its assaults had broken on the city's massive defences. In 1453, optimists in the city found encouragement in this 'victory', and argued that Constantinople, the Queen of Cities, could hold out indefinitely, especially since the encircling walls had been strengthened. Moreover, there were promises that Christian Europe would rally to the defence of their co-religionists. These optimists ignored the most pronounced quality of the Turks: their doggedness. It had taken Osman ten years to take Bursa, but he had won in the end. The Turks never conceded defeat: they had failed once against Constantinople, but they would return again. If they lacked siege-engines to batter down the walls, then they would make them. If they required ships to control the narrow Sea of Marmara, the city's lifeline to the west, then they would build them. The city would fall once the Turks were determined to take it.

☾

In 1453, the city was besieged by a man more determined than any of his ancestors to accomplish the long-awaited conquest. Mehmed II was in his twenty-second year, 'of middle height but strongly built. His face was dominated by a pair of piercing eyes, under arched eyebrows, and a thin aquiline nose that curved over a mouth with full lips. In later life his features reminded men of a parrot about to eat ripe cherries'.[2] Mehmed was the third son of the sultan Murad II, and had never been expected to come to the throne. But his two elder brothers, Ahmed and Ali, had died unexpectedly, and Mehmed became the heir. In 1444 his father had abdicated, and the boy succeeded him briefly, only to be deposed in 1446 at the insistence of the great magnates of Anatolia. It was said that they objected to his plan for an assault on Constantinople. Murad was recalled to the throne, and his heir began a fearful life at Manisa, far from the capital, daily expecting a visit from the palace executioner. Mehmed's position became even more precarious when in 1450 one of his father's concubines gave birth to a baby boy. But in February 1451, after Murad had died of apoplexy at Adrianople, Mehmed occupied the throne without opposition from those who had deposed him before. But he took the precaution of having his infant half-brother smothered, so that there should be no future focus for rebellion.

Mehmed possessed two dominant traits. The first was patience. The second was cruelty. He never forgot an insult or a slight, but would wait for years to exact his vengeance. His childhood had taught him the value of wariness. These traits conditioned the manner in which he moved against Constantinople. After months of exchanging pleasantries with the Byzantine court, in the autumn of 1451 he found a pretext for breaking off relations. During the winter he assembled thousands of masons and labourers, and set them to work building a fortress on the European shore of the Bosporus directly opposite an old Turkish fort at Anadolu Hisarı. His intention was clear: once the new strongpoint (named Rumeli Hisarı) was complete and guns were mounted in both fortresses, the Turks would control all traffic up and down the straits. The emperor Constantine wrote in protest, and as a contemptuous response Sultan Mehmed cut off the heads of the Byzantine envoys. All the signs were of war.

By August 1452, three huge cannon were mounted on the ramparts of Rumeli Hisarı and the Turks closed the straits to all ships which had not sought permission to pass. Most of the ships passing through the straits were from Genoa and Venice. Genoa had a colony at Galata, on the far shore of the Golden Horn, while Venice was still a great power in the Aegean and on the Greek mainland. A few intrepid commanders ran the blockade, but finally a Venetian ship was sunk by cannon fire and her crew were captured. The seamen suffered the same harsh fate as the Byzantine envoys, but worse was reserved for their captain: he was impaled. This terrible death was intended as a message to the city of Constantinople, and to the doge and council of Venice far away to the west. Mehmed had signalled that it would be a war without mercy.

In January 1453 the sultan told his generals and ministers that the time to conquer the city had arrived, and immediately the well-oiled machinery of Ottoman war-making slid into action. Fleets of Turkish ships suddenly appeared in the Sea of Marmara during March 1453; meanwhile the Ottoman army was mustering near Adrianople. By European standards, it was a huge force – about 100,000 in total. But, of these, fully a fifth were wild irregulars (bashi-bazouks) who were useful only to blunt the enemy defence at the cost of their lives. The spearhead of the final assault would be the sultan's crack troops, the janissaries. He possessed about 12,000 of these incomparable foot-soldiers, armed, trained and equipped to an exceptional standard. These janissaries were not Turks: they were the children of Christians who had been taken from their parents and trained to serve in the armies of the sultan.

Severed from their Christian origins and converted to Islam, these personal slaves of the sultan displayed a fanaticism in battle that overawed all their enemies.

The bulk of the army was made up of the feudal levies, mostly horsemen (*sipahis*), who were fearsome warriors in the open field but wasted in a siege in which they could only serve as foot-soldiers. Apart from the janissaries, the key to Ottoman success was artillery. Cannon were still a relative novelty in Europe, but Mehmed was quick to appreciate their potential. With artillery, the balance of advantage would swing from the defenders of a walled city to the attackers. He had employed a Hungarian called Urban, who had found no employment in Christendom, to cast cannon in a foundry at Adrianople for the fortress at Rumeli Hisarı. He now directed him to make a gun to be used not against the ships plying in and out of the Golden Horn but against the city itself. Urban did not disappoint him. He created a prodigious weapon, bigger than anything in the West. With a barrel over twenty-five feet long, it fired a quarter-ton stone cannon-ball for over a mile, to impact with terrifying force. Not even the great walls of Constantinople could withstand such a monster.

On 5 April, Mehmed joined his huge army before the walls of the Queen of Cities. The task that faced him was unique in the annals of war. Constantinople had been besieged more than twenty times but had been taken by force only once, by the crusading armies in 1204. But they had captured the city by treachery, scaling the low walls on the harbour side of the city from their ships at anchor in the Golden Horn. These were the weakest part of the defences. Constantine knew how the city had succumbed in 1204, so he had a great iron chain supported on floating pontoons to seal off the Golden Horn from attack. The chain would keep out the Turks while a section could be lowered to allow Christian ships to move freely. The other two sides of the roughly triangular peninsula on which the city was built posed much greater difficulties for an attacker. On the other seaward flank, the walls were built on steeply rising ground which made any assault difficult and dangerous. To the north, in front of the Turkish encampment, were the main walls of the city, a masterpiece of military engineering.

Even today, with the fortifications but a shattered fragment of their former strength, the triple walls of Constantinople are awe-inspiring. Built in the fifth century, in the reign of the emperor Theodosius II, they ran from the Sea of Marmara for about four miles, stopping just short of the Golden Horn. The defences embodied all the skills which Rome had learned in a thousand years of war. On the city side was a massive wall some forty feet in height, with a parapet running along the top behind deep battlements and loopholes. At regular intervals there were tall towers, either square or octagonal, which the defenders used as strongpoints. In front of the Great Wall and its towers was an area of flat ground, which separated the Great Wall from the Outer Wall. The theory was that any invader who overran the Outer Wall would be trapped in this killing-ground, while the defenders showered stones, spears and boiling oil on them from above.

The Outer Wall was less massive – it was about twenty-five feet high, and its towers were spaced at intervals of between fifty and 100 yards – but to reach it an attacker had to overcome a series of obstacles. The first was a deep ditch, sixty feet wide and some fifteen feet deep, sections of which could be flooded to form a moat. Once across the ditch, the attacker would have to scale a stone rampart, which towered more than twenty feet above the bottom of the ditch and would be heavily defended. Any invader who captured this first line of defence would find himself standing in bare open ground in front of the Outer Wall, where he would be battered by arrows and other missiles from both walls and towers. No other city in the world had such comprehensive protection.

There were, however, three points of vulnerability in the city's defences. Two were obvious to Mehmed as he made a careful survey of the walls. The triple line of fortifications did not reach as far as the Golden Horn: a royal palace and the fashionable Blachernae quarter had been built between the great walls and the harbour. The palace and the other buildings were protected by a moat and a single wall, but this corner was a weak point in the defensive perimeter. As Sultan Mehmed rode along the line of the triple walls, he also saw that the walls (which followed the lie of the land) were lowest at the point where a stream, the river Lycus, flowed underneath them. His heaviest artillery would be emplaced so that it could batter this low point.

Constantinople's greatest weakness was concealed from the sultan. The Christian forces numbered only 7,000 fighting men, to defend fourteen miles of towers and walls. Soldiers from Venice and Genoa had come to the aid of the city, while the pope had sent money, arms and food. The most valuable addition to the defenders' ranks were the 700 men-at-arms brought by the able Genoese soldier Giovanni Giustiniani Longo, who quickly became a key figure in the emperor's military council. A number of individual paladins, like the Spaniard Don Francisco de Toledo, also came to Constantinople to fight a personal crusade. But the high quality of these soldiers could not make up for their lack of numbers. The triple walls were effective only when fully manned, with troops standing shoulder to shoulder along their length. Constantine had only enough soldiers to man one of the walls, and even this minimal concentration of forces was achieved only at the cost of denuding the sea walls of their defenders. The emperor's lack of troops was hidden from the Turks by an elaborate subterfuge. Men were constantly moved back and forth along the Great Wall to give the impression that it was fully manned. Troops were inspected and trumpets sounded; flags were flown from all the towers, and camp fires were lit, all to give an impression of a large garrison making ready to resist the armies of Islam.

By 7 April the Turks had surrounded the city by sea and land. The sultan's plan was to harry Constantinople from every side. On 12 April the Ottoman guns had been dragged up to the very edge of the ditch and began a bombardment which continued remorselessly day by day. The very largest guns were so heavy and so difficult to aim that they could be fired only seven times a day, but they slowly demolished the walls in front of them. After five days the outer wall and two of the towers facing the valley of the Lycus were in ruins. The defenders tried to reduce the shattering impact of the huge stone cannon-balls by hanging bales of wool and bundles of wood over the walls to absorb the impact, and, as fast as the Turkish guns demolished the walls, the Christians built stockades of wood and earth in the ever-growing holes in the stonework. The defensive line remained unbroken. The stockades were unimpressive to look at, but they defeated every Turkish assault.

On the night of 18 April, Mehmed launched his first full-scale assault on the weak points in the walls. The fighting was desperately hard, but the defenders threw back all the assaults. Not a single Turk crossed over the low earthworks plugging the gaps in the great walls. The sultan determined on another approach. On the day following the assault on the land walls, the Turkish fleet attempted to break the iron chain protecting the Golden Horn. They failed. Two days later, four Genoese ships ran through the blockade to safety in the Golden Horn. Spectators crowded the sea walls of the city to watch this gladiatorial combat between the four tall vessels with the cross of Christ emblazoned on their sails and the hundreds of smaller Turkish craft milling around them like insects. The sultan rode along the shore close to the Golden Horn to watch his ships triumph over the Christians. As the combat went against the Turks, he could be clearly seen from the city walls, spurring his horse into the water, splashing through the shallows until his fine robes were soaked through. His shouts of encouragement turned to threats and curses as his seamen failed before his eyes.

The failure of the first assaults by sea and land made it clear to Mehmed that the city would not yield easily. After the Christians had held off the initial assault, there were murmurs in the Turkish camp that Constantinople would never be taken. The sultan responded by tightening his grip around the city. The iron chain still protected the mouth of the Golden Horn, so Mehmed decided to outflank it. In the greatest secrecy he created a rough slipway from the Bosporus up over the steep heights of Galata to the Golden Horn, a distance of some seven stadia (1,400 yards). This slipway was made of planks and tree-trunks laid side by side, sometimes roped together where the incline was steepest. All the planks were greased with sheep's fat and oil. At the same time his carpenters built large cradle-like sledges on which the keel of a ship would rest. On the morning of 23 April, eighty ships were dragged out of the water on to the cradles, then, with hundreds of soldiers and teams of oxen straining at the ropes attached to the forward corners of the sledges, they were dragged up the greased slipway. As the ships were hauled by brute force up the steep slope, their crews sat at their oars and the sails were unfurled, giving the impression that they were sailing up the hill and on to the plateau above. The commanders even ran along between the ranks of oarsmen whipping them and shouting at them to row harder. As the chronicler put it, 'It was a strange spectacle and unbelievable in the telling except to those who actually did see it – the sight of ships borne along the mainland as if sailing on the sea.'[3] But it was real enough. Within a few hours a Turkish fleet was slithering down the hillside into the waters of the Golden Horn. Now the Turks could attack the city on every side.

By the end of the second week of the siege a stalemate had

been reached between attackers and defenders. The guns battered away at the walls, and the defenders attempted to repair the breaches. Christian and Turkish ships skirmished indecisively in the restricted waters of the Golden Horn. Both sides tried to undermine their opponent's morale. The Turks impaled some captive sailors in full sight of the triple walls, so the Christians responded by hanging all their Turkish captives, and dangling them from the battlements opposite the place where the sailors' bodies lay swollen in the heat. The stench of rotting flesh from the hundreds of corpses overlay both the city and the Turkish camp

There were dangers for both sides in this stalemate. Disunity threatened the Christians. The garrison was made up of many discordant nationalities, and, as the siege continued and conditions became harsher, violent tensions rose between Greeks and Italians, and between traditional enemies like the Venetians and the Genoese. The Turkish side was just as riven by factions, with the sultan and his closest supporters facing the now open opposition of the great families of Anatolia. The sultan's will was absolute so long as he was successful, but if Mehmed failed to capture the city he would be deposed. Once deposed, he could then expect a visit from the executioner, who would strangle him in time-honoured Turkish fashion.

As April moved into May, both sides tried every trick to break the deadlock. The Turks attacked the boom, and launched repeated attacks on the walls. At midnight on 12 May 50,000 Turks poured towards a gap battered in the wall at the weaker, northern, end of the fortifications. The situation seemed desperate for the Christians, and 'most of us believed', the Venetian surgeon Nicolo Barbaro wrote in his diary, 'that they would capture the city.' But, miraculously, this Turkish attack was driven off, as were all the Turks' other assaults from land and sea. When the Turks attempted to mine underneath the walls, the Christians dug countermines;

fourteen mining attempts were made, and all were frustrated. The stalemate continued.

Both Turks and Christians began to look for omens of heavenly intervention. The Christians were dismayed when a statue of the Virgin fell to the ground during a procession through the streets. An unseasonal cloud of mist settled over the city, and was immediately taken as an omen that God had withdrawn his light from his people. The sultan Mehmed was similarly despondent when he saw a mysterious shaft of sunlight which seemed to suffuse the great church of St Sophia (Aya Sofya) with a golden glow; this he interpreted as a sign of divine intervention on the side of the city. As the siege stretched into its sixth week, with no sign of a relieving Christian fleet from the west, the defenders came to rely more and more on a miracle. They realized that, as each day passed, their reserves of powder and shot, as well as food and other supplies, were dwindling. Their confidence, likewise, was ebbing away. The shaft of light which so disturbed the sultan was taken within Constantinople as the fulfilment of an ancient prophecy that the city would perish in a pillar of fire, God having abandoned his people.

Constantine and the Genoese commander Giustiniani read other signs as they surveyed the Turkish camp from the walls of the city. There was great evidence of activity in the Turkish camp and on board the ships in the Golden Horn. The cannons were being manoeuvred so as to concentrate their fire on the temporary stockades and fortifications with which Giustiniani's soldiers had filled the gaping holes in the walls. Turkish irregulars were to be seen collecting branches and vines, both of which were used to make scaling-ladders and fascines (large bundles of brushwood). The fascines would be piled one on top of the other, against the rampart and the stockades, to give attacking troops a foothold. The alert Christian commanders also noticed the sultan in the dawn of

Monday 28 May as he rode slowly around the walls and along the line of the Golden Horn, surveying the city for new points of weakness. All the evidence pointed to a major attack in prospect. Before noon, Constantine's spies in the Turkish camp had confirmed his surmise. They told him that Mehmed had summoned all the commanders to his tent at sunset. The Christian war council concluded that the great assault would not be long delayed.

The Turkish plan was to attack along the whole line of the walls, by land and sea simultaneously. The bashi-bazouks would go first. Then the Anatolian feudal levies were to attack on the southern sector of the land walls, while the janissaries were to be massed in the centre opposite the most damaged section of the fortifications, which was the weak point in the Christian defence. The Turkish ships were to mount a concerted assault all along the sea walls. The flotilla in the Golden Horn was to shower the defenders with spears and arrows, to prevent any reinforcements being drawn from the sea walls to the main battle. The Turkish ships cruising endlessly back and forth in the Sea of Marmara were loaded with soldiers and scaling-ladders ready to exploit any weakening of the Christian defence.

After sunset on 28 May an unnatural silence fell over the Turkish camp, broken only by the sound of the evening prayers. The Venetian Barbaro saw how both Turk and Christian now put their trust in God, 'each side having prayed to its God, we to ours and they to theirs, the Lord Almighty with his mother in heaven decided that they must be avenged in this battle of the morrow for all the sins committed.' In Constantinople it was now the eve of St Theodosia. In her church on the Golden Horn a curious air of normality prevailed. The church was filled, as for centuries past, with an abundance of roses and wild flowers. The worshippers began gathering as normal, although it was noted they were now mostly women: the bulk of the men were serving on the walls.

But this year there was a Turkish fleet anchored within hailing distance of the church, and plainly making ready for battle.

The congregation's prayers were now for the deliverance of the city. Throughout the day the icons and holy relics of the city had been brought out from their shrines, paraded through the streets and up on to the walls to invoke the aid of God and his saints. The churches tolled their bells, and the words of the Kyrie Eleison were chanted endlessly. At sunset, the emperor and the notables formed a long procession to the great church of St Sophia. Before he entered the tall bronze doors of the church, the emperor Constantine turned and spoke to his people for the last time: 'The Turks have their artillery, their cavalry, their hordes of soldiers. We have Our God and Saviour.'

As the night drew on, the Turkish camp came to life. Cannon and huge war machines were dragged closer to the walls. Their fire was pinpointed on the weak points. Long lines of bashi-bazouks came forward carrying fascines to fill the ditch in front of the rampart. Many of these 'expendable' irregular soldiers were killed by the Christian soldiers firing from the walls, but more came forward to replace them, all apparently oblivious to the hail of missiles around them. About half past one in the morning, the sultan, now satisfied with the preparations, ordered his war banner to be unfurled. At this signal, the word went out along the line: begin the main attack.

In the centre of the line, Giustiniani and his soldiers had agreed to man the stockade and the Outer Wall. Behind them the gates through to the city were locked. Giustiniani and his men were trapped between the advancing Turks and their own fortifications. They had to win or die. Through the darkness they heard an explosion of sound, of drums beating, a clamour of cymbals and cries of 'Allah, Allah', as the bashi-bazouks rushed forward in a confused mass. Flares were lit, and cast a flickering light over the pulsing Turkish horde

below them. The Christians poured a devastating fire down
on to the irregulars battering against the rampart. The fiercest
attack came along the valley of the Lycus. Like Giustiniani
and his men, the bashi-bazouks were trapped and unable to
retreat, because Mehmed had placed his janissaries behind
them, with orders to kill any who fell back from the walls.
After two hours, the sultan judged that the irregulars had
sapped the strength of the defence and allowed them to retire.

The Anatolians and the janissaries pushed forward over the
bodies of the fallen bashi-bazouks. Where the irregulars had
wavered under fire, the janissaries advanced file by file in a
solid disciplined mass. When one fell, another took his place.
But even they could find no chink in the Christian defence.
Some succeeded in lodging their scaling-ladders against the
stockade, and a few even reached the top, but none survived
for more than a few seconds. The sultan, who had led his
crack troops to the edge of the ditch, finally ordered them to
withdraw. As they fell back, the Turkish guns began to batter
away again at the defences, drowning out the church bells
now tolling over the city. For four hours, until just before
dawn, it seemed that a miracle might be accomplished. Every
Turkish assault had been thrown back. The temporary
stockades of wood and earth had proved an effective barrier
– as good as the walls themselves. But the unrelenting pressure
of the attack eventually uncovered a weak point. At the
northern end of the walls, close to the Golden Horn and the
imperial palace, a small side-gate called the Kerkoporta had
been used to launch night attacks on the Turkish lines. After
the last raid, it had not been properly secured. At the height of
the battle, some alert Turks noticed that it was open, and
burst through. They were eventually killed, and the gate was
shut, but not before they had pulled down the Christian flags
from the towers and raised Turkish banners in their place.
Roughly at the same time, in the heart of the battle, a chance
musket shot wounded Giustiniani. He decided to leave the

battle. The emperor begged him to stay, for he had inspired the defence, but he refused. Constantine reluctantly unlocked the gate through the Great Wall, and Giustiniani was carried away by his men-at-arms to a Genoese ship in the Golden Horn.

The simultaneous loss of their leader and some of their best soldiers dismayed the remaining Christians. Some shouted that the Turks had taken the city, as they saw the enemy banners flying over the towers near the Kerkoporta, and Constantine galloped off along the space between the walls to rally the troops on the northern flank. Rumours spread that the Turks had broken through the walls, and the fighting around the stockade slackened. This sudden weakening was noticed by the sultan, who was close to the fiercest part of the battle. He pushed the janissaries back into the attack, promising riches and fame to the first man into the city. This time a huge janissary named Hassan clambered up the stockade and held the defenders at bay while more Turkish soldiers joined him. Eventually the Christians cut him down, but the defensive line had now been breached. Once the janissaries had secured a foothold on the Christian side of the stockade, their discipline began to overwhelm the exhausted defenders. They pressed the Christians back to the Great Wall. There the janissaries' scimitars rose and fell remorselessly. Soon a heaving pile of dead, dying and wounded Christians was piled up shoulder high at the foot of the Great Wall.

The tenor of the battle changed immediately. The Turks clambered up the Great Wall unopposed, and broke open the Military Gate of St Romanus; long lines of janissaries trotted through into the defenceless city. Within a few minutes, the Turks had penetrated the walls in two other places and were pouring through into the city beyond. Dawn was breaking, and along the sea walls the Turks saw their flags replacing the Christian banners on the towers and high buildings to the north. They pressed their attack forward with increased zeal.

The defenders began to abandon their posts, running home to protect their families. The Turkish scaling-ladders were no longer pushed away, and the attack triumphed in every sector.

The emperor Constantine preferred to die with his city rather than survive as a captive. He threw away his helmet with the imperial eagle, and his emblazoned surcoat, and sought an anonymous death in the heart of the fighting. The city finally fell: as Edward Gibbon expressed it, 'after a siege of fifty-three days, that Constantinople, which had defied the power of Chosroes [the Persians], the Chagan [the Avars], and the caliphs [the Arabs], was irretrievably subdued by the arms of Mohammed the Second.'[4]

The consequences of the Turkish victory were horrifying. In April, with his army gathered before the walls, the sultan had summoned the city to surrender and had guaranteed the lives and property of all within. When the offer was turned down, he promised his soldiers, in accordance with the customs of warfare, that they should make free with the city for three days after its capture. Their passions were already inflamed, both by the prospect of plunder and by a desire for revenge. The Turkish troops had suffered from the long siege almost as much as the Christian defenders, and they had not forgotten the bodies of Turkish prisoners hanging from the towers and battlements. The chronicler Kritovoulos tells how the janissaries and other soldiers killed 'without rhyme or reason', because they had been roused by the 'taunts and curses' hurled at them from the walls all through the siege. Once they had entered the city, 'they killed so as to frighten all the City and to terrorize and enslave all by the slaughter'.[5]

Of all the Christian writers, Kritovoulos is the most balanced, the most willing to see the Turkish point of view. It was perhaps easier for him to remain the detached historian, because he had spent the final days of the city far away from the battle on his native island of Imbros. Yet even he was overwhelmed by the enormity of the city's fate. It is the casual observations which best indicate the extent of the killing. One writer noted how blood ran down the gutters towards the Golden Horn, staining the waters of the harbour. The Venetian Barbaro saw hundreds of severed heads bobbing up and down near the shoreline, reminding him of the rotten melons which sometimes clogged the canals of his native city. Many felt that the worst violation was not the killing, which was an out-pouring of blood-lust quickly assuaged, but the ravishment of defenceless women and children, and the pillage of homes and churches. All the eyewitnesses talked of women 'dragged by force from their chambers', and

other women sleeping in their beds, had to endure nightmares. Men with swords, their hands bloodstained with murder, breathing out rage, speaking out murder indiscriminate, flushed with all the worst things – this crowd made up of men from every race and nation, brought together by chance, like wild and ferocious beasts, leaped into the houses, driving them out mercilessly, dragging, rending, forcing, hauling them disgracefully into the public highways and doing every evil thing.[6]

The same language of ravishment described the treatment of the churches:

And the desecrating and plundering and robbing of the churches – how can one describe it? Some things they threw in dishonour on the ground – icons and reliquaries and other objects from the churches . . . some were given over to fire while others were torn to shreds and scattered at the cross-roads. The last resting-place of the blessed men and women of old were opened and their remains were taken out and disgracefully torn to pieces . . . and made sport of the wind while others were thrown in the street.

Chalices and goblets used to hold the holy sacrifice, some were used for drinking and carousing, and others broken up and melted down and sold. Holy vessels and costly robes richly embroidered with much gold or brilliant with precious stones and pearls . . . were consigned to the fire and melted down for the gold.[7]

The first church to suffer had been Theodosia's shrine, on her final festal day. The chronicler Ducas recorded how in the 'terrible darkness' of that last night 'the church of St Theodosia, ablaze with lighted tapers, gleamed like a beacon of hope. An immense congregation ... filled the building and prayers ascended to heaven with unwonted earnestness.' But even the saviour of the Queen of Cities could work no final miracle. 'Suddenly the tramp of soldiers and strange shouts were heard. Had the city fallen? The entry of Turkish troops into the church removed all doubt, and the men and women who had gathered to pray for deliverance were carried off as prisoners of war.'[8]

The Turkish host, which had been promised all the riches of Constantinople, 'poured into the city from daybreak and even from early dawn to the evening. They robbed and plundered it, carrying the booty into the camp and into the ships ... Thus the whole City was deserted, despoiled and blackened as if by fire. One might easily disbelieve that it ever had in it any human dwelling.'

The Turks were the soldiers of Islam, but most had come for the booty. As they gained possession of the various parts of the city, each district was systematically stripped of everything of value. The citizens were consigned to the slave market, and their possessions were looted even down to the last pots and pans in the kitchens. Some of the people vainly sought a final refuge in the church of St Sophia, shutting the heavy bronze doors behind them and celebrating one last liturgy to implore God's grace. The Turks battered down the doors, and enslaved those at prayer. The very young and the very old were killed on the spot, because they had no value in the slave market. Men were roped together, and many of the younger women were knotted in groups of two or three by their long hair, or with their girdles. Byzantine eyewitnesses told how young girls and boys were raped on altar tables, and the great church echoed with their screams. Only those few who managed to slip away to the ships in the Golden Horn escaped the universal catastrophe.

CHAPTER 2

At the Gate of Bliss

THE SHAPING OF OTTOMAN POWER

On the ninth day of June 1453, three small ships sailed into the harbour of Candia on the island of Crete, their decks crammed with people. As they passed the Venetian fortress guarding the anchorage, a crewman shouted to the sentinels on the rampart that the Queen of Cities had fallen to the Turkish Antichrist; the few Christian souls aboard the ships were all that remained from the slaughter. That same evening a monk in the monastery of Agarathos, hearing the refugees describe the atrocities they had witnessed, wrote in despair, 'Nothing worse than this has happened nor will it happen.' On the distant shores of the Black Sea, a similar scene was being enacted, and a Georgian monk listening to the story of the last day, recalled how 'on the day when the Turks took Constantinople, the sun was darkened.'[1]

Far away in western Europe, the doge and senate of Venice learned of 'the darkest day in the history of the world'. On 29 June messengers had arrived from the Venetian towns on the Greek mainland and told them the gruesome accounts of massacre and enslavement recounted by Christian fugitives. On the same day, the Venetians sent dispatches to Pope Nicholas V in Rome and to their network of agents scattered through Europe. By the end of July the doleful story had reached the courts of Scandinavia and Scotland. Priests announced the catastrophe from their pulpits, and masses were said for those who had died as martyrs in defence of the city.

The first Western response was outrage, but expedience followed quickly in its wake. Those who had the closest involvement with Constantinople sought to negotiate with the triumphant Ottomans. Within a month of the capture of the city, the doge had dispatched an ambassador to recover the 300,000 ducats which Venice had invested in the city. Genoa, with even more at stake in the trading settlement at Galata, had everything to gain from a sensible agreement with the Turks. Other states were equally reluctant to undertake a reconquest. When Pope Nicholas V called for a holy war in September 1453, his appeal was answered by forthright declarations of support. The duke of Burgundy, the richest prince in Europe, even staged a lavish masque in which a huge man dressed as a Turk threatened a young boy disguised as a defenceless damozel, who mimed the sorrows of Our Lady Church. As one man, the guests rose and took the crusader's oath. But it was merely a gesture: no nation offered tangible support, and the proposed crusade collapsed.

These contradictory responses to the fall of Constantinople presaged the ambivalent relationship between the Ottoman empire and western Europe. Christians abominated the Turks and believed that the Ottoman sultan was 'the cruel enemy of God, the new Mohammed, violator of the Cross and the church, despiser of God's law and prince of the army of Satan'.[2] Yet they were forced to respect their enemy's power and competence. Turkish armies were better trained and equipped than anything which Europe could put against them. The *Pax Ottomanica*, imposed by force and sustained by savage punishments, gave more peace and security to its citizens than many Christian states could provide. A French traveller in Turkish lands wrote, 'the country is safe and there are no reports of brigands or highwayman ... the Emperor does not tolerate highwaymen or robbers.' It was more than could be said for some regions of Italy and much of Spain. Some theologians resolved the ethical ambiguity – of evil outdoing good – by explaining the Ottoman triumph at Constantinople as a God-given retribution for the sins of his people: 'we must not be amazed if God is now punishing the Christians through the Turks as he once punished the Jews when they forsook their faith . . . for the Turks are today the Assyrians and Babylonians of the Christians and the rod and scourge of God.'[3] Like storm and pestilence, the Turks were an affliction sent to test God's chosen.

From the moment when Constantinople fell, Europeans regarded the Turks with a mixture of horror and fascination. They were outside the bounds of society, and almost beyond the realm of humanity. John Lyly, writing in *Euphues, The Anatomy of Wit* (1578), described the Turk as 'vile and brutish'.[4] Other authors made much of the Turks' supposed addiction to unnatural vice: 'The Bassas [pashas] of the Court, great in dignities . . . plunge themselves in all sorts of voluptuousnesse, and their spirits mollified in the myre of filthy pleasures, they seek them in a contrary course and demand of nature which she hath not.'[5] Only a few writers and travellers regarded the Ottomans as neither superhuman nor subhuman. A young Venetian called Giacomo de' Languschi met Mehmed only days after the conquest of Constantinople: he presented an alternative image of the 'Terrible Turk', who ate children alive – a stereotype rapidly becoming universal in the West, and one which mothers found useful for terrifying naughty children. The Venetian described the sultan in the terms which, used of a Western monarch, would have portrayed a paladin. Mehmed was depicted as

noble in arms, of an aspect inspiring fear rather than reverence, sparing of laughter, a pursuer of knowledge, gifted with princely liberality, stubborn of purpose, bold in all things, as avid for fame as Alexander of Macedon. Every day he has Roman and other histories read to him . . . chronicles of the popes, the emperors, the kings of France, the Lombards; he speaks three languages, Turkish, Greek and Slavonic. Diligently he seeks information . . . on the

Pope, of the Emperor, and how many kingdoms there are in Europe, of which he has a map showing the states and provinces. Nothing gives him greater pleasure than to study the state of the world and the science of war. A shrewd explorer of affairs, he burns with the desire to rule. It is with such a man that we Christians have to deal.[6]

But whether the Turks were monsters or paragons, the reality was that they intended to conquer the world for Islam. For Mehmed the capture of Constantinople was the beginning and not the end of his advance. As he said to de' Languschi, 'he would go from the East to the West as the Westerners had gone to the East. The Empire of the world, he says, must be one, one faith and one kingdom. To make this unity, there is no place more worthy than Constantinople.'[7]

The Ottoman empire was, traditionally, ruled from 'wherever the sultan pitched his tent'. Mehmed intended to make a more permanent centre for his empire. He had built his first palace in the heart of the city. The Eski Saray ('Old Palace') was not one building but many, set amid trees and gardens in a great park surrounded by a high wall. But the sultan found it impossible to settle there, preferring the wider vistas and the greater tranquillity of his palace in the old capital, Adrianople. In the Eski Saray the sense of the chaotic, noisy streets of the city outside was ever present.

The sultan planned to build a new palace, one which would be an ideal world in miniature. In his entry for 1459, the chronicler Kritovoulos noted, 'He gave orders for the erection of a palace on the point of old Byzantium which stretches out into the sea – a palace that should outshine all and be more marvellous than the preceding palaces in looks, size, cost and gracefulness.'[8] For his 'New Palace', or Yeni Saray – to be known as the Abode of Bliss or the Abode of Felicity – Mehmed chose the isolated, wooded grounds of the old Byzantine acropolis, to the south of Aya Sofya which had been the first part of the city to be settled almost a thousand years before. The work proceeded with astonishing speed, and regardless of cost, for the sultan determined to confound those who said it would take twenty-five years to build the palace he had in mind. By 1465 the chronicler could write of its completion:

The sultan, passing the winter at Byzantium, among other interests, occupied himself with repopulating and rebuilding the city. Also he finished the palace, the most beautiful of all the buildings, equally for the view, for usefulness, for pleasure, for ornamentation; it left nothing to be desired even by comparison with the most ancient and most marvellous edifices of the world . . . There was also a very great wall which surrounded the palace. The whole was built as I have already said, combining variety, beauty, grandeur and magnificence; on every side, inside and out, shone and glittered gold and silver, ornaments of precious stones and pearls in abundance . . .

On every side extended very vast and very beautiful gardens, in which grew every imaginable kind of plants and fruits; water, fresh, clear, and drinkable, flowed in abundance on every side; flocks of birds, both of the edible and of the singing variety, chattered and warbled; herds of both domestic and wild animals browsed there.[9]

Within this earthly paradise, contradictions abounded. Mehmed was a passionate gardener, and many accounts talk of him at work planning, digging and planting his gardens. He took special pleasure in the sound and smell of running water under the trees, mixed with the scent of flowers and fruit. Rare plants were sent at his command to the palace gardens from distant parts of his domains, to create a garden which a later visitor described as 'a most wonderful confusion of exquisite trees, fruit trees and others, and with all sorts of flowers and herbs'.[10] Yet this Arcadian vision was often sullied by moments of savagery: the sultan, finding one of his prized cucumbers missing, ripped open the stomachs of his gardeners to discover which of them had eaten it. These *bostancıs* (gardeners) had another and more sinister role: when not tending the plants and gardens, they were the executioners within the palace walls. A visit from the head gardener and his burly assistants carrying a sword or a silken cord was a token of imminent doom.

The overwhelming sense was of isolation and separation from the city beyond. The palace, or rather palaces, were hidden behind a massive wall some thirty-five feet tall. Janissaries patrolled along the battlements, and at each gatehouse there was a strong guard of gatekeepers. On the landward side there were four great gates, but the central or Imperial Gate (Bab-ı Hümayun) was the only point of entry. Visitors were freely admitted, 'men and women, Jews and Christians, poor and rich alike',[11] and the whole huge quadrangle was alive with different activities. All the various services which were used by the palace had their quarters around the perimeter of the first great courtyard, which occupied some 500,000 square feet. There were stables for the royal horses and for the cavalry, barracks for the guards and gatekeepers. Almost 1,000 gardeners tended the grounds of the palace, while about 600 craftsmen – goldsmiths, workers in amber, armourers, potters, upholsterers, sabre-makers, weavers and many others – worked to sustain this symbol of Ottoman magnificence. Yet even in the first courtyard, despite the thousands who lived inside its walls or who came as visitors and petitioners, there was an unnatural, almost religious stillness; Westerners who visited Turkish war camps noticed the same unexpected silence, quite unlike the bedlam in European bivouacs. The artist Nicholas de Nicolay, who accompanied the French ambassador in 1551, found the atmosphere oppressive: 'notwithstanding the number of people coming together from all parts is very great, yet such silence is kept, that yee could scarcely say that the standers by did either spit or cough.'[12] More than a century later, the same point was made even more emphatically: 'Anybody may enter the first court of the Seraglio . . . but everything is so still, the Motion of a Fly might be heard in a manner . . . nay, the very horses seem to know where they are, and no doubt they are taught to tread softer than in the streets.'[13]

While the great mosques, thronged each day at the hours of prayers, were the overt focus of the city's life, the palace was its hidden heart. The outer, public part of the palace was as open as the mosques. On holidays or on the day when the sultan's divan, or council, was in session, 10,000 people or more would crowd through the gate into the first courtyard. There were other attractions. Formal public executions took place beside the Executioner's Fountain, near the fortified gate to the inner palace on the far side of the great court. The severed heads of the unfortunates would be displayed on two marble columns beside the fountain, or placed on spikes above the gate. Others were disposed of less publicly within the inner sanctum. Every Friday and on the great festivals of Islam, the sultan rode out in procession under the eyes of a vast crowd gathered in the first court, to pray at one of the imperial mosques in the city or at the mosque of Eyüp outside the walls.

The looming Gate of Salutation, set in a high blank wall, marked the real boundary between the outer and the inner worlds. If all humanity flowed in and out of the Imperial Gate, few of the sultan's subjects passed through the gatehouse into the inner palace except by invitation or for the ceremonial occasions of state. The thousands of palace servants or guards in the outer court rarely penetrated into the invisible domain beyond. The gate to the inner palace was a strongpoint, some 150 feet long and thirty-five feet deep, pierced with gun loops and arrow slits. The two sets of doors were sufficient to resist a siege, with a massive iron pair of doors on the outside and a second, equally massive, wooden set within.

But once past the gatehouse, the mood changed entirely. Any impression of a fortress vanished. The visitor stood under an elaborate wooden canopy, intricately pierced and decorated, which rested on ten substantial pillars. From the entrance gate, a broad portico set on slender columns extended to right and left around the great open space. Doors led off this covered arcade to the hidden parts of the palace within. The impression upon visitors was less of a set of solid buildings than of tents set up in a park or garden. One visitor remarked on 'certain stretches of lawn where the growing grass provides pasture for a number of gazelles which breed and are regarded with pleasure'.[14] Cobbled paths radiated out from the gate, through lawns studded with fountains and plane and cypress trees. Facing the great gate was another, smaller, entrance, surmounted by a tiled cupola which shimmered in the sunlight. This, called the Gate of Bliss or the Gate of Felicity, was the entrance to the innermost heart of the palace, the sultan's own quarters. But, dominating the Gate of Bliss and the little pavilions or 'kiosks' which dotted the quadrangle, was the burnished tower of the Divan.

The Hall of the Divan was the outward, public face of the Ottoman system. Its visual message was of the wealth and power of the sultans. The floor was gilded, and covered with a carpet of cloth of gold. The dais on which the throne was set was also covered with a golden cloth, richly embroidered. The walls were emblazoned with jewels set into an intricate tracery of golden lines, and the whole opulent spectacle shimmered in the strong sunlight flooding in from the tall windows and the glazed panels beneath the dome. It was the seat of majesty.

For almost 300 years the same unfailing ritual was observed. Just after daybreak, on Saturday, Sunday, Monday and Tuesday, all the members of the imperial divan – the senior officials, judges, and men of religion who advised the sultan – gathered in the first court of the palace. One by one, accompanied by an entourage of guards and clerks, they processed slowly across the first court to the Gate of Salutation. When all the members of the divan had gathered before the gate, they marched as a body into the second court, watched from the colonnades to left and right by thousands of janissaries, gatekeepers, and *sipahis*. On some occasions, the onlookers silently flanking the courtyard could number ten or twelve thousand. When the sultan or the grand vizier arrived, the officials formed a long double line outside the golden chamber, each one standing with his hands crossed and his eyes averted as a token of submission.

The sultan might be present in person to act as the supreme judge of his people, but more often than not he would listen behind a 'wicker-work grille, with a curtain of crape or black taffeta, and it is called the "dangerous window", because the prince may . . . listen to and see all that takes place, without being seen'.[15] After 1475, Mehmed rarely attended a meeting of the divan, preferring the secret control which the 'dangerous window' gave to him.

The Hall of the Divan was the final intersection between the inner and the outer world. The whole palace, from the outer walls and gates, through the two great courtyards, with its vast kitchens and stables and its thousands of guards, gardeners and craftsmen, existed to support the third court, the inner sanctum. Few ever penetrated more than a few yards inside the Gate of Bliss. But beyond that gate was another, separate world, where more than 3,000 people spent their entire adult lives. This palace within a palace was the Abode of Bliss, third court of the seraglio (a word originally referring to the whole palace complex but in the West later becoming synonymous with the harem) and seat of the sultan's happiness and harmony. If the outer palace excluded the hubbub and rank odours of the city, the innermost palace was detached entirely from the realities of life. The whole area, from the portal stone which was kissed by all who passed it, to the sea walls which bounded the Abode on its southern flank, was '*haram*', or forbidden. It was forbidden territory because it was filled with the spirit of majesty.

Mehmed the Conqueror had at first conceived of the Abode of Bliss as a summer retreat in the capital, but it quickly became the political centre of his empire. He was quite specific as to which departments of the old palace were to be transferred to the new. Most notably, his large harem, the female household of concubines and servants, was left behind. With the sultan went his treasury and armoury, those men closest to him and a few women. It was predominately a male world.

The *iç oğlan* (royal pages) were among the first to make the journey from the old to the new palace. These young men were the body servants and guards of the sultan, mostly culled from among the subject Christian peoples of the empire. They were part of the *devşirme* or slave tribute which the Ottomans exacted to fill the corps of janissaries. These pages were carefully selected and tested to fulfil a higher role. The court was their school and university: their real duties were to undergo a rigorous training which would fit them to be the future governors, soldiers and administrators of the empire. All became *kul* or slaves of the sultan; all were circumcised and converted to Islam. To be a *kul* implied no servility, for the greatest men in the empire began life as slaves. As an Italian writer described them in 1537, the *kul* was 'one who blindly and unquestioningly obeys the will and the command of the sultan'.

The slave system was a source of great strength to the Turks. In the centuries after the conquest, the human tribute was abandoned, and the influx of new tribute boys dried up. Thereafter the *kul* status was transferred from father to son, as a badge of honour. To be a slave of the sultan was a privilege and an opportunity. Many free-born Muslims, in theory debarred from the status of *kul*, bribed or cajoled their way into the sultan's household, where, by accepting the status of slave, they became Ottomans – of the tribe and stem of Osman. To be an Ottoman was to accept the duties of a caste: absolute loyalty and obedience. In return the sultan provided a career, a status and a salary for life.

Gia Maria Angiolello was a young Venetian captured at the siege of Negropont in 1470. He served as a translator in the palace from 1473 to 1481 and described the system as it operated at the time of Mehmed the Conqueror. He wrote of the *iç oğlan* as

sons of Christians, in part taken in expeditions with foreign countries and in part drawn from his own subjects . . . in accordance as they conduct themselves the pages are assigned to the offices of the royal household to attend upon the Grand Turk and after they have been in his service a certain time, when in the opinion of the lord he can trust them, he sends them out of the palace with salaries which are increased as he thinks fitting . . . thus the greater part of the lords, captains and great men in the service of the Grand Turk, receive their education in the Royal Palace . . . and there are few that do not accomplish their duties, because they are rewarded for the smallest service to their lord, and also because they are punished for the smallest fault.[16]

The pages were trained by white eunuchs. These geldings were mostly bought from dealers in Christian Europe and Circassia (Vienne in France was the main centre of production), for the laws of Islam prohibited castration. They guarded the Gate of Bliss and organized the day-to-day life of the third court. The first Ottomans had eagerly adopted the Byzantine practice of using castrated men for guarding their women, and the white eunuchs (so called to distinguish them from the black Africans who came later to the palace) rapidly extended their activities into administration. Like the pages and the other slaves in the sultan's household, they were isolated from Turkish society; shunned and feared because their mutilation divorced them from normal social relationships, they were, of necessity, loyal to their master. Eunuchs never gained the power in Ottoman society that they had wielded in Byzantium, where patriarchs, and generals and many lesser officials were drawn from their ranks and some offices of state were reserved for them alone. In the Byzantine civil service 'the castrated bearer of a title took precedence of his unmutilated compeer'.[17] In the Yeni Saray their power was largely invisible, as was the subtle shift in authority from the white to the black in the reign of Suleiman (1520–66).

The harem in the Eski Saray was traditionally guarded by black eunuchs, who had suffered the most radical form of castration and were thought most suitable for employment in the women's world. They became the point of contact between the imperial harem and the outer world, and administered the estates and properties which were owned by the sultan's mother and the mothers of his children. Their power was considerably enhanced when in 1541, after a fire in the old palace, Suleiman broke with tradition and permitted his favourite (and later legal wife) Roxelana to move into the kiosks in the gardens of the Yeni Saray. Thereafter, the transfer of the harem from the old to the new palace was gradually accomplished. But from the time that Roxelana came from the Eski Saray – with 100 ladies in waiting, a guard of black eunuchs, cooks, dressmakers and all her own servants – the character of the palace was altered irrevocably. The Yeni Saray was transformed from a seat of government to the centre of the sultan's personal life; once the harem had moved from the Eski Saray to the new palace, the Africans monopolized the principal positions of power. The *kizlar ağası* (chief black eunuch) became the sultan's most trusted servant, with a seat in the imperial divan; he wielded immense power within the palace, because he had an unrestricted right of access to his master. In 1595, the Africans' supremacy was recognized and the right to administer the holy mosques in Mecca and Medina (and the vast revenues which went with them) was transferred from the chief white eunuch to his African rival.

1. *Women and Children Leaving a Bathhouse*, Camille Rogier (1810–48)
An imaginary scene, though Rogier spent the years 1840–43 in Constantinople.
Unlike many Western depictions of the bathhouse, this lacks the hothouse
sensuality of Ingres' equally imaginary *Le Bain turc*.

2. *The Turkish Letter-Writer* (Arzuhalci), *1855*, Amadeo, Count Preziosi (1816–82)

4. (Opposite) *The Eating-House*, c. *1810*, Anon.
Set in Pera, and overlooking the Golden Horn, this shows with great accuracy a
traditional Ottoman eating-house. This and other images show how deserted were
the city streets in the heat of the day.

3. (Above) *The Coffee-House, 1854*, Amadeo, Count Preziosi (1816–82)
This, one of the most magical but accurate water-colours by Preziosi, shows
Constantinople as the crossroads of the empire.

5. Janissaries in the Second Court of the Yeni Saray, c. *1810*, Anon.
European visitors described the unseemly rush of the janissaries for their pay in the
second court, but it was a time-honoured formula – almost a military drill.

6. *The Chief Eunuch*, Anon.
The chief eunuch (*kizlar ağasi*) headed the
sultan's household. Always a black man,
he was feared both for his powers of life
and death within the harem and for the
supposed tendency to extreme cruelty
resulting from his altered state.

7. *The Aga of the Janissaries*, Anon.
By his uniform this is certainly a senior
janissary officer, and most likely the
commander (aga) of the janissary
regiments. But officers rarely held their
command for very long.

8. (Opposite, above) *The Turkish Courier*, after Sir David Wilkie RA (1785–1841)
Wilkie was in Constantinople when the news of the Anglo-Turkish victory over the
Egyptians in November 1840 arrived in the city; but he died on the voyage home, in 1841,
so his paintings were prepared for the lithographic press by Joseph Nash.

9. (Opposite, below) *Mehmed Ali, 12 May 1835*, David Roberts RA (1796–1864)
Mehmed Ali, *vali* of Egypt, is shown receiving the British 'viceroy' of Egypt in his palace.

10. *Interior of the Dome of the Rock, Jerusalem, 1863,* C. F. H. Werner (1808–94)
A holy place for both Muslims and Jews: where the Prophet Muhammad ascended to
heaven on his horse, and the site where Abraham offered Isaac up for sacrifice.

Suleiman and his immediate successors brought only their favourites to live within the Abode of Bliss. But by the middle of the seventeenth century all the sultan's women were installed in the seraglio, while the relicts of former sultans were relegated to live out their days in the old harem behind the walls of the Eski Saray. The harem was much misunderstood by the Christian West, who conceived of it only as a furnace of lust, in which the sultans indulged their passions, and the women gratified each other's desires. In fact its origins arose from Islam's preoccupation with female purity, which meant that women were to be separated from all men except their husbands and young sons. The world of women was 'haram', forbidden, to all other males. In the hands of the Ottomans this system of seclusion became a political and social institution as well.

The imperial harem was designed for the sexual gratification of the sultan, but it was also a training school – parallel to the institution which educated the royal pages. Indeed, after a page had ended his training and was sent out to his first administrative appointment, he would be given a wife from among the harem women, who like him was a slave of the sultan. Both shared the common experience of palace life, and even the unique dialect spoken in the Abode of Bliss.

The female world of the harem soon became the new centre of palace life, but its separate and inferior status was evident in the buildings created to house it. One of the first twentieth-century visitors to the harem, Dr Barnette Miller, was struck that 'The Harem of the Grand Seraglio is not at all the spacious and splendid edifice which one would naturally expect, but a congeries of separate buildings, annexes, suites, and rooms which are closely huddled together, and which are, almost without exception, small and dark.'[18] It was a warren of narrow passages, and blanked-off corridors; often it was impossible to gain direct access between adjacent rooms, except by a roundabout route under the watchful eyes of the black eunuchs, who superintended every aspect of the women's lives. Even access to the fine park which lay between the third court and the sea was prohibited, except on occasions of special celebration, although the women had their own small private gardens.

The contrast with the male part of the palace, both the ceremonial public rooms and the private quarters, was startling. In the male rooms (*selamlık*) the rooms were airy and open, with one room leading directly into another. The eye was drawn outwards, to the gardens and to the world beyond the walls. Even the pages lived in spacious dormitories with many windows and high ceilings, which looked out over the court or the gardens of the palace. The women's world was confined and claustrophobic. Only the valide sultan (the mother of the sultan) and those women fortunate enough to bear him children lived in some style and with a vista out over the world beyond the harem

The transfer of the harem from the Eski Saray changed the balance of power within the palace. It created a parallel hierarchy centred around the person of the valide sultan. She began as a harem girl, but, through the lucky chance of giving birth to an heir to the throne, achieved an exalted status. When her son became sultan, her power and influence was enormous. Only the most determined sultan was willing to defy his mother and if necessary to imprison or execute her. The valide sultan formed an alliance of interest with the chief black eunuch, and when the sultan was young, or enfeebled, the real power within the palace rested with his mother and her entourage. Against them, the grand vizier and state officials were often powerless, unless they bribed the harem politicians or themselves entered the murky world of faction fighting.

Few of the sultans was more grossly manipulated than Ibrahim, 'the Debauched'. Saved from the dying order of his brother Murad IV (1623–40) for his execution, his sensual passions were encouraged both by his mother and by his ministers:

At the beginning of his reign, when he was still the only descendant of the race of Osman, all the viziers felt they should encourage his fondness for women, and competed in their eagerness to offer him beautiful slaves ... At the age of twenty-four the passionate and robust young man had a large harem, and his strength so faithfully kept pace with his immoderate desire that twenty-four slaves could visit his couch successively in the space of twenty-four hours. His whole system soon began to feel the results of such excess ... he designed a robe for orgies with sable outside and inside; he created another, the buttons of which were inlaid with precious stones ...

But when his indulgences threatened the balance of power within the palace, drastic action was taken to redress it:

Once while riding near Scutari, he decided that the degree of sensuous delight must be proportional to physical size. Messengers were immediately sent out to find the biggest and fattest woman possible; they found a gigantic Armenian ... the new favourite rose so fast in the sultan's favour that she soon overtook her rivals ... But the Valide Sultana, jealous of the increasing influence of the Armenian, invited her to a feast and had her strangled.[19]

Ibrahim's career of indulgence was ended by a realignment of the factions. He had exiled his mother at the behest of his favourites, and she enlisted the support of the janissaries to depose him. Under the laws of Islam, the sultan was all-powerful so long as he ruled in accordance with the precepts of religion. His mother obtained a fatwa (declaration) from the Islamic judges that a madman could not reign, and his madness had been to 'ruin his empire through murder, shame and corruption'. Ibrahim was deposed and shortly afterwards murdered, and his mother set her eight-year-old grandson in his place.

Sultan Ibrahim was both created and destroyed by harem politics. His mother had saved him from execution, but eight years later she replaced him with a pliant child when he moved beyond her control. The dominance of the harem was a cancer within the Ottoman system. The valide sultan retained her power only while her son (or grandson) was incapable of exerting his own will, or had no interest in governing. The imperial mothers ensured that this period of infancy was prolonged. They encouraged their sons into debauchery and drunkenness, and discouraged them from all activity beyond the confines of the palace.

From early in the seventeenth century, it was not merely the women who were imprisoned beyond the Gate of Bliss. Whereas once the sultans had ridden out on campaign, they now abandoned the outer world to their viziers and their generals. It became a matter for comment when a sultan like Murad IV (1623–40) or Mustafa II (1695–1703) showed any ambition to lead his armies in battle. Ottoman princes grew up within the harem, living in a small suite of rooms called The Cage which was entirely cut off from the rest of the palace. When one of them became sultan, he was released to enter the rest of the palace for the first time. This was a device to prevent young princes from becoming a focus for conspiracies, a humane alternative to the practice formalized by the Conqueror whereby all the sultan's brothers and cousins were murdered at the accession of a new sultan. But, humane or not, the practice gave the Ottoman empire a succession of rulers who had no experience of the world beyond the confines of the palace.

When the Conqueror built the Abode of Bliss on Seraglio Point, he created more than a building. The palace was the apex of Ottoman society: all power flowed out from it, carried forth by the sultan's servants sent to govern in his name. In their distant provinces, they modelled their own households on the pattern of the seraglio, following the *kanun-name* or law codes in which were codified all the procedures and ceremonials within the palace, defined the roles and

duties of officials, and even laid down the dress and accoutrements for every member of the ruling caste. The colour of
their robes, the cut of the sleeves and the shape of the turban
were all prescribed in the greatest detail. The length of the
beard and the colour of the costume defined every official.
The viziers wore green, the chamberlains scarlet. The religious
dignitaries – the *ulema* – were resplendent in purple, while the
mullahs wore light blue; only the master of horse was dressed
from head to foot in dark green. Even the shoes provided a set
of symbolic distinctions: officers of the Sublime Porte – the
grand vizier's offices, just outside the palace walls – wore
yellow shoes, while the court officers all wore light red. The
same strict distinctions applied to non-Muslims: the Greeks
wore black shoes, the Armenians violet, and the Jews blue
slippers.[20]

Within the silence of the palace, colour and form had their
own eloquence, and costume possessed a subtle grammar.
Europeans in pursuit of Oriental exoticism delighted in the
'outlandish' variety of Ottoman dress, with some understanding of the complex social and political gradations which lay
behind the sumptuous display. But over the centuries the
deeper meanings were lost even among the Ottomans themselves: the code could no longer be deciphered. What remained,
though as more than a mere residue, was a common language
of ornament and display, imperfectly spoken but still eloquent.
When Ottoman sultans wished to reassert their authority,
they showed their determination by enforcing the old edicts
concerning dress and ornament. The great modernizer
Mahmud II (1808–39) applied the ancient codes with the greatest
rigour. When Mahmud sought to move the Ottoman empire
from its ancient Oriental past towards its modern Occidental
future, he reshaped the costumes and uniforms of the nation.
Out went the robes and turbans of the past, to be replaced
by the uniform black frock-coat (the stambouline) and the
conical red felt fez which typified the nineteenth-century

Ottoman. The symbolic power of the change was evident far beyond the confines of the palace; there were riots and demonstrations against the abandonment of 'Islamic' costume for the godless habits of the West. Only the clergy were allowed to retain their old flowing robes and huge turbans, indicating that there were limits to the power of even the most determined reformer.

The sultans of the nineteenth century left the palaces of their ancestors and moved into more modern and more palatial residences, designed along Western lines; but they brought the old palace system with them into the cold new marble halls. Théophile Gautier was taken round the vast Dolmabahçe palace while it was still under construction in the 1850s. He visited the wing of the palace allocated to the imperial harem: 'The rooms succeed each other in line, or open on large corridors; the harem, among others, has adopted the latter style of arrangement. The apartment of each lady opens, by a single door, upon a vast hall or passage, as do the cells of a nun in a convent. At each extremity of this passage is an apartment for a guard of eunuchs or *bostanjis*.'[21] Forty years later, a British naval officer, William Spry, visited Turkey on his ship HMS *Antelope*. In the company of admirals and diplomats, he was taken on an official tour of the 'new palace' of Dolmabahçe, and to the other new palaces of Çirağan and Beylerbey. By that time, the harem in Dolmabahçe had been in use and his Turkish guide pointed out the great closed door which he described as 'the Gate of Bliss' marking the boundary of the 'Abode of Felicity'. Even Spry's group of eminent visitors were not permitted to pass beyond it, although they ranged freely through the rest of the palace. In fact the harem was empty, and the sultan and his women resided elsewhere. But their former quarters had become *haram*: no strange man could pass through into the rooms which Gautier had once seen. The architecture was new and Western, but the instincts and attitudes were those of the Yeni Saray, four centuries before.

CHAPTER 3

Strangled with a Silken Cord

THE CONSTRAINTS OF OTTOMANISM

Beyond the walls of Constantinople, near a poor district of the city called Davut Paşa, lay a rough grass pasture. For most of the year the Cyrpyci Meadow was a wasteland where nomads grazed their sheep and goats. But, throughout the fifteenth to nineteenth centuries, once the fast of Ramadan had ended, the field was suddenly transformed into a temporary city. A small army of gardeners, tent-makers, upholsterers, seamstresses and carpet-makers, worked by day and night, levelling the ground, creating paths and roads, and then slowly assembling the streets and squares which would make up the sultan's tented war camp.

'Tents' suggests something temporary and makeshift, and far removed from the sumptuous reality. The merchant Paul Rycaut described the war camp as 'rather . . . Palaces than tents, being of a large extent, richly wrought within . . . and in my opinion, [they] far exceed the magnificence of the best of their buildings.' The walls of the pavilions were made of canvas or heavy felt, suspended by multicoloured silken cords from massive posts, as thick as a man's waist. On the exterior, the rough fabric was concealed by colourful silk hangings, embroidered with arabesques, flowers, or stripes; inside, the floor was covered with carpets, and the walls with fine hangings or kelims. The camp followed the structure of an Ottoman town, with the size and location of each tent according precisely with the status and importance of those who would live within. The intricate hierarchy of the seraglio was recreated, if only for the space of a few days, within a palisade of red silk, symbolizing a fortress wall.

Finally the tent-makers departed, and the new city stood empty. Janissaries raised a stout gilded pole before the entrance of the sultan's pavilion, which was capped by a huge golden crescent, bearing the sultan's war standard or *tuğ* – an array of six black horsetails that seemed to dance in the steady spring breeze. Suspended below them was an array of tiny bells which sounded continuously, like wind-chimes. Visitors to the camp compared them to the sound of water in the gardens of the palace. Beyond the imperial enclosure, another city – a teeming suburb – was quickly growing. Once the war banner was raised, contingents began to converge from all parts of the Ottoman empire, following orders and requisitions sent out many months before, ordering them to send their levies to meet after the fast on the plain by Davut Paşa.

As the snows melted in the passes of Anatolia and from the mountains of Europe, each *beylerbey* (provincial governor) mustered a contingent of *sipahis*, armed horsemen who held their *tımars* (fiefs) in return for military service. Each *sipahi* provided his own horse and equipment; many bore weapons inherited from a father or grandfather. In battle they were used as a heavily armoured shock force. Most carried both a sabre and a long straight sword, and eighteenth-century *sipahis* still wore a steel breastplate over a long mail coat, and a plumed steel helmet. Over many weeks, long columns of horsemen – some *sipahis*, some irregular lightly armed *akıncıs* (raiders) – converged on the capital. *En route* they passed companies of *seğmens* (sharpshooters), armed with matchlock carbines and short swords, and *tüfekçis* (musketeers), easily recognizable in their short red coats and tall red conical caps. Great bands of Tartar horsemen, each leading a string of ponies and armed with the small powerful bow of the steppe cavalry, trotted down the hills towards the Golden Horn, to join the sultan's array.

The war camp was both the emblem of war – the symbolic gathering of the host of Islam, ready to make war – and a muster which would be recognized by a commander in any army. Each detachment would be listed and checked against the muster roles. Each *sipahi* would be inspected, to see that he had brought all the equipment and levies that his fief demanded. Every gun and musket was carefully checked; all the rations and supplies were sealed and certified by the sultan's officials. But the rituals which accompanied the war camp were more ancient, a tribal ceremony that even antedated the conversion of the Turks to Islam. As the sultan's *tuğ* was carried through the streets, the crowds prostrated themselves in its path, as they had when the pagan hordes had gathered for battle. But the advance of Islam was a sacred task, so the presence of the symbols of the Faith magnified the atavistic summons of the horsetails. When the sacred banner of the Prophet was removed from its forty silk coverings in its chamber at the heart of the palace and, unfurled, was carried slowly through the outer courts, men bowed before it as in prayer, calling on the name of Allah. As the Children of Israel carried the Ark of the Covenant before them in battle, so the symbols of Islam made the war camp a holy place, and the war which was its purpose became a most holy duty for even the most distant regions of the empire.

The war camp grew daily, and soon its districts and divisions mirrored the many elements of the empire. First came the janissary quarter, representing the heart of the Ottoman institution. The janissaries and the sultan's personal troops surrounded the imperial enclosure, and their camp was neat, uniform, silent and orderly. They drilled at set hours each day, not with the textbook manœuvres of European pikemen or musketeers, but with a single-minded determination, rushing forward over obstacles, and discharging their muskets close to the 'enemy'. European observers said that they behaved as though they were but a single body. A Venetian ambassador, Gianfrancisco Morosini, visited an Ottoman war camp in 1585. He wrote to the doge, 'I walked through the whole army and carefully observed every detail about the calibre of their men, their weapons and the way they organized and fortified their camp. I think I can confidently offer this conclusion: they rely more on large numbers and obedience than they do on organization and courage.' He went on to say that '10,000 Christians could defeat 30,000 Turks, but that it would be harder to govern 2,000 Christians than 100,000 Turks – much harder if the Christians were Italian.'[1]

Each regiment, or *orta*, set up its tents in a grid around its commander – an echo of the sultan's own encampment – and at the heart of each was the regimental cooking-pot. Each regiment had its own distinctive badge, sometimes a flower or plant, and its banners and its muskets were stacked in piles close to each tent. This contrasted with the normal chaos and filth of a European military camp. The same sense of calm and order continued with the sultan's household (*kapıkulu süvarileri*) cavalry, all heavily armoured, well mounted on excellent horses and impressively well equipped, all at the sultan's expense. Equally skilled with lance, sword or bow, with their heavy chain-mail coats sweeping down over their horses' flanks, their turbans wound round their tall, pointed steel helmets, they seemed to those watching them at drill like a steel-mailed tide that flowed and ebbed around their 'enemy'. The imperial ambassador Ghislain de Busbeq was mightily impressed by their 'brightly painted shields and spears, their jewelled scimitars, their many coloured plumes, their turbans of the purest white, their garments, mostly of purplish or bluish green, their splendid horses and trappings'.[2]

On the battlefield, the Turks fought with the same verve and *élan* they had displayed before Busbeq. Where Western cavalry relied on shock and mass, the Turks used speed and precision in attack: a blunt Christian broadsword versus a slashing, razor-edged scimitar. The sultan's trained *sipahis* would surge forward, seemingly a many-headed, undirected mob, but then, at the crucial moment, and at full gallop, they would launch a lethal shower of arrows which would punch gaping holes in an opposing line of infantry. Some sophisticated Europeans were dismissive of the armour, the spears, bows and arrows. For example, an Austrian envoy, Count Alberto Caprara, sent to Istanbul in the spring of 1682, described in his letters the Turks' 'weakness, disorder and almost ludicrous armament'. He poured scorn on the notion that the Ottomans could mount an assault: 'I cannot believe that the Vizier intends to go to Vienna, and that so ambitious a design can be based on such mediocre forces. It is possible that brutal resolutions of this kind may be inspired by sheer pride, but the judgement of God will fall upon them.'[3]

Perhaps Ambassador Caprara, an elderly professor of moral philosophy at the University of Bologna, was in no position to make professional military judgements. One who was, Prince Eugène of Savoy, victor of many battles against the Turks, admired his enemies for their bravery, skill and undaunted determination. It was he who, a century after other Western troops had effectively abandoned armour for use on the battlefield, insisted that Austrian armies facing the Turks still clank about in cuirasses and leg armour – a precaution born from a bitter experience of the Ottoman style of war.

The Ottomans' was, above all, a horse army – more than 100,000 horses were used in some of the campaigns of the late sixteenth century. But only a few of these were the fine beasts of the household cavalry: the reality of the Ottoman army lay beyond the tents of the janissaries and the spruce horse-lines of the cavalry. Here the impression of order disintegrated, with clusters of shaggy ponies tethered close to myriad campfires, a panorama of almost 25,000 tents looking like nothing so much as a vast nomad encampment. The army had responded at the call to arms like its *gazi* (warrior) ancestors, from the lands of the sunset (*maghrib*) on the shores of the

Atlantic, to the mountains of Yemen, looking down over the Red Sea. Christians always claimed that the ready response was because the Muslim paradise was peopled with alluring houris, who would delight the endless hours of the warriors who died on the field of battle, their tireless bodies knowing no end to pleasure; but for Muslims the emphasis was on duty and not on pleasure. Even the humblest nomad was equal to a sultan in the eyes of Allah, and he shared with the sultan himself the responsibility to advance the boundaries of the Faith until the whole world acknowledged Allah. The *gazis*, soldiers of the True Faith, who gathered on the Cyrpyci Meadow, were honoured by all.

Ottoman officers tried to impose some discipline on the holy warriors; on the horde of feudal *sipahis*, and their levies, both mounted and on foot; on the irregular cavalry, *akıncıs*; and on the mass of foot soldiers – some, *azaps*, equipped with spears or muskets, even armour; others, *delis*, wild, near-naked dervishes. They sought in vain to create unity from a kaleidoscope of different styles of dress, customs, languages and weapons, and from races ranging from the blond musketeers of the Balkans and Hungary to the desert warriors of Arabia and North Africa. The army that gathered behind the horsetail banner mirrored the chaotic, multinational reality of the empire.

Most Europeans could not understand how Ottoman armies functioned. There were no ranks in the precise, hierarchical sense that they knew them, and no real premium was placed on military experience – the commander might be a palace official, the grand vizier, with little experience of war. The council of war did not plan a battle or campaign in the same way that the sophisticated, professional Western armies did by the late eighteenth century. There was no school of military lore, and no sense of military history as a means through which to understand the eternal verities of warfare. While Western commanders would know, at the least, the campaigns of Julius Caesar, and perhaps even some more modern battles, the Ottomans knew only the legends of their own heroes, praise-poems in honour of their courage, sagacity and bravery. Where a European army was directed, from the head, by the commanding general, an Ottoman host was organic. The *serdar*, or commander, would define his objective – the defeat of the enemy, the capture of a town – and would then 'loose' or 'unleash' his eager troops. Of course, the reality was not quite so heroic, and on many occasions Ottoman troops were herded unwillingly into battle by their officers. But the act of loosing or unleashing implied a loss of control – like an arrow flying to its target, beyond the influence of the bowman. Ottoman soldiers knew how to fight, and needed no training save in the particular skills at arms. But they did not manœuvre: they only charged, boldly, directly, at the enemy; or, in defence, they held ground to the death.

The exceptions were the professional corps – the sappers, artillerymen, miners, bombardiers, supply and commissariat staff. These were skilled in the particular technologies of their trades. Many fewer in number than the cavalry or the janissaries – rarely more than 5,000 men – but perhaps the key to the Ottoman success in wars which involved so many sieges, was an artillery corps (*topçu*) created by Mehmed and enlarged by his son Beyazid and then by Suleiman. Its field cannon stood ranged wheel to wheel close to the imperial enclosure, with the gunners, recognizable by their tall hats, standing before them. For almost a century since the conquest, no army in Europe had been able to match the Ottoman's fire-power on the battlefield. Their field guns were lighter and more manœuvrable than those of the West, able to keep pace with the advance of the janissaries and the cavalry. The heavier pieces – cannon, bombards and mortars designed to pulverize the walls of cities – were not on display. Some stood at the edge of the camp, their barrels and carriages lying in specially designed wagons drawn by teams of horses or oxen. Others were already far away in frontier citadels, with their crew of *topçus* waiting for the advance of the army.

The annual marshalling on the Cyrpyci Meadow (or on the other, Asiatic, shore above Üsküdar (Scutari) if the host was to be sent against Iran, or into Egypt or Arabia) was the ultimate emblem of Ottoman power and its seemingly limitless reserves. Every point of the ceremonial was pregnant with political symbolism. On a day declared propitious for war, the sultan left the heart of the Yeni Saray and processed through the city to take up residence in his war camp. With him from the sixteenth century, brought from the palace Treasury, were the most sacred relics of Islam, talismans for a successful campaign. The banner of the Prophet and the twin-pointed sword of Omar were an exhortation for every good Muslim to advance the cause of the True Faith by fire and the sword. They reminded the Faithful that the Prophet himself had fought against unbelief; under his banner, those who died in battle would pass straight to paradise.

Foreigners watching the parade marvelled at the size and good order of the vast force as it marshalled before them. But the Ottomans' real (and unique) strength was not visible there. *Pace* Morosini, sheer weight of numbers was not the key to their success in war: rather, no other contemporary nation (save perhaps Manchu China) approached the process of conquest so systematically. Wars in the West before the seventeenth century were random and confused, a jockeying for power and advantage between roughly equal adversaries. The Clausewitzian dictum that war was politics carried on by other means was not wholly true for the Ottomans, for in their empire war was a by-product not so much of politics but of religion. A common faith provided the cement that held the Ottoman host together. It was the duty of every Muslim to extend the 'Domain of Peace' – *dar ul Islam*, the lands where Islam reigned supreme – into the 'Domain of War' – *dar ul harb* – where Allah was not honoured. The very presence of the sacred relics at the start of a campaign made the religious duty plain to every soldier from the humblest scavenger to the most refined commander. Since the wars were driven by the demands of an advancing faith, the enemy was also clear, and unvarying. In the west, and at sea, it was Christendom; to the east, it was the heretic Shiah empire of Iran – judged 'worse than the infidel', and hence its subjects more worthy of death than any number of Christians. The claim to be advancing the boundaries of the Faith was elastic enough to embrace more strictly political Ottoman objectives, as when under Selim I, known as 'the Grim', the Ottomans absorbed Egypt and the Levant, wresting them from the control of the orthodox Sunni Mamelukes of Egypt.

The advance of Islam had suffered frequent delays and reverses. There were crushing defeats, as in July 1456, when Mehmed failed to take Belgrade, the last major Christian bastion before the great plain of Hungary, and the highroad to the West. For the Christians, their victory at Belgrade seemed a sign from God. Sixty thousand Turks had besieged the city, and, as at Constantinople, the Ottoman cannon had reduced its walls and towers to rubble. The defenders fought bravely against huge odds, but, after a battle which extended over seven days, the janissaries finally broke through. The repeated assaults had cost them many dead, and they swore revenge on the people of Belgrade.

The Christian soldiers and civilians were well aware of the ghastly fate which awaited them all if the Turks won, so, even after the Ottoman army had broken through the walls, the defenders continued to fight desperately from house to house. Finally the janissaries faltered, and the defenders pressed them even more fiercely. Gradually they drove the Turks back along the streets towards the breaches in the walls. Then, from the top of the battered walls, the Christians hurled blazing bundles of staves and branches soaked in sulphur and oil down on to the milling janissaries below. Eyewitnesses described a long wall of fire which fell upon the Turks, who panicked under this assault from the sky. The Turkish army retreated in disorder, leaving thousands of charred bodies in the ditch below the walls. On the following day, 22 July, St Mary Magdalene's Day, the Hungarian army under the regent John Hunyadi attacked the Turkish camp and drove the Turks away in disorder. Mehmed himself was badly wounded in the savage hand-to-hand fighting. This victory was a sweet revenge for the ravishment of the Queen of Cities.

Christendom rejoiced. The pope, Calixtus III, described it as the happiest day of his life. All the church bells in Rome rang out together, while the cathedrals resounded with the celebrations. The churches were filled even in far-away England, where a solemn mass was held in Oxford. The English scholar Thomas Gascoigne wrote of the battle that Mehmed, 'who planned to obliterate the name of Jesus Christ from the face of the earth' had been defeated upon St Mary Magdalene's day by the Army of God, 'led by John Capistrano [the Franciscan friar who had commanded the defenders] carrying a huge cross and shouting "Jesus, Jesus, Jesus." Hunyadi's army carried the huge cannon abandoned by the Turks back in triumph to the royal palace in Budapest.

If the Turks lost a battle, however, they generally returned to win the war. For war was not a single campaign but a state of being until the whole of the Domain of War was embraced within the Domain of Peace. War was a season of the year, like winter or summer. So, while Mehmed failed to capture Belgrade, his great-grandson, Suleiman, succeeded sixty-five years later. The island of Rhodes resisted Mehmed, but succumbed to Suleiman in 1522. For fifteen years the Ottomans suffered raids into Anatolia by Iranians and Mamelukes from Egypt. Then, in 1515, Selim, Mehmed's grandson, moved to the offensive, turning the Ottoman armies south. In two years, he checked the advance of the Iranian empire at the battle of Chaldiran (1515) and smashed the Mamelukes at Merj-Dabik, just to the north of Aleppo in Syria. Within six months Selim's army had marched across the Sinai desert at Gaza, and on 25 January 1517 it captured Cairo. In the Egyptian capital, Selim hanged the Mameluke leader, Tuman Bey, from the city gates, and resistance quickly subsided. The sultan received the submission of local rulers, among them the chiefs of the Bedouin tribes of Arabia and the sherif of Mecca, guardian of the holy places of Islam.

As a direct consequence of this conquest, Selim and his successors gained immense prestige as the 'Servant and Protector of the Holy Places'. Attempts were even made to buttress his rights of conquest by constructing a pedigree which 'proved' that the sultan – a born Turk – was a lineal descendent of the Prophet. He received the keys to the Holy Kaaba in Mecca and the sacred relics of the Prophet and his family – the robe, the sword of Omar, the sacred banner – which were dispatched immediately to the palace in Constantinople. With the title and the emblems of Islam, the Ottoman sultans assumed the unquestioned leadership of the Islamic world. Legitimacy was ultimately less important than the capacity to defend and then advance the boundaries of the Domain of Peace.

War was thus the *raison d'être* of the Ottoman state. The Ottomans planned systematically for each campaign. They garrisoned all the key strategic towns with detachments of janissaries and special fortress troops, partly to control the countryside, but principally to provide the staging-posts for the advancing host. Year after year the army marched the same route, going north-west from the capital to Adrianople, through the Balkan mountains to Sofia, and onward into Serbia. After Suleiman captured Belgrade in 1521, that city became the last Ottoman stronghold, before the army set out along the line of the Danube into the Domain of War, through the debatable lands of Hungary, towards Vienna and the west. If the sultan had decided to wage his campaign in the east, the process was reversed. The host would then gather at the heights above Üsküdar, on the opposite shore of the Bosporus to the Yeni Saray. The long procession which wound through the city towards the Cyrpyci Meadow for the war against Christendom was transformed into a string of caiques and barges heading from the Golden Horn to the opposing shore. After pausing to pray at the shrine by the shore, the sultan would appear before his army and launch them on their march eastwards. Thereafter, the host would head towards Erzerum, Van and Diyabakir, which were the traditional departure points for the campaign against Iran; or the army might meet the fleet (and its supplies) at Aleppo or concentrate its forces farther south at Mosul. But, either in the north or the east, there was a limit to the extent and duration of any campaign. The Ottomans did not spend winter in the field – that would be almost impossible in the harsh wastes of Anatolia, and difficult in the extreme in the eastern recesses of Europe. The Army of the Divine Light that left the Cyrpyci Meadow or Üsküdar in the spring returned in late autumn. Leave it too late, ran a Turkish proverb, and all the horses would die.

No amount of planning, however, could overcome the malign forces of nature, and the logistical problem of moving large bodies of men in both the east and the west. The first difficulty came with the size of the forces involved and the distances to be covered. The extent of the Ottoman host should not be exaggerated. Despite the wild calculations of Western observers, Ottoman armies rarely exceeded 60,000 to 70,000 men; the vast force of more than 100,000 that the grand vizier Kara Mustafa led to Vienna in 1683 was wholly exceptional. As a point of comparison, the Spanish army of Flanders, late in the sixteenth century, usually totalled 65,000 trained fighting men, mostly pikemen and musketeers. In the Ottoman army, by contrast, two-thirds or more were cavalry: both the disciplined household troops and the *sipahis* performing military service as a feudal duty. The wild men were left out of the account. But the whole army needed to be properly provisioned – something which Westerners were notoriously more inclined to leave to chance. The horses consumed vast quantities of fodder, even if the cavalry tried to forage when on the move. Then the army could only advance at the pace of its huge artillery train – in 1526 Suleiman left the capital with more than 300 cannon and then collected more *en route* from the depots closer to the frontier.

The guns, a vital component in the Ottoman battle plan, also posed an insuperable logistical problem. Roads and bridges in the Turkish-occupied Balkans were kept in relatively good order, and it was part of the responsibilities of a *sancakbey* (regional governor) to draft in peasants to prepare the road surface for the army's advance, and to clear other traffic out of the path of the advancing host. But beyond Belgrade, into the no man's land of Hungary, there were no roads capable of bearing the weight of the heavy cannon wagons, and the great rivers like the Drava and the Sava had no bridges across them. Other means of crossing had to be found. When Suleiman advanced into Hungary in 1526, the governor of Belgrade had collected a fleet of 800 river craft to carry the heavy equipment and the army's stores. But there had been so much rain during April and May that the roads were a quagmire and the currents on the Danube (swollen with flood water) made it virtually impossible for the flotilla of ships to make any headway upstream. Where the Ottoman engineers built temporary bridges across the torrent, the rushing waters broke them apart. Small wonder, then, that Suleiman's diary of the campaign is dominated by notes on the ceaseless rain and the piercing icy winds.

The Ottoman army arrived at the front with whatever it could carry. The Austrian general Montecuccoli compared it to a mobile fortress, 'which drags around with it everything that enables it to live and fight'. The Turks usually followed a well-tried route, so that at least the conditions of the ground would be known, and also because the host could not adapt to rapid change. When the army left Belgrade in 1526, it followed the southern bank of the Danube, so that it would not have to cross further upstream deep within enemy territory. Some equipment was left behind at the crossing of the Sava, and the marshes through which the Drava flowed swallowed many cannon, until an elaborate wooden bridge and causeway almost 6,000 yards long allowed the army to cross dry-shod. Just to the north of the crossing-point, the Hungarian king Louis, with a hastily gathered army, blocked their further advance on his capital city of Buda. At a crucial battle on 29 August the two armies confronted each other on the plain of Mohács, a strip of land sandwiched between the Danube marshes on one side and a range of low, wooded hills on the other.

Like its opponents, the Hungarian army had a preponderance of armoured horsemen, but they were heavily armoured cavalry. With the infantry, they stood in three solid phalanxes with the town of Mohács at their back and with about twenty cannon emplaced before the front rank. The Ottoman host, in its chain-mail and flowing robes, looked fragile by comparison.

The Turks appeared from the wood and began to move down on to the plain below. A contemporary painting depicts quite accurately what happened. The front ranks of a Turkish army were filled with the most expendable troops, the irregulars. When the Hungarians spurred their horses forward, the bodies of these unfortunates absorbed the impact of the charge. Although the Hungarians successfully smashed through them to reach the line of guns chained wheel to wheel in front of the ranks of janissaries (and, behind them, the sultan himself), the momentum of their attack had by then dissipated. Finally the charge faltered, and one by one the Hungarian knights were dragged from their horses or were shot from the saddle. As the residue slowly withdrew, they were pounded by the remorseless fire from the Turkish light field guns, massed at the edge of the wood, and by the musket shots of the janissaries, who were now slowly advancing as a mass on to the plain. From the opposite flank, the *sipahis* raced down on to the demoralized Hungarian infantry, turning a retreat into a rout. Then, as the Ottoman chronicler described it, 'at the orders of the sultan, the fusiliers of the janissaries, directing their blows against the cruel panthers who opposed us, caused hundreds, or rather thousands of them, in the space of a moment, to descend into the depths of hell.'[4]

The Hungarian guns and musketeers had played almost no part at all after the initial fusillade. They were deployed defensively, and could not be moved forward to keep pace with the Hungarian advance. The fluidity of the Ottoman tactics and their lighting exploitation of enemy weaknesses rendered the Hungarian guns useless. The artillerymen, like all the other Hungarians, paid with their lives for their king's failure. The Turks took no prisoners, and Suleiman recorded in his diary for 31 August that, 'seated on a golden throne', he received the applause of his army, amid the torrential rain. On that day 2,000 captives were killed, and two days later the Turks buried the bodies of 20,000 foot-soldiers and 4,000 cavalry; all those who had survived the battle were put to death by order of the sultan.

Mohács was a disaster for Hungary's Magyar nobility – the 'tomb of the nation', as one historian described it.[5] Throughout Europe the battle was portrayed as the destruction of a tiny band of Christian paladins by the overwhelming hosts of Islam. The truth was very different. The effective strengths of the two armies were very similar, since most of the conscripts and the *akıncıs* and *delis* who made up the bulk of the Ottoman army were of little value. The Ottomans were also weary, after eighty days on the march before they joined battle at Mohács, while the Hungarians had been fresh and eager for a fight. In fact to the Turks, on the day after the battle, it appeared something of a pyrrhic victory, since the piles of dead on both sides were roughly equal. Most Ottoman battles were like that, showing little evidence of tactical or strategic skill but an astonishing power of endurance.

After the battle the Ottomans took the capital, Buda, and then slowly retreated, pillaging. By November 1526 Suleiman was back in Constantinople, displaying the two vast Turkish cannon which the Hungarians had carried off in triumph from Hunyadi's victory over the Ottomans, and, more privately, enjoying the remarkable library assembled by the scholar-monarch Matthias Corvinus in the castle at Buda. Behind him, Suleiman left chaos along the Danube following the virtual elimination of the Hungarian élite. The vacuum was slowly filled by the triumph of the Habsburg candidate, Ferdinand of Austria, for the vacant thrones of Hungary and Bohemia.

Austria, Hungry and Bohemia, united, threatened the Turkish position, and by the early autumn of 1528 the sultan was planning a new expedition to the north – this time aimed beyond Buda, at the city of Vienna itself.

On 10 May 1529 the horsetail standard was carried forth from Davut Paşa, and the army moved north. By 16 August it had reached Buda, where Suleiman received the Hungarian opponents of the Habsburgs, who flocked to join the Ottoman host pressing on to Vienna. As three years before, the weather was atrocious, the river in spate, and the roads almost non-existent. Many of the heavy siege-guns had to be left behind, creating what proved a mortal weakness in the Ottoman capacity to take a great fortified city. The army advanced slowly, either forcing Habsburg-held fortresses into submission or bypassing them. A month after the Turks reached Buda, the first parties of *akıncıs* crossed the frontiers of Austria and ravaged the province of Burgenland up to the walls of Vienna itself. On 27 September, Suleiman pitched his camp before the city, and by the end of the month he had cut it off from the outside world.

The Ottomans' siege-craft was far in advance of their tactical skills in open combat. The sultan's armies had already successfully besieged two substantial cities – Belgrade in 1521 and the island fortress of Rhodes in the following year – but neither had been so well defended as Vienna, where the medieval walls of the city had been rebuilt (although there were some weak points) and a garrison of more than 20,000 men now crammed the city. There was feverish activity as the Viennese cleared the ground around the city walls, demolishing the ramshackle buildings which had grown up against the walls, which might provide cover for the advancing Turk. The few gun ports in the medieval walls were strengthened and enlarged, and, with a grim sense of realism, the Viennese began to dig trenches inside the walls to delay the advance of the janissaries if they broke through. The sense of alarm grew as pamphleteers began to publish wild stories of Ottoman atrocities and to compare the impending siege to that of Constantinople three-quarters of a century before. But the situations were not the same. In 1453 Mehmed surrounded an isolated outpost in the heart of his own territory; Suleiman was operating at the extremity of his lines of communication. Moreover, the walls of the Queen of Cities had been systematically battered by the huge cannon which Mehmed had had cast for the purpose. The light and medium guns which Suleiman had emplaced before Vienna could only sweep the walls with a constant hail of fire, and wreck the houses within the ramparts.

When an Ottoman army invested a city, the defenders could see the Turks' whole plan unfolding before them. First they could observe huge excavations which began in the distance, outside missile range. The earthworks became enormously elaborate. Trenches and mines were dug by conscript peasants, without any protection, and, as they came closer to the walls, the conscripts died in their thousands from the guns, spears and arrows of the defenders. But they were expendable and easily replaced. As the military commentator the Marshal de Tavannes observed, 'the defenders become weary with killing and their muskets become unusable from excessive shooting – truly the Turks have learned to extinguish fire with blood.' In some sieges, the slaughter was sickening. At the siege of Rhodes in 1522, the defending Knights of St John, expecting the assault, had measured the distance to all the points where the Turks might attack, so that they could produce accurate, aimed fire at known and measured objectives. The killing was continuous as the conscripts slowly advanced their trenches through the rocky ground. European sappers zigzagged their trenches so that defenders could not fire down on the diggers; but the work of digging took longer, as more excavation work was required. The Ottomans placed speed above the human cost and dug a broad straight trench directly towards the wall of the fortress. The enemy could pour fire into this trench at will, and sometimes so many bodies of the dead and dying were heaved out of the trench by the other diggers that they looked like the spoil thrown up by some demonic mole. The advance was inexorable. While the conscript peasants dug, the Turkish guns pounded the walls and bastions of the city – more than 3,000 stone cannon-balls were fired in a single month.

As the network of trenches came closer to the wall, the mood changed. The conscripts disappeared, and the final lines were built up more elaborately, parallel to the wall, and protected with buttresses and field fortifications. An observer watching from the walls described how 'the ditches and shelters are so many, and so well arranged, that the whole army could be drawn up within, and though quite close to the city, every man would be under cover, buried as it were among these mounds of earth.'[6] The visible line of advance had stopped, but the digging continued: now a skein of tunnels inched forward towards and below the walls, the work being carried out in silence by the skilled Turkish miners (*lağimciyân*), while, above, the defenders desperately dug countermines in a last-ditch attempt to preserve their defensive line. Inevitably some of these counter-attacks were successful and Turkish tunnels were destroyed. But the Ottoman system relied on multiple assaults, with many trenches and explosive charges, so that at least some would succeed. At Rhodes, for every one sap that was intercepted and destroyed, several more reached their target. When the miners laid their charges and exploded their mines, much of the city wall crumbled in a moment.

Suleiman's assault on Vienna depended on the success of these mining operations. The siege-guns which would rapidly have reduced the old walls to rubble had been lost for ever in the marshes. Spies inside the city, who had observed the desperate strengthening of the fortifications, sent messages to the sultan to inform him that the weakest point was the section of wall on the southern side by the Carinthian Gate (Kärntner Tor). The Turkish saps, moving forward towards the walls, slowly garrotted the city by pressing remorselessly on that weak point. The defenders' only hope lay in relieving the pressure, if only for a moment. Each day, a rag-bag of infantry and a few horsemen would mass inside one of the gates. The heavy doors would be unbarred and they would rush out towards the enemy lines, pouring fire into the trenches and hacking at the sweating sappers. The results were pitifully inadequate: on one day they came back with thirty Turkish heads and ten prisoners. Their valiant surges from the Carinthian Gate and from the narrow sally-port by the Hofburg achieved almost nothing. And, since the Turks, now regularly informed by their spies, had identified the most vulnerable sector, they could mass their assault accordingly. The Viennese commanders could only watch with growing despair as the trenches close to the Carinthian Gate began to fill with the paraphernalia of a major attack – ladders and fascines to pile up at the foot of the walls – and, as the unmistakable tall conical caps with white neck-flaps of the janissaries began to predominate among the antlike figures below the walls, they knew that an assault would not be long delayed. In the afternoon of 9 October a huge Turkish mine blasted the defences, leaving a gap through which two dozen men could have marched in line abreast.

But the attack did not come as expected, and all through the day and the following night the Austrians piled the rubble from the shattered walls to make a fragile but continuous defensive line. On successive days the janissaries rolled forward, but, instead of launching an attack at many points, forcing the defenders to spread their slender resources, they confidently placed all their hopes on the vast breach in the wall by the Carinthian Gate. But the technology of firearms had advanced since the days when Mehmed had taken Constantinople, employing very similar tactics. The Austrians massed their muskets and light cannon all around the gap in the walls, and when the janissaries rose from the trenches and poured into the breech they were assailed by a devastating fire, not only from the remaining walls above but from the earthwork in front of them. The distinctive janissary banners – emblems of dogs, cooking-pots, brooms, elephants, candles – bunched closely like tulips into the breach, and then fell like so many broken stalks. On the next day, they launched another attack in the same place, with the same inconclusive result, and on 12 October a third. Each time, the Austrian defence line held – although on the third day the situation seemed impossible: just before the Turks rose from their trenches, another huge mine was exploded, which brought down most of the remaining wall. But, miraculously, once again the assault failed, although the defenders feared they could not withstand another.

They did not know that the Turks were also in a desperate

position. At the council of war held before Suleiman that evening, the troops were given a cash payment of 1,000 aspres, and it was proclaimed throughout the camp that the first soldier to pass through the walls would receive 30,000 aspres and immediate promotion. In an effort to rally his troops, the sultan himself came close to the walls to inspect the breach, and then declared that the gap was large enough to make one final, and triumphant, assault. On the morning of 14 October three massive columns surged towards the ruined defences, to the accompaniment of all the Turkish bands and with the sultan's own banner flourished. Behind the troops came their officers, with drawn swords to prevent any retreat. But after a half-hearted attack the troops turned and ran, some crying that they would rather die at the hands of their own agas than face the long Austrian harquebusses again.

The sultan ordered another mine to be blown and the demoralized troops to make one final attack. This too was thrust back, and Suleiman decided to end the attempt. At about midnight the janissaries struck their tents and burned everything they could not carry away. The darkness around the city was punctuated by innumerable bonfires; by morning, they had died down and the vast Turkish host had gone. The city awoke to a victory. The Viennese then discovered the charred corpses of captives who had been thrown into the flames, while the bodies of more than 1,000 women and children, killed because they were not worth carrying into slavery, were huddled in clusters with their throats cut.

The siege of 1529 has been described in some detail because it displayed the fundamental problem faced by the Ottomans, and in the sixteenth century – at a time of their greatest success – rather than in a moment of renewed but temporary energy during the seventeenth or eighteenth centuries, after a period of decline. It was, as a historian of the Ottomans, Joseph von Hammer-Purgstall, observed, 'The first of Suleiman's enterprises which was not crowned with success',[7]. The true turning-point in Ottoman fortunes is set by most Western historians at the point where defeat became habitual, with the attempt by the grand vizier Kara Mustafa to take Vienna in September 1683. His catastrophic defeat by a relieving Christian army led by the king of Poland, John Sobieski, is the first entry in a catalogue of woe which continued through the eighteenth century and into the nineteenth.

From 1683, the Ottomans' failure was blamed on their inability to accommodate Western technology. Each defeat at the hands of the Austrians or Russians was held to be fresh evidence of their backwardness. Foreign experts despaired at Ottoman complacency. A French mission sent to Turkey to improve fortifications in the European provinces reported:

Lafitte Clavier had proposed to plant the rampart with storm poles and palisades in the European style, but the Turkish engineer who replaced him . . . and who was merely the head gardener of the seraglio, had no idea at all of fortifications. He found immense quantities of palisade stakes in store, and he could think of nothing better to do with them than set them up in the middle of the parapet, instead of planting them point downwards on the exterior face, which would have made escalade almost impossible.

The contemptuous reference to the 'head gardener' reflects the European misunderstanding as to the distribution of power in the Ottoman lands: the *bostancis* did care for the sultan's gardens, but they also commanded troops and the police of the city, and carried out capital sentences. But the incident also reveals the lack of curiosity or interest among the Ottomans in the affairs of foreigners. The Turkish engineer cooperated with the Frenchman because he had been ordered to do so, but he found Lafitte Clavier's commands and objectives as pointless and meaningless as the Ottoman's rank and duties were to Lafitte Clavier. Asked to prepare a fortification in the Ottoman style, the engineer would not have displayed such lack of competence; asked to learn from a European, his mind closed. In the Ottoman empire it was often safer not to exercise initiative.

The defeat before Vienna was a consequence not just of inferior technology but of a more fundamental weakness: the Ottomans' unwillingness to learn or change. In some areas they excelled: the Austrians had been amazed at the accuracy and rapidity of Turkish fire. Nor was Europe a synonym for modernity. The relieving army which swept down from the hills above the Austrian capital on to the hapless *sipahis* and janissaries below was led by the *Husaria*, the élite Polish heavy cavalry:

Each rider was helmeted and plumed; his breastplate encrusted with gold and gems; cloaked with leopard-skins; winged with great arcs of eagle-feathers rising over his head; mounted on a magnificent charger caparisoned in silk and velvet embroidered with gold. Each *husarz* carried sabres and pistols with jewelled handles, and a twenty-foot lance with streaming pennant. As they broke into a lumbering canter and lowered their lances, the pennants and wings on their backs set up an evil hiss while the ground shook with the pounding of fifteen thousand hooves.[8]

By any judgement these *husarz* were an anachronism – more so than the *sipahis* whom they drove from the field – but they were recognized as the survival from some heroic past, no longer a pointer for the future. By contrast, the Ottomans had no sense that their style of war was equally outmoded. Reformers wished to purify the old order of janissaries, equip them with new arms, buy new guns, build new ships; but they did not demand change.

The consequences of this conservatism were recognized only slowly; the great battles against the Austrians, and later the Russians, which resulted in the steady shrinking of the empire were not simple triumphs of superior Western equipment, as many Ottomans liked to think. After this last defeat before the gates of Vienna, the Domain of Peace began to

contract. In the century which followed, the Ottomans lost
Hungary, Croatia and Transylvania to the Austrians; Podolia
to the Poles; parts of Greece to Venice; Bessarabia and the
Crimea to the Russians; while the resurgent power of Iran to
the east absorbed the provinces of Azerbaijan and Dagistan.
There were occasional victories – the Russians were forced to
surrender to the Ottomans at the river Pruth in 1711, and the
Greek provinces were recovered from Venice in 1715 – but
whenever an Ottoman army met a European army on roughly
equal terms the result was invariably a defeat for the Turks.
The Ottoman style of war, once far in advance of that of
Christian Europe, could no longer match the improved training, technology and tactics of the West; by the end of the
eighteenth century, the sultan's soldiers had not varied their
equipment or methods of war for more than two hundred
years.

It was not that the system was incapable of alteration. In
war, as in other aspects of their government, the Ottomans
mixed rigidity with the capacity to adapt. Faced with walled
cities, they had embraced artillery and the 'gunpowder age'
more systematically than any Christians. They quickly learned
the crafts of mining and bombardment, partly from the
Mongols and partly from European experts. But, having understood both the theory and the practice, they created their
own system. To Western eyes, their techniques might seem
capricious and wasteful of human life, but they could be dev-
astatingly effective. Nowhere was their capacity to adopt new
techniques more evident than in building their naval power.

By origin a people from the steppes of Central Asia, the
Ottomans had no tradition of naval warfare. But, as their
empire grew during the fifteenth century, they faced powerful
maritime powers such as Venice and Genoa; the Turkish ships
played an important part in the capture of Constantinople.
When the need dictated, they became a sea power. Indeed, it
was their assault from the sea that instilled the greatest terror

throughout the Mediterranean and Adriatic. Just as the inhabitants of the Austrian province of Styria traumatized their children with stories of Turkish marauders stealing them in the night, all along the Mediterranean coast there were tales of the sudden attack by 'Turks' or 'Moors'. The archives of the Alhambra in Granada are full of accounts of Turks being guided ashore by local spies. They tell of raids on villages being led by 'Moriscos' who had fled from Christian Spain to the more welcoming shore of Morocco. At first the Ottomans employed pirates from the Barbary Coast of North Africa – indeed their greatest commander, Khair-ed-din, known as 'Barbarossa', was a former corsair – but soon they began to build their own ships, and, although the dockyards at the Queen of Cities could never rival Venice's arsenal, they produced ships at a remarkably high rate. The catastrophic losses at Lepanto in the Gulf of Corinth in October 1571 – more than 300 ships – were made up within two years. Whenever a new pattern of Christian ship was captured, it was taken to the capital, careened, and minutely examined so that the naval designers could learn any new lessons in ship design.

In Spanish political mythology, Lepanto symbolized the decisive shift of power in the struggle for control of the Mediterranean. This triumphalism was enhanced by the close association of the house of Habsburg with Lepanto. Don John of Austria, the commander, was half-brother of King Philip II of Spain, and his victory was depicted, in pamphlets and paintings, as part of the apotheosis of the Habsburgs. But, rather like the Spanish recovery after the destruction of the Great Armada by the English in 1588, the victory was less clear-cut. Both Ottoman and Spanish naval power continued, but the process of aggressive expansion was halted.[9]

By the end of seventeenth century, however – in naval design just as in firearms technology – an early lead had been allowed to wither away. Islam allowed a good Muslim to use the arms of the enemy to advance the cause of the Faith. The Ottomans' traditional arms were swords, bows and spears, like the weapons of Mehmed now displayed in the Topkapı museum. But, when handguns became of increasing import-ance, the role of the firearms increased within the sultan's armies and they created ever larger numbers of specialized troops – Bosnian *panduks* and *eflaks*, sharpshooters and musketeers. But all these changes were assimilated within a traditional system of control and command: the new detach-ments were used in exactly the same way that the old had been. Instead of using musketry *en masse*, as was developing in the West, or massed pikemen acting in unison, the Ottomans looked upon each musketeer or sharpshooter as a warrior risking his life for a place in paradise. Individual bravery and daring were the most valued attributes: janissaries and other soldiers vied for the badges of courage they could pin on their turbans. Indiscipline was considered only a venal offence, provided it stemmed from an act of courage.

Consider one of the last battles where the Ottoman army overcame a Western force in the open field, at the river Pruth in 1711. The victory was won in the most traditional and time-honoured fashion:

A janissary coming before the Vizier's tents, and crying out, shall we lie here to die of sickness and misery? Let all true Musselmen follow me to attack the infidels, he snatched up one of the colours that stood before the Tents and went forwards. He was immedi-ately followed by others, who seized other Colours, and in this tumultuous manner the Janissaries, Serdenghestis and Delis gathered together and with their usual cries moved towards the enemy. They were repulsed three times with the loss of about 8000 men and forced to retire to some distance where they cast up a retrenchment.[10]

What the Ottomans ignored was that the supreme courage of janissaries and others who gave their lives was in vain: the

Russians, riddled by disease, were on the point of surrender:

And it is written me by a friend, who is now in the army that he understood from judicious persons, who were present and saw the action, that the Turks were certainly beaten, if the Muscovites had known the consternation they were in, and could have pursued their advantages by continuing their fire and sallying out of their camp among them. The next morning, when the Turks began to play their canon, the Czar sent out officers with a white flag . . . tis said the Muscovites did not lose above 800 men in the attacks; but the sicknesse was so great among them, that there died 3 or 400 men daily.[11]

Like the Highland clansmen of Scotland – another society of renowned warriors who fell before the organized volleys and the massed bayonets of modern European armies versed in military science and under firm discipline – the Ottoman armies failed not so much from outdated equipment but because they trusted only the traditional ways of waging war. Deep down, they did not believe that they had anything to learn from Europe in this respect.

But certainty about the superiority of the 'Ottoman way' was mixed with doubt. This was the central (and unresolved) ambiguity of Ottomanism in its attitude towards the West. At many points throughout the eighteenth century the sultan's governments hired Western soldiers to teach their army the new disciplines. In 1729 a French officer, Count Alexander de Bonneval, began to modernize the Ottoman engineer and bombardier corps, but, after his departure in 1742, all his reforms were gradually eroded by Ottomans opposed to change. By the time that the most effective of the foreign instructors, the Baron François de Tott, arrived in 1768, almost all evidence of Bonneval's work had vanished.[12] Consequently, de Tott too had only a partial success. He showed officials and some of his troops that organization, enterprise and initiative could overcome almost any obstacle.

He built new cannon, erected new forts and trained troops, but ultimately to little avail. The soldiers felt that his military science turned them (as it did) into automata – creatures without honour and bravery. The officials expressed enthusiasm, and seemingly accepted the miracles of improvisation, but they nevertheless resisted his demands for proper equipment and support. In the end, his initiatives were smothered in the soft embrace of Ottoman traditionalism: the military officials and army commanders preferred the old ways.

A single episode recorded in de Tott's memoirs seems to sum up the whole experience of trying to build a modern army within the Ottoman context. Once, after many delays, de Tott had arranged a meeting to plan the seaward defence of Constantinople against a threatening Russian fleet. He was greeted politely and assured that all his needs would be met – in full, and instantly. Yet, while he talked, the Ottoman official with whom he was dealing seemed wholly preoccupied with the problem of finding two canaries that could sing the same tune.

The sacred laws of Islam were, by definition, incapable of improvement, and the Ottoman government, which was the political expression of those laws, was also immutable. That did not mean that the system was immovable, but it placed strict limits on any reforms. One means of achieving change was by 'restoring' a debased institution to its ancient purity. This was the tactic which Murad IV used when he accused his janissaries and *sipahis* of corruption: 'the lure of office has increased the number of malcontents among you, who refusing to listen to the words of the elders and wise men of the troops, like yourselves spend their time oppressing the people, devouring the pious foundations, and giving you a disastrously bad name for tyranny and rebellion.' To this accusation the soldiers could only reply with the time-honoured formula 'We are the slaves of Padishah; we do not protect rebels; his enemies are our enemies.'

Since the Ottoman state was part of the divine order – above any human imperfection, and beyond any need for innovation – certain consequences logically followed. If the state apparently failed in any respect (as before Vienna), this could only be because of human error and treachery. If the Ottoman power seemed to have declined from the great days of Suleiman (although even he had proved fallible, as at Vienna), this was because of the corruption wrought by evil men. This doctrine could be as dangerous for the rulers as for the subjects. If a sultan was deposed – a frequent occurrence in the turbulent conditions of the seventeenth century – this was because he was fated to suffer deposition. Many commentators wrote of the need to reform the Ottoman order, but their aim was, universally, to restore the solidity of the state as they imagined it had existed under Mehmed the Conqueror or Suleiman. Almost until the last days of the empire in the twentieth century, those who wished to change the system harked back to some golden age.

Of course, the notion of the 'good old days' was not exclusive to the Ottoman empire. It is striking how similar the complaints of first Ottoman critics of the system are to those put forward by those reformers – *proyectores* – who inveighed against the decline of Imperial Spain early in the seventeenth century. But the antipathy to innovation – and the Ottoman Turkish word for this, *bida*, carried the sense of 'an event to be avoided if at all possible', akin to heresy – was markedly different to the attitudes prevailing in the West. There was a saying attributed to the Prophet that 'the worst things are those that are novelties, every novelty is an innovation, every innovation is an error, and every error leads to Hell Fire.'[13] The quality of timelessness which Western commentators attributed to the Ottomans, with nothing seeming to alter over decades or even centuries, was exaggerated, but it came close to the truth. When Ottomans began to travel to the West, as they did in the eighteenth and nineteenth centuries, they were shocked by the sense of change and mutability that seemed to dominate every aspect of life. Sheikh Rifaa Rafi al-Tahtawi, a teacher at the university of al-Azahar, was sent from Cairo to Paris in 1826, learned French, and ultimately spent five years in the French capital. He understood and admired the West, but even he found it hard to come to terms with the rootlessness of European life: 'One of the characteristics of the French is their avid curiosity for everything that is new and their love of change and variety in all things and especially in the matter of dress. This is never fixed with them and no fashion or adornment has remained with them until now.' For an Ottoman, rooted in a society where dress made a fixed statement about rank and status, and remained unchanged – the subject of rigorous controls and even capital punishment for misuse – the concept of fashion was completely alien. Westerners were infinitely more curious, and thus better informed about the empire than Ottomans were about the world beyond their frontiers. Only the Chinese exhibited a similar lack of concern (as the first British embassy discovered) for anything that took place outside *their* 'heaven-protected domains'.

By the late eighteenth century the West had a clear if not wholly accurate perception of the Turk's strengths and weaknesses. They saw that the Ottoman army that gathered at Constantinople was only the most visible evidence for the vast resources that the sultan could command. As the Venetians shrewdly noted, 'The security of the Turkish lands depends first on the abundance it has of all the necessities of life.'[14] From the hinterland of Asia, Europe and North Africa flowed a torrent of goods: wool, leather, furs and cambric through Constantinople; food and spices from the Levant; textiles from Greece; iron from Anatolia; gold and precious stones from India and the Far East. The empire stood astride all the traditional trade routes from East to West, and controlled a coastline of more than 3,000 miles, which encompassed some of the greatest ports of the Mediterranean – Alexandria and

Tripoli. Even the great Christian centres – Ragusa (Dubrovnik), Genoa and Venice – although past their peak, traded with the Ottomans more regularly than they fought with them, and were integrated into the Ottoman trade network.

The sultan ruled over thirty kingdoms, and drew taxes from all of them. The Ottoman empire did not interfere with the traditional practices of its subjects: it merely taxed them with increasing rigour and efficiency. The poll tax on Christians, which allowed them the privileges of practising their faith and maintaining their own patterns of authority (bishops, patriarchs and synods), is well known; but it was part of a broader pattern. While non-Muslims paid the capitation tax, Muslims paid *zekât* – originally the alms tax ordained by the Prophet, but used simply as a source of general revenue under the Ottomans. And, in addition to these individual taxes, almost every commercial transaction produced money for the state. Every household was taxed; each farmer (in many parts of the empire) was charged according to the fertility of his soil. Even nomads were taxed, by the size of their flocks and the time that they spent on pasture land. The fees and duties fell on everything, from a tax on bridegrooms to a scale of payments for the recovery of stray animals.

Many of these taxes were 'customary', and had been collected for many generations; the Ottoman administration provided a channel through which the money could flow to the sultan's Treasury. Officials were sent from the capital to all the larger cities and main markets to administer tax-collection. They were paid a state salary (but supplemented their pay by *bahşiş*, the traditional payment made by suppliants for government services). These commissioners (*emins*) collected the bulk of the revenues in the main centres, but it was not economical to collect the rural revenues directly, so the rights to collect taxes were rented out to the highest bidder – the system of tax farming, or *mültezim*, which guaranteed a set return to the Treasury in the capital. This was an effective system, practised in Europe until quite late in the nineteenth century.

The Ottomans were more rational in dealing with their subjects than were their European contemporaries. All subjects who were not members of the ruling Ottoman caste were called '*rayas*', a word meaning 'flocks'. As the descendants of nomadic shepherds, Ottomans knew that livestock should be both conserved and exploited. Each year, a percentage (the weak and unproductive) would be culled, and the rest shorn; but there was nothing to be gained from slaughtering the flock. Europeans were preoccupied, by contrast, with the human soul. The medieval Christian church had sought to obliterate dissent with fire and sword. The wars of religion which ravaged Europe for much of the sixteenth century and the first part of the seventeenth were fuelled by the demand that rulers and ruled should be of the same faith: *cuius regio, eius religio* – the ruler determines the religion of his people. Late in the seventeenth century, Catholic France, the richest country in Europe, expelled the Protestant Huguenots, its most industrious and skilled citizens, because they would not conform to this principle. To a Turk, this was the equivalent of killing the most fecund ewes.

The Ottoman approach was wholly pragmatic. Jews and Christians within the empire were allowed free practice of their faith, but were required to pay a special tax for the privilege. By paying this, however, they were also exempt from the military conscription which was suffered by Muslim subjects. The levy of Christian children in the Balkans as slaves of the sultan – the *devşirme* – was abandoned in the first half of the seventeenth century, when it was found to be unnecessary: more than enough volunteers could be found to staff the palace and the janissary corps.

Although Christians were exempted from compulsory military service, many served voluntarily in the ranks of the army of Islam. Wallachians, Albanians and Bosnians were recruited as auxiliaries in the Turkish armies from the first days of the Ottoman occupation of the Balkans. Many of the border Slavs converted to Islam, but those who did not were equally acceptable. Similarly, many of the new corps of musketeers were Christians, or villagers from Anatolia who had become mercenaries, and received a daily wage like the janissaries (rather than depending on plunder like the *delis* and many Western soldiers). The Ottoman government had at first resisted the development of these irregular forces, fearing that they would become a focus for rebellion, but by the mid seventeenth century they had been incorporated into the sultan's army, paid and equipped by the treasury. The non-Muslim troops were considered trustworthy, much as the janissaries had been before they gained a feel for their political power in the state. But the janissaries had posed a potential danger to the state ever since their formation. Mehmed the Conqueror had faced janissary revolts, and their sense of power and importance grew immeasurably when they became a form of praetorian guard for the sultan after the reforms of Mehmed and Suleiman. Only constant war kept them in check, and even the call to arms might not be obeyed enthusiastically as they became more accustomed to the comforts of urban life.

Not surprisingly, as the seventeenth century advanced, the military power of the central government in Constantinople declined, and its capacity to enforce its will in distant provinces weakened considerably. Yet the Ottoman empire continued to provide a sense of legitimacy and true order. Much of Asia Minor was dominated by rebels, bandits and others outside the control of the state. The power to execute the sultan's orders often depended as much on the interests of local magnates (notably in Syria and Rumelia) as on any armed force which could be sent out to enforce them. But the ultimate and unquestioned power was obedience to the sultan.

Even if the authorities could not enforce the sultan's writ, his right to command was never denied, and there are many records of bandits submitting to authority and becoming loyal Ottoman officials. This effective consent, sustained by the power of Islam, was the root of Ottomanism. Even overmighty subjects – some even more powerful than the sultan himself, like the ruler of Egypt, Mehmed Ali (1805–49) – preserved the fiction of imperial control. For the subject peoples, the *rayas*, the Ottomans offered a codified and relatively honest system of justice, imperfect though it was, and a structure for trade and economic life, even if clogged with venal administrators and corrupt practices. And, at a time when Europe was riven by social and religious hatreds, the Ottoman empire offered sanctuary to the persecuted, whether Spanish Jews, Huguenots or (it is said) rebel Scots fleeing English justice after the 1745 rebellion. (One 'Campbell' became a valued military adviser, accepting Islam and becoming known as 'Ingeliz Mustafa'.) Thus, despite all its failings, the 'heaven-protected domain' continued to provide a refuge for the persecuted.

The phrase 'turned Turk' was a term of opprobrium in Europe, signifying a renunciation of all the values and social codes of the West. But it also indicated the ease with which the transition was possible, and how much some on the margins of their own societies might gain by it. Turning Turk meant entering a world fundamentally different from any society in western Europe. But observant strangers noted how the weight of custom bore heavily on all. To be an Ottoman meant acquiring privilege, visible to the outer world in the multitudinous distinctions of official rank. The life of a state servant, military or civil, was unquestionably more comfortable than that of those who stood outside this charmed circle. And yet, with the benefits came burdens – lightly borne for much of the time, but silken cords none the less.

For an official, a silken cord carried a sinister meaning, for this (or a bowstring) was the instrument of doom borne by the sultan's executioners sent to end the lives of failed ministers or commanders. This, too, was in its way a mark of respect, just like the silken rope with which a condemned peer of England had the right to be hanged. It spared the victim the ignominy of a public execution, although his head would be severed post-mortem and exhibited as a warning to others. Kara Mustafa at Belgrade, after his armies had failed to take Vienna in 1683, became a model of the old Ottoman virtues. He received his executioners with courtesy, and, when shown the cords, praised the sultan's honour and generosity, prayed briefly, and submitted silently to his doom. Then, as an Ottoman historian put it, 'His head rolled at the feet of the sultan.' So too, almost two centuries later, did the head of the great Ottoman reformer Midhat Pasha, exiled in Arabia and visited by the sultan's executioners, although some said that Midhat struggled fiercely against his fate, resisting Abdul Hamid II to his last moments.

Over four or more centuries, the virtues of an Ottoman remained largely unchanged. He was to be obedient but not servile, dedicated to those around him, his official family who relied on his patronage (intisap), as well as to the sultan. It was almost an equal imperative that he should seek to accumulate wealth and power, but he should accept demotion or even death with resignation. And, although the laws of Suleiman expressly forbade it, it was also accepted that he would act in the interest of his blood family and, especially, seek to advance the fortunes of his sons. To his subordinates, he should behave with justice and restraint, without excessive greed for presents and bahşiş. These and many other of the financial practices later considered corrupt in Europe were not looked upon in the same light within Ottoman society, but nor were they in Europe (except perhaps in Prussia) until the great bursts of nineteenth-century reform.

But beneath the calm and equanimity with which Ottomans faced the world lay fear. Success or failure would be governed not by merit but by chance – such as the good fortune of having impotent or divided enemies, or the opportunity to achieve modest success. A great triumph could be as dangerous as defeat, as it was for the commanders who defeated the Russians at the battle of the river Pruth in 1711. Sir Robert Sutton, the English ambassador to the Sublime Porte, revealed the mysterious logic of the Ottoman court when he wrote in his dispatch of 21 November 1711:

Vizier Azem Mehmet Pasha being deposed, . . . the late Vizier's creatures and confidants, viz. Omar Efendi (his Chief Secretary), the Secretary of the Corps of Janissaries, the commander of the Sipahis, and his reporter, were cast into prison . . . three days after Osman Aga who was his Chief of Staff . . . was imprisoned here. It is believed that none of them will be punished with loss of life but only with drawing their purses.'[15]

One month later he was writing, with some surprise, 'On the 14th instant afternoon Osman Aga, who was the late Vizier Azem's Chief of Staff at the Conclusion of the Peace, and Omar Efendi, his Chief Secretary, were beheaded before the Great Gate of the Seraglio, and the bodies left exposed.'[16] They had the misfortune to serve a sultan who had come to the throne through the deposition of his brother and who feared a victorious army more than he feared a defeated one.

Office-holders balanced opportunity with risk. Ottomans were often rapacious because they feared that their opportunities for gain might suddenly be cut off, and they sought to protect their families by bequeathing their property to religious trusts (vakf) which were immune from the sultan's confiscation. Although the empire's servants began as kul – slaves of the sultan – many outside sought to share in the benefits provided by the system, either for themselves or for their children. Long after the devşirme ended in the seventeenth century, parents sought to enter their children into the sultan's slave household. As late as the early twentieth century, many of the young women proffered to the imperial harem or to those of the viziers and other high officials were sent by their families, eager to share even at the humblest level in the benefits of being Ottoman. (Others were captured in war, a few were kidnapped, some bought. They would be sent to the palace by Ottoman officials seeking to carry favour or by slave-traders drumming up business.) This entry of outsiders into the closed ranks of the Ottoman system was one of the commonest complaints of Ottoman reformers from the beginning of the empire. Muslims, officially outside the narrow bands of entry to the system, were first adopting Ottoman lifestyles, in dress and behaviour, and then gradually infiltrating themselves as local or provincial officials within the ranks of the chosen. In the provinces furthest away from the effective control of the centre, in Syria and in Egypt, powerful local families soon assimilated themselves to the new ruling caste; in conquered Europe, the process was never effectively or actively prevented.

So, while the outward forms of Ottoman rule were legally unalterable, and nothing seemed to change, the substance behind them was mutable. For the Ottoman world had two aspects. The two worlds, public and private, were often incommensurable: what took place in the official arena was governed by the strict rules, while the domestic world had its own quite different limits and constraints. The doctrine of separation – of official from private, of male from female, of Ottoman from *raya* – was effectively sustained not by law (although elaborate codes were drawn up and refined) but by a sense of propriety. All Ottomans were able to decipher the apparent ambiguities with which the system was riddled. The model of virtue was Suleiman the Lawgiver, who tempered severity with justice, and warlike accomplishment with a love of culture. The elaborate structures established by Mehmed and then Suleiman were soon eroded, however. Indeed, they may never have worked at all as they intended, for the divisions between civil and military government, the restrictions of official government positions to the formerly Christian slaves of the sultan's household and the many ordinances controlling the janissaries were being undermined even at the apogee of 'Ottomanism' under Suleiman. But the system survived.

In the two decades after the Turkish failure at Vienna, the Ottoman territories in the Balkans were gradually reduced by the advance of Austria. But the Ottomans saw their victory over the Russians in 1711 and the recovery of parts of Greece seized by Venice as a sign that the old ways of war had been vindicated; they mounted a new assault into Hungary, with an army of 100,000 men marching north in the summer of 1715. But at Peterwaradin, on the Danube, the great army was routed and the survivors streamed home much as they had in 1683. The nadir of the Ottomans' fortunes came with the Austrian capture of Belgrade in 1717. It seemed to justify the gilded slogan emblazoned over the Hofburg Gate in Vienna, through which a victorious Prince Eugène passed in triumph: 'The Turkish Power Totters ... God always does Wonders against the Turk.'

After 1717, peace rather than war became the normal state. Ahmed III and his vizier, Damad Ibrahim Pasha, sought to avoid conflict. This was in part made possible by constant purges of the janissary corps (which had deposed Ahmed's brother Mustafa II in 1703, and placed Ahmed on the throne). Ahmed was renowned as a man who loved peace and pleasure, but his policy was built on the traditional Ottoman pattern: the noose, and the executioner's sword. The 'Tulip Era' was sustained by an active sultan – or, more precisely, by the sultan and his grand vizier – reclaiming power into his own hands.

The Tulip Era, named after the sultan's passion for the tulip, created its own ceremonial – an echo (conscious or unconscious) of the summons to Davut Paşa – which, like all Ottoman ceremonies, lasted long after its original purpose had been lost in the past. A French visitor described how in 1766, many years after Ahmed's death, the court was summoned to view the tulips and to walk in the gardens of the palace:

It takes place in April. Wooden galleries are erected in a courtyard of the New Palace. Vases of tulips are placed on either side of these rows in the form of an amphitheatre. Torches, and from the topmost shelves, cages of canaries hang with glass balls full of coloured water, alternating with the flowers. The reverberation of the light is as lovely a spectacle in the daytime as at night. The wooden structures around the courtyard, arbours, towers and pyramids are beautifully decorated and a feast to the eye.[17]

The sultan 'camped' in an elaborate kiosk prepared by the tent corps and erected in the third court, where he received the tributes and accolades from his courtiers and foreign dignitaries.

In his long reign, from 1703 to 1730, the Tulip Sultan and his courtiers built kiosks and pleasure gardens along the banks of the Golden Horn, abandoning the rigours of the battlefield for the lists of love and the pursuit of sensual pleasure. He dispatched embassies to discover the secrets of the West – to Moscow, Vienna and Poland, and above all to France. He even permitted the introduction of a printing-press, which could produce texts in Arabic script – a near-heretical device. The spirit of the Tulip Era found poetic expression in a line by Ahmet Nedim, a great favourite of the sultan: 'Let us all laugh and play, let us enjoy the world's delights.' For the first time, 'the world's delights' were not restricted to those within the Domain of Peace. Many Ottomans quickly understood the delights to be found in Europe, and beyond. Others did not, and continued to look back to the old customs as a means to restore Ottoman glory. In 1774 an 'old Ottoman', Jankili Ali Pasha, wrote a long memorandum, lamenting defeat by Russia but saying that the way forward was to go back, to the tried and tested customs of the past, rejecting foreign innovations.[18]

Yet Ahmed ultimately failed to control the forces of tradition. In September 1730, an Albanian janissary, Patrona Halil, stood up in the courtyard of the Beyazid mosque in the capital and declared that the sultan and the grand vizier had broken Islamic law by surrendering part of the Domain of Peace to the infidel. He found a ready audience in the janissary barracks at Et Meydan, and the insurrection became the focus for all those who opposed the new ideas of the Tulip Era. Faced with a janissary revolt, Ahmed made concessions to the mob that surrounded the palace, even yielding his grand vizier, Damad Ibrahim Pasha. However, in token of the vizier's long and faithful service, he sent him the silken cord and then delivered only the corpse to the rebels. The gesture cost him his throne.

His successor, Mahmud I, took almost a year to recover from the turbulent conditions which brought him to power. Eventually, the rebel janissaries, who had terrorized the city – rioting, burning and destroying many of the new palaces and buildings erected by the wealthy, as well as demanding protection from traders and merchants – alienated many of those who had formerly supported them. There was general relief when the new sultan invited Halil and the other leaders to a conference in the palace, then had them bound and strangled. Their severed heads were displayed in the first court on the same day. Mahmud behaved like a true sultan – cunning in lulling his enemies, then acting with ruthless speed – and there was no impropriety in the sultan exercising the full severity of punishment that custom allowed him.

Through the remainder of the eighteenth century a series of sultans and grand viziers either made no attempt to halt the opening to the West or actively encouraged it. Invariably they wanted to strengthen the army and navy, grafting Western technology on to the old Ottoman structures, reforming a corps here and there, building new shipyards or cannon factories. But, as all the Western technicians discovered, there was no deep commitment to change. When a grand vizier supported innovation, it flourished while his support was obvious and active. When his support was withdrawn, or was merely reduced, then the pace of reform first slowed, then halted. And, given the turbulence of Ottoman politics, many viziers lost their heads. Change and tradition existed in parallel, with first one then the other being in the ascendant. Consequently, no official who valued his head was likely to commit himself too firmly in favour of one cause or another.

This dichotomy, of parallel institutions, seemed a natural development to many Ottomans, since it echoed the concept of separation at the heart of Islam, and the Ottoman system. It was expressed most clearly within every Ottoman household. The master of a household had absolute rights over all within his family – slave and free – subject only to the laws of God. Yet it was considered improper for any man to interfere too directly in the affairs of the female half of his household – that was the responsibility of his mother and his wife. The division into the male, public, part – *selamlık* – and the female, private, part – *haremlik* – was absolute and unbridgeable. They were certainly not equal, for power and outward display – the best furniture, the finest decoration – were concentrated in the public, *selamlık*, rooms. Of course, the division of public and private also appeared in Western houses, where the 'rooms of parade' reflected the male attributes of power and prestige, but few nineteenth-century English visitors, critical of the separation of spheres in the Ottoman lands, drew any analogy with their own experience, where 'the household was divided into family, guests and servants; the servants were divided into upper and lower servants; the family into children and grown-ups; the children into schoolroom and nursery. It was considered undesirable for children, servants and parents to see, smell or hear each other except at certain recognized times.'[19]

The barriers in the West were not formalized along strict

gender lines, as they were under Islam. Ottomans of the same period, used to easier relationships within the family, would never exclude children in the Western manner, and certainly Ottoman slaves had a more secure status within a household than English servants. By the beginning of the nineteenth century it was not law but a sense of custom and propriety that controlled the way in which households were organized, and a similar shift was taking place in the outer world. The silken cords were soft and flexible, providing, it seemed to outsiders, no restraints or curbs at all. In practice, all Ottomans, in private and public, from the sultan downwards, were bound by this gossamer web, which they burst at their peril. The relationship between the theory and the practice of Ottomanism became increasingly fluid. The clear limits or boundaries laid down in the regulations of Suleiman were vanishing; the rigidity of law was transmuted into the more elastic (but still binding) restraints of custom and tradition.

CHAPTER 4

'The Auspicious Event'

THE EXTIRPATION OF THE JANISSARIES

The prevailing wind in Constantinople blew from the east, down the Bosporus from the Black Sea. In winter it brought rain and snow, and in the coldest years it pushed ice floes down the narrow straits to block the Golden Horn. But in summer the moist air filled the city with morning mists and, through the hottest part of the day, gave a steady cooling breeze that made the fetid streets bearable. June was noted for its sudden shifts in wind and temperature; it was consequently a time of year when tempers were short and crimes of violence and passion became more common. At the height of summer, a change in the wind was sufficient to alter the mood of the people from tense irritability to an outburst of fury and rage.

The winds from the west, off the land or gusting in from the Mediterranean, were hot and dry, and they carried a foul smell. On the days when there was a strong breeze from the north-west, noses puckered at the stench of the tanneries just outside the walls. When it blew across the city from the Sea of Marmara it carried another taint: not the rank stink of the tanneries, but a cloying, sweet smell of blood. Its source lay in the heart of the city, close to the Mosque of the Conqueror. The muezzin calling the faithful to prayer from the minarets of the mosque could look down into a great open area surrounded by tall wooden buildings, with a huddle of pens and lean-to shacks built up against their walls. A traveller out walking in the early morning would meet flocks of sheep being herded towards the square, and, as he approached closer, the terrified bleating and the warm odours of butchery announced a slaughterhouse. It was Et Meydan – 'the place of meat'.

Et Meydan was not a square in the European sense, although it was commonly known as Meat Square (and often confused with At Meydan the old Byzantine Hippodrome close to the Yeni Saray). The dusty expanse of open ground was dotted with groups of people, tents, horses and cooking-fires. The butcher's stalls clustered in the central area of the square sold joints of beef and lamb, as well as bundles of live chickens tied by their legs. In an arcade beneath the tall lodging-houses, shops offered boots and shoes, bales of cloth and all the profusion of goods to be found in the other markets of the city. But Et Meydan was no ordinary market. It was called Meat Square because here the sultan's regular soldiers, the janissaries, received their daily rations, cooked in the huge cooking-pots which were the proud symbol of each *orta* (regiment). It was the centre of the janissaries' quarter of the city. Their many barracks, houses and vegetable plots covered the western slope of the fourth hill, down as far as the sluggish waters of the river Lycus.

Et Meydan was not only a barracks: it was also a place of business. Many of the soldiers were craftsmen, working as cobblers, joiners and cabinet-makers, metalworkers or saddlers. They traded from small shops in the streets around Et Meydan or in the crowded alleyways which led down to the Golden Horn. They looked little different from all the other artisans in their workshops, but their true business was the profession of violence. Other janissaries in baggy trousers, short waistcoats and white turbans, with long knives and pistols in their sashes, swaggered through the streets. No one was quite sure how many there were in the city, since those claiming their daily rations in Et Meydan, and their quarterly pay in the second court of the palace, far outnumbered the possible total of active soldiers. When they were summoned to go to war in 1811, 13,000 paraded. But when the column set out to march north to the war, the number had dwindled to 1,600. The commonly accepted figure that there were 20,000 janissaries in the capital was probably not far wrong, since it included their children and families, as well as old soldiers retired on generous pensions.

The Ottoman name for the corps of janissaries was the *ocak*, meaning the communal hearth of an encampment. The symbolism of cooking and eating was deeply ingrained in their customs. The officers were given titles, like that of the colonel, *çorbası* (soup cook), which related to the provision and cooking of food. The soup-kettles were the most prized possession of the janissaries, the emblem of their corporate life: any regiment which lost its soup-kettles to the enemy was permanently disgraced. When the janissaries rioted or mutinied, they ceremoniously turned over the great copper kettles to signify that they no longer accepted the sultan's rations and renounced their obedience.

In the tradition of the East, the act of sharing food day by day, eating communally from the same pot, bound each individual to the community. Invitations to eat in the janissary messes were eagerly sought, because it brought the guest under the protection of the *ocak*. Some enlisted officially as *yamaks* – auxiliary janissaries, who were responsible for manning the fortresses along the Bosporus – while many of the porters, pedlars and street criminals of the city enlisted in one of the *ortas* to claim its privileges.

In 1821, the Revd Robert Walsh described the janissaries and their hangers-on as:

a motley group of boys and old men, without any settled uniform except for a large, greasy, very awkward, felt hat or bonnet . . . It is so ungainly that it is continually falling off. The colonels are distinguished by most extraordinary helmets which are so tall and top-heavy that they are sometimes obliged to keep them on their heads with both hands; indeed, every covering for the head among the Turks seems remarkably ill-adapted to convenience. The turban in its best state is unmanageable, and some resemble wool sacks, constantly balanced on the head like milk pails.[1]

Walsh further reflected the general opinion among Europeans, and one widely held by many Ottomans: that the janissaries had become corrupt and dangerous, and were a threat to the safety of the state. They were no longer the soldiers once renowned for their discipline in battle and their sobriety in time of peace. Until the seventeenth century, the recruits had been the *devşirme* boys who had come to Istanbul as the new slaves of the sultan. Circumcised and converted to Islam, they grew to manhood as labourers on the farm lands in Anatolia. By the age of seventeen or eighteen, they were strong and fit, ideal raw material for the regimental recruiting-officers. The *ocak* became their new family.

The sultan's service seemed a paradise to the farm boys. They were given fine uniforms, a long caftan over a short coat, full Turkish trousers, and heavy boots or sandals. They became *kapıkulu* – slave soldiers of the sultan. Some were trained as cavalry, but most became infantry janissaries, allocated to one of the 150 *ortas*. Each *orta* had its own insignia, which was painted on the doors of its barracks and embroidered on the white silk regimental banners and on the round tents in which each *boluk* (squad) of young soldiers lived on campaign. Within a few weeks of admission, most young janissaries had rubbed gunpowder into their arms or face and had tattooed themselves with that same insignia as an outward and visible sign of belonging to the honourable order of janissaries. The tall janissary cap, with its soft white neckcloth, was their badge of privilege.

In battle, the janissaries fought for the honour of the sultan and their order. The *kapıkulu* were trained to be brave rather than skilful soldiers. Each young janissary chose his own favourite weapon – the regimental armoury in the former church of St Irene was crammed with whips, flails, battle-axes, maces, halberds, billhooks, and a profusion of swords, daggers and light sabres – but they were expected to be familiar with all missile and hand-to-hand weapons, and during the sixteenth century the squads were trained in the use of firearms. Weapons changed, and so did the traditional uniforms, but the janissary approach to war remained the same. They used their long-range weapons – bows, crossbows or their long matchlock muskets – to keep up a continuous if ragged fire on the enemy, until they were ordered to close. Then the guns were put aside, and the janissaries drew their sabres or unsheathed their yataghans (long heavy short-swords). The strongest soldiers hefted their maces or *nacaks* (short-handled crescent-headed axes backed with a stout spike). The officers straightened the ranks and took their place beside their men. From the rear, the regimental *mehter* (military band) struck up a steady, insistent rhythm on its fifes, drums and horns.

A janissary assault was relentless, like an incoming tide. The advancing ranks shouted their battle-cries, and called on Allah to give them victory. Christian commanders noted that the janissaries would advance into an inferno of fire, climbing over piles of their dead, and would instantly exploit any flaw or weakness in the defence. If the first assault failed, a second and a third would follow. By the eighteenth century the janissaries' weapons and tactics were primitive by the standards of western Europe, but their steadiness in both attack and defence still frightened their opponents. The Austrian Marshal Ernst Laudon wrote admiringly of the janissaries defending a fortress against his attack in the campaign of 1788:

It is beyond all human powers of comprehension to grasp how strongly these places are built and just how obstinately the Turks defend them. As soon as one fortification is demolished, they merely dig themselves another one. It is easier to deal with any conventional fortress and with any other army than with the Turks when they are defending a stronghold.[2]

All janissaries looked with contempt on the disciplined ranks of Western armies, which loaded and fired their muskets like automata. They despised the elaborate drills and manœuvres which were the Western way of war; janissaries fought as individuals, and trained by slashing with their sabres at felt hats mounted on poles, and by bombarding large targets with their muskets. They saw no honour or bravery in the methods of the West. Despite defeat after defeat on the battlefield, they remained convinced that their way of war, hand to hand with the enemy, was right – the true Islamic path. Buried deep beneath their efforts to preserve their privileged position at all costs was this bedrock of principle. The janissaries could not be transmuted into Western-style soldiers without abandoning the customs which had grown up over two centuries and become the core of their regimental identity. The *ulema* – the religious leaders – had supported their refusal to adopt Christian ways of war, suggesting that *gazis* should fight as they had always done, with the weapons and tactics of their ancestors. Tradition became a religious duty.

The regimental pride and implacable determination which made the janissaries so fearsome in battle made them a menace in time of peace. The demands of war swelled the *ocak* far beyond its original limits. Until 1574 the corps had rarely exceeded 20,000, its size being limited by the number of boys brought in by the *devşirme*. But in the 1580s the conditions for admission were relaxed. The sons and more distant descendants of former janissaries were permitted to join the *ortas*. (The original prohibition on janissaries' marrying had long been ineffectual.) By 1591 the *ocak* had increased to almost

50,000. Reforming viziers and active sultans like Murad IV purged its ranks, but the total crept inexorably upwards. The *devşirme* was abandoned and the ranks were opened to volunteers: 30,000 became janissaries in this way during the war with Austria of 1687–98. By 1826 the government was giving rations and wages to 135,000 janissaries each month.

However, there were not 135,000 trained soldiers available for active service in the field. The muster roles were grossly inflated, either by officers' continuing to collect the pay of dead janissaries, or by the dead janissaries' wives and children who lived on the weekly rations of mutton and bread; in 1805 the number on the register had been 112,000, and there were no more soldiers available for service in 1826 than there had been twenty-one years before. The *ocak* had great benefits denied to the ordinary citizen. As soldiers, the janissaries were exempt from the taxes which weighed heavily on the peasants and townspeople; their privileged status gave them an advantage in all business dealings. Although their power was most evident in the capital, where the janissaries deposed and elevated sultans at will, or murdered officers and officials who opposed them, they dominated the provincial cities as well. Most of the 150 regiments were stationed in the provinces or on the frontiers. They had originally been placed there late in the sixteenth century, to protect the empire from internal rebels or raiders from outside the borders, but, once settled in comfortable billets, the janissaries refused to return to the field army. They remained in the same region for generations, building family ties and creating flourishing businesses. By the early nineteenth century they would fight only in defence of their own cities or privileges.

The traditions of the *ocak* bound one janissary to another; by 1800, these clan loyalties had virtually replaced allegiance to the sultan or to the Ottoman state. Adolphus Slade, a British naval officer, wrote that, 'No man who was not of them, no property that was not theirs was safe; and habituated to lawless excess, they knew no crime but what aimed at their privileges.'[3] The *ortas* stationed in the capital were even less keen to fight than the provincial janissaries, and the sultan was forced to rely on mercenaries or irregulars to fill out his armies. There was a steady flow of volunteers, who went by a variety of names. In the seventeenth century they were called *tüfekçis* (musketeers); other groups, some Christian and some Muslim, were called *seğmens* and *saricas*. In the eighteenth century they were known as *yamaks*. For them, military life meant regular pay and provisions, and the privileged position which the janissaries enjoyed. But in battle they were little more than a rabble, since they had no training and little incentive to fight.

It was an old problem, going back to the origins of the Ottoman state. The janissaries – the 'new troops' (*yeniçeri*) – had been created in the fourteenth century to provide a disciplined, loyal and selfless alternative to the erratic Turkish levies. Four centuries later, it was clear that, while the janissaries would fight like tigers to defend their homes and families – as the Russians and Austrians had discovered to their cost – they would no longer risk themselves in battle against the superior firepower and tactics of the Western nations.

By 1800, the janissaries, once Constantinople's protectors, had become its predators. Two or three times each day, squads set out from Et Meydan to patrol the city. They were armed with heavy clubs, and short-swords, but they rarely had to use them: fear of the janissaries was sufficient to quell most disturbances. Walsh described how the crowds scattered at their approach.[4] Patrols carried the instruments of punishment, the *feleke* and the bastinado, to administer summary justice. The *feleke* looked like a heavy bow loosely strung. The string was twisted around the bare legs of a victim and tightened like a garrotte. The pain was excruciating, but the real purpose of the *feleke* was to immobilize the criminal while a janissary beat the soles of his feet with a heavy stave, the bastinado. This was administered freely, and for the most trivial offences; a lavish bribe was the only means of avoiding pain and humiliation. Adolphus Slade wrote of the janissaries:

Lords of the day, they ruled with uncontrolled insolence in Constantinople, their appearance portraying the excess of libertinism; their foul language; their gross behaviour; their enormous turbans; their open vests; their bulky sashes filled with arms; their weighty sticks; rendering them objects of fear and disgust. Like moving columns, they thrust everybody from their path without any regard of age or sex, frequently bestowing durable marks of anger or contempt.[5]

Security was available to those who could pay. All the European embassies employed janissary guards, as did any wealthy Stamboulu who could afford their wages and bahşiş (bribes). The janissaries were also responsible for fire-fighting, which in the crowded conditions of the capital usually meant creating a fire-break by demolishing the wooden houses close to the outbreak. This too was a profitable field for extortion, with householders paying heavily to have their property left intact.[6] It was well known that in quiet periods the janissaries would themselves set buildings alight, unless the owners paid protection money. In the reign of Abdul Hamid I (1774–89), more than 140 fires were started in this way.

The janissaries' oppression fell most heavily on the Christians and Jews living within the city. They were forced to clear the ordure and offal from the streets around Et Meydan, although it was the janissaries' duty to sweep the area of their barracks. Oppression of the infidel was both a pleasure and a duty. The Baron de Tott noted that, 'The pleasure of knocking down and beating the Christian is so a high a regale [pleasure] for the Turks.'[7] Jews were sometimes killed when they failed to pay large bribes for their protection.

The sultan's kapıkulu were fanatical Muslims, and there had traditionally been an unspoken and informal alliance

between the mosque and the barracks. The religious authorities saw the janissaries as the protectors of the True Faith.
The *ortas'* silk war banners were inscribed with sentences
from the Koran, and their battle-cries glorified the name of
Allah. But even this close alliance of interests was being
undermined. In 1811 a gang of janissaries assaulted an elderly
imam, and its *ocak* then closed ranks around the offenders
when the religious authorities demanded exemplary punishment. In subsequent years there were regular street battles
between janissaries and the *softas* (theological students) attached to the imperial mosques. Students were subsequently
executed on the orders of the janissary commander, while
soldiers escaped without punishment.

Some of the *ulema* began to assert that the janissaries were
tainted with heresy, because of their close links with the
powerful Bektaşi order of dervish mystics. From their first
foundation in the fourteenth century the janissaries had been
connected with the Bektaşi, and the dervish *tekkes* (lodges)
were clustered around the janissary barracks and encampments
in the field. The mystics took a relaxed attitude towards some
of the traditional prohibitions of Islam, permitting wine-
drinking and allowing women to mix freely with men. The
janissaries found it a convenient creed, and Bektaşi dervishes
accompanied the janissary *boluks* on campaign, often to the
virtual exclusion of the official chaplains provided by the
ulema.

The regiments were out of control. The *ocak* was commanded by the aga of the janissaries – one of the great
officers of state, appointed directly by the sultan or the grand
vizier – but his orders were simply ignored. None of the other
senior officers, bearing resounding titles like Master of the
Harriers, Master of the Bear Hounds, Master of the Cranes,
was much more successful. Only the *kaimakam* (adjutant),
who was elected by the janissaries themselves and acted as
their spokesman, understood how to manage his difficult and

dangerous troops. The junior officers were appointed by senior-
ity from the ranks of the janissaries; even the colonels identified more closely with their men than with their commanders.
Many senior officers served very briefly: under Mahmud II,
most janissary agas lasted only a few months, as, one after
another, they failed to bring their soldiers to heel. Other high-
ranking officers had bought their positions, as they were
permitted to do after 1740, and were interested only in achieving a return on their large investment.

The opportunities for corruption were legion. The aga and
his senior officers received a percentage of the pay and allow-
ances for the whole *ocak*. Presents and bribes were expected
at every level. The colonels in particular were deeply involved
in the many fraudulent practices which swelled the payroll.
They invented the names of new recruits or forgot to report
the death of old janissaries; the estates of dead janissaries
were forfeit unless the families agreed to share the proceeds.
Colonels were responsible for supplying rice, butter and

vegetables to their men, and many profitable deals were organized with the quartermasters and city traders, at the expense of the Ottoman treasury. But the regiments looked after their own. Pensions were paid to the widows and families of loyal soldiers, while janissaries' children who did not themselves join the *ocak* were apprenticed as tradesmen. Girls were found husbands, and disabled veterans were given sinecures to provide a small income.

Contemporaries condemned the janissaries as cowards, swaggerers and scoundrels. The situation was absurd: soldiers simply refused to answer the call to arms, and the Ottoman state was forced into the position of hiring troops while its own well-paid regulars refused to step outside their barracks. In wartime, the sultan was forced to beg the support of the provincial pashas (governors), who recruited and armed their own troops. So too did powerful local magnates (*derebeys* – literally 'lords of the valleys'), and these would also provide men – but at a high price. The power of the local leaders increased as the authority of the central government declined. Officials like Ali, the pasha of Janina in northern Greece, simply ignored any government edict of which they did not approve. Until the sultan could command an army which would fight willingly against all his enemies, internal and external, he was condemned to impotence.

Every attempt to create an army which would fight met with stubborn resistance from the janissaries. All through the eighteenth century, the sultans and grand viziers had sought to persuade the janissaries that the nature of war had changed. They offered them weapons as good as those possessed by their European enemies, and instructors to train them in their use. They ordered them to adopt the bayonet, which had proved so devastating in the hands of the Russians and Austrians. The janissaries accepted the bribes and inducements, but refused to use the new 'infidel' weapons. Their refusal had a simple explanation: better weapons meant that they would have to fight, and they had no interest in dying on the battlefield. But their obstinacy had deeper origins.

They were the soldiers of Islam – 'the warriors favoured by Allah', as the Ottoman decrees described them. Their skill in battle had advanced the Domain of Peace from Asia into the heart of Europe: 'for a long time the enemies who presented themselves before the tight ranks of our battalions succumbed to the mace and the Muslim heroes, laden with booty, have had the right to vaunt themselves in the arena of glory.' Each janissary fought for his faith, assured like any *gazi* who fell in battle that he would be translated directly to heaven. He fought for the sultan, whom he served as his slave. But most immediately he fought for his regiment and the honour of the corps of janissaries.

They were a community united against the world outside. Each regiment gathered regularly around the great copper cooking-pot that symbolized its common life, and in assembly each individual janissary had a voice in the affairs of the regiment. Momentous decisions were frequently taken in this democratic fashion, as when they resolved to mutiny against the orders of the sultan, or to take vengeance on some enemy. In such discussions the lead was often taken by ordinary soldiers, or respected veterans, with the officers as powerless spectators. Only an officer whom the men respected could influence them: rank alone had no magic.

The regiment was a home for life. Even a janissary retired on a pension remained a member of his *orta*. The only way out was by desertion, death or, for a colonel, to take command of another *orta*. The janissary district, filled with the janissaries' wives and children, as well as the *yamaks* and the camp-followers, looked to a Westerner more like a village or a small town than a European regiment. Janissaries lived in their own houses or lodgings, and only rarely in barracks or billets. In the capital, and in the main centres in the provinces, like Baghdad and Belgrade, large sections of the city were given over to the janissary district, which was notable for being cleaner and more orderly than the surrounding streets.

Every great city of the empire – Aleppo, Damascus, Salonika, Adrianople, Bursa – had its contingent of janissaries, who over generations had established their own closed community, with its separate zone within the city. The first detachments had been austere young celibates, but by the early seventeenth century the janissaries had married and entrenched themselves within the local communities. And, faced with the irregularity of their pay from the capital, they had taken up trades, although officially forbidden to do so. By the end of the eighteenth century, the janissaries in many cities had abandoned all pretence that they were a fighting force: rather, they formed the centre of a network of powerful interests in each of their strongholds. The invitation to join an *ocak*, and more especially the right to a janissary meal-ticket, was the means by which many rural Muslims entered the life of the city.[8] Natives of particular regions congregated within particular regiments and companies.

But it was not only the porters, auxiliaries, and other hangers-on of the *ocak* who had an interest in the continuance of the janissary order. In 1735, in order to raise money for the war against Austria, the sultan decreed that it was legal to buy and sell the janissary paybooks (*esames*). These entitled the owner to eat at the sultan's expense from the common cooking-pot and (more important) to claim a daily payment. Speculators accumulated janissary paybooks like stock certificates, and drew an excellent revenue from them. A janissary aga of the mid eighteenth century whose goods were confiscated by the sultan was found to have paybooks in his possession which produced a daily revenue of 12,500 ackhes, while his banker was found to have another 9,000 at his disposal.[9] Many of these paybooks were, of course, from 'dead souls' – janissaries who had died but whose names had never been removed from the muster-books. Every attempt to purge the false returns seemed doomed to failure. Even the device of demanding that all janissaries muster in person to the sultan's war camp to make their claim and have their paybooks certified was undermined by the cunning of the paybook holders.

The system invited deceit and peculation, to the frustration of many brave and religious janissaries. Promotion was based not on merit but on connection – the Ottoman network of mutually sustaining clientage (*intisap*). Yet, time after time, this rotting carcass roused itself to action. In battle, especially in defence of their own interests, as when they fought off the French at Acre in 1799, the local janissaries displayed all their former courage and even impressed Sir Sidney Smith, the British commander in the city, by their steadiness under fire.[10]

To foreigners, their behaviour frequently seemed paradoxical, almost quixotic. Their refusal of European weapons was not based on self-interest, for many recognized that it would enhance their status and power in the state. The changes which they opposed most consistently were those which clashed with their self-image: that depended on the primacy of hand-to-hand conflict. Their sense of honour, as a warrior caste, was bound up with the use of swords, spears, daggers and maces. Even their nemesis, Sultan Mahmud II, declared how 'the enemies who presented themselves before the tight ranks of our battalions succumbed to the mace and the Muslim heroes.'[11] Here, heroism is bound up with the ethos of individual combat. The honours (the three or four feathers or *çelenk*[12]) which janissary heroes bore on their turban could be achieved only by great bravery in contact with a *superior* enemy. The value system of the *ocak*, the stories told each night, was founded on raw courage in battle. Just as the bravest warriors among the plains tribes of North America were those who 'counted coup' on the bodies of their enemies, so among the janissaries the longest tales told around the cooking-pots were of those who had been first into the breach

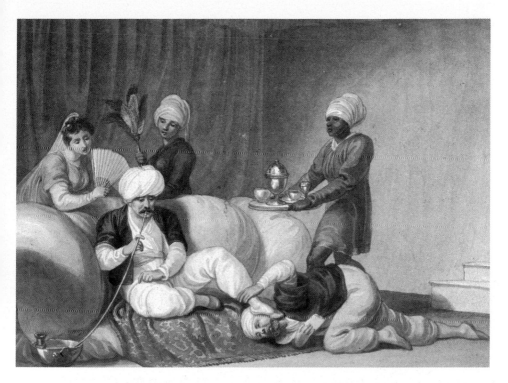

11. *Turkish Pasha Receiving a Petition,* William Craig
This engraving, published between 1810 and 1820, embodies almost every Western
stereotype of the Ottomans.

12. *View of Constantinople from the Hills behind Scutari, 1829,* Anon.

13. *The Streets of Stamboul,* Anon.

This provides an unusually realistic view of Stamboul. The relative emptiness of the
streets off the main thoroughfares was partly dictated by the difficulties of getting around
a city with muddy tracks that became a quagmire in winter. The streets were cleaned
by scavenging dogs, who would pick up the scraps dropped by the kebab vendor.

14. (Opposite above) *The Men's Bathhouse,* c. *1810,* Anon.

Painted from life rather than the imagination, by the 'Turkish Anonymous' who produced
the collection for Stratford Canning, it entirely lacks the air of sexuality which dominates
most 'Orientalist' images and which is even present to an extent in Rogier's image of
women leaving the bathhouse (plate 1)

15. (Opposite below) *Wrestling at the Yeni Saray,* Anon.

The Turkish passion for wrestling was as powerful in the Ottoman empire as it is
in modern Turkey. Here the sultan views from his kiosk while the wrestlers perform,
with women separated from the male spectators.

16. *Travelling in the Ottoman Empire, c. 1800,* Luigi Mayer (*c.* 1750–1803)
Luigi Mayer, widely known as an artist of Egypt and the Holy Land, left this sketch
of his journey in the Ottoman domains. The European-style coaches lurch across the
ill-made roads, bracketed on either side by the impaled corpses of malefactors.

17. *Costume of the New Troops, 1828,* J. Clarke
The new troops of Mahmud II, wearing their unique 'Islamic' uniforms.

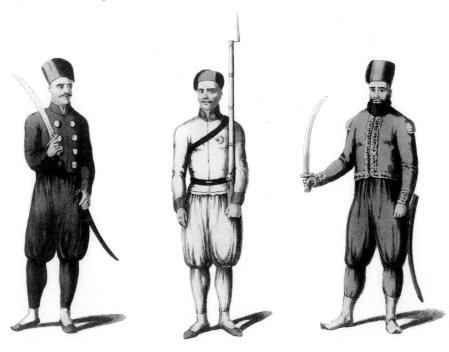

18, 19. *Ottoman Women,* Anon.
This traditional dress of women
changed more slowly than that
of men, but once the harem adopted
Western styles the transformation
was the more profound.

20. *Turkish Houses of the Bosphorus*, J. C. Bentley
In this plate from Julia Pardoe's *Beauties of the Bosphorus*, Bentley shows the old wooden houses to which Ottomans escaped in high summer from the stifling heat of the city. During the nineteenth century, more and more leading Ottomans abandoned the city for the 'rural' life along the Bosporus.

21. (Opposite) *The Mosque at Eyub*, J. Carter
The mosque of Eyüp (or 'Eyub') was a sacred shrine outside the capital; here the sultan ceremonially girded himself with the sword of Osman at his accession, symbolizing his determination to be a warrior of Islam.

22. (Above left) *The Sultan's Gardener* (Bostancı), Anon.
The Ottoman love of gardens and gardening elevated the status of the palace gardeners.
Sultans used them as bodyguards, secret messengers and executioners, as well as for
their more formal duties of tending the gardens and, above all, preparing for the annual
tulip ceremonies. Here a head gardener stands resplendent in his heavy red felt head-dress
and scarlet robes.

23. (Above right) *The Grand Vizier*, Anon.
The imposing figures of the vizier, with his white robe, heavy furs and dignified mien,
was appropriate for the most senior official of the Ottoman hierarchy. Under a weak or
incompetent sultan, the grand vizier was the monarch in all but name.

and lived to tell the tale. The emphasis on personal courage determined the way in which the janissaries were willing to fight, to the despair of commanders who wanted to deploy them in a different fashion. (By a curious parallelism, the Austrian army was also to be handicapped by their young officers yearning to win the equivalent of the janissary feathers, the *Maria Theresin Orden*, which similarly demanded an act of reckless individual courage.)

For the janissaries, the missile weapons – whether bows, muskets or rifles – were merely preliminary to the main business of a battle. They believed that European armies had abolished individual courage in handing each soldier a musket and a bayonet. They objected particularly to the bayonet, since they saw it as perverting the ethos of cold steel. The bayonet was a device that kept a soldier as part of a line, quelling his 'natural warlike ardour'. The Turks had never developed the antecedent of the bayonet, the long pike, which, massed both defensively and offensively, gave rise to the characteristic form of western-European battle in the seventeenth century. The consequences for the individual combatant were that 'by the end of the Thirty Years War, European armies were no longer a mere collection of individually well trained and bellicose persons . . . nor a mass of men acting in unison with plenty of brute ferocity, but no effective control once battle had been joined.'[13] The process of what William McNeill has aptly called 'the bureaucratization of violence' created

a consciously cultivated and painstakingly perfected art of war allowing a commanding general, at least in principle, to control the actions of as many as 30,000 men in battle. Troops equipped in different ways and trained for different forms of combat were able to manoeuvre in the face of an enemy. By responding to the general's command they could take advantage of some unforeseen circumstance to turn a stubbornly contested field into lopsided victory. European armies, in other words, evolved very rapidly to the level of the higher animals by developing the equivalent of a central nervous system, capable of activating technologically differentiated teeth and claws.[14]

The janissaries knew at first hand what the European style of war meant on the battlefield, and they wanted no part of it.

Their perception of the implications of 'reform' was thus doubly correct. Financially, once they no longer had the monopoly on organized violence, it was inevitable that their market value would decline, and even their basic security would be threatened. But, if they went along with the demands for change, they would cease to be the 'heaven-selected warriors', the chosen of Allah. Nor was this only the janissaries' belief, because all the dozen or so reform plans in the eighteenth century aimed to *restore* them to their old quality rather than seeking any radical innovation. Indeed, the traditional Ottoman skills of war could still produce dramatic successes, and a single victory would make up for many defeats. Thus the recapture of Belgrade in 1739 (after its loss in 1717) seemed an omen: the Ottoman tradition could still overcome all the military arts of the infidel.

Their links with the Bektaşi dervishes, who counted more than 7 million adherents in Anatolia and more than 120,000 in the capital, gave the janissaries a popular base of support. Many janissaries were converts to Bektaşi beliefs, a particular brand of Islamic zealotry:

We are the believers since the beginning of the world. Since that time we have recognized the unity of Allah – we will sacrifice our heads for this belief . . . We have been the intoxicated ones from all eternity – we are butterflies in the divine light – we are in this world a legion forever in ecstasy before the grandeur of Allah – we are so numerous that we cannot be counted on the fingers – our spring is inexhaustible – the profane ones can never know our state.[15]

Beneath the florid language, the fervour of their self-image as the 'heaven-chosen soldiers of Islam', unyielding in the face of all heretic innovations, was beyond question. Only the ascetic Wahabis of the Arabian desert also spoke with such intransigent ferocity. Corrupt, avaricious, deceitful though they had become, the janissaries still embodied the warrior, the *gazi*, the ideal of all Ottomans. Although they were much more loath to fight than they had been in the days of Suleıman, less willing to leave the comforts of the city for a campaign, once roused they fought as bravely as ever. The single janissary who had led the attack at the river Pruth in 1711 (see page 67) epitomized their traditional spirit and courage. Thus, although there was universal hatred for the illegal exactions and corrupt practices that had become almost synonymous with their name, there was a widespread belief that the order could and should be reformed, and restored to its former glory.

The first comprehensive programme for reform came from the young sultan Selim III, who succeeded his uncle Abdul Hamid I in the spring of 1789. He inherited a war with Austria and Russia which, despite one or two remarkable victories, ended in disaster. Both his father, Mustafa III, and his uncle had favoured change, and as a young man he had been taken to inspect the new artillery developed by de Tott. The experience of humiliating military failure by the Austrians during his first year on the throne made him all the more determined to move ahead with change. But, instead of pressing ahead by the traditional means of sultanic fiat, he revived the long-neglected concept of the state council (*majlis*) to consult the leading figures of the empire. Apart from Koça Yusef Pasha, the grand vizier, few of the advocates of reform whom he invited to submit written reports had much experience of war; and none (other than the two Europeans asked for their advice: a French artillery officer called Bertrand and the Armenian D'Ohsson, who was the chief dragoman (interpreter) at the Swedish Embassy) had any extensive knowledge of European armies.

Bertrand limited himself to commenting on a tendency in

Ottoman administration to equate the issuing of a firman, or decree, with accomplishing the desired result. Too little was done to ensure that the theory would be translated into practice. D'Ohsson suggested that reform would not work if it resulted only in the creation of 'parallel institutions' – the expensive and impractical tendency to create new modernized forces which would coexist ineffectually with the old unreformed corps. While the old intractability of the janissaries was left untamed, nothing substantial could be achieved. The Ottoman officials proffered much more conventional advice, although the suggestion of an Anatolian militia which would guard the homeland, while the reformed janissaries advanced the boundaries of Islam, aroused the sultan's interest.

Within a few months of the consultation, a torrent of decrees for the reform of the old corps, the *sipahis* and the janissaries, began to pour forth. They seemed to follow the least realistic and most conventional advice given to the sultan: that if the janissaries were properly honoured and esteemed they would automatically return to discipline and would, the advisers confidently asserted, once more be the loyal and fearsome troops of yore. They should be given regular and better pay, and, if they were to be instructed by European officers, then it was essential that those officers accept Islam, since the janissaries, as true believers, could not be expected to accept the statements and teachings of infidels.[16]

As a result, the janissaries' pay and living conditions were dramatically improved: the sultan was seeking to achieve by kindness what compulsion had failed to accomplish. For the first time in half a century, salaries were paid without deductions. and promptly every quarter, as stipulated by the regulations. The janissaries' barracks in the capital were enlarged and improved, and the sultan even paid them the traditional accession tax which had fallen into abeyance. They responded as they had in the past to every other proposal for reform: by rioting. Janissaries protested every time attempts were made to issue them with rifles and bayonets on the European model. Any foreign instructor, convert or otherwise, risked his head if he attempted to instruct them in the use of new weapons. Moreover, the attempt to purge the corps of its non-existent or non-functional members had no positive effect. Indeed, with the greater regularity of pay, the janissary paybooks became an even better investment, and the numbers in service grew to a high point of 109,000 just after Selim's fall in 1807 – almost double what it had been at his accession.

There is a sense of a routine traditionalist appeal to 'restoration' in the sultan's handling of the janissaries, as if he had no expectation of success. Certainly most of his energy went into the creation of an army of the New Order (*Nizam i-Cedid*), the 'Trained Soldiers [*Talimli Askeri*] of Allah'. Its origin lay in a group of German and Russian deserters taken by the grand vizier Koça Yusef Pasha while he was on campaign against the Russians in the north. They were offered privileges (and their lives) if they trained together as a drill troop, using captured Russian weapons and wearing costumes modelled on an approximation of European military dress. They formed platoons, fired by line and by volley, and practised bayonet drills, countermarches and the other evolutions of the European military manuals.[17] They had no purpose, except perhaps as the equivalents of the entertainers who had once accompanied Ottoman commanders as part of their baggage train.

On the conclusion of the war, the grand vizier returned to the capital with his toy army, and the sultan saw its manœuvres and volley-firing for the first time. In late 1792 the first Turks were recruited for this little army – about 100 taken from the streets of the capital. Deliberately, the vizier's men chose only those with no previous military experience, and certainly avoided those who had contacts with the traditional corps. They were spirited out of the city to a place called Levend Çiftlik, a flat piece of ground about ten miles north of the city, once used by de Tott as a training-ground for his artillerymen. Here they were placed under the command of those Germans and Russians who had formed the grand vizier's toy army and were drilled remorselessly. Meanwhile builders began work on barracks to house the new recruits, and it was clear from the scale of the construction work that many more could be expected.

To keep the existence of this small (but potentially highly controversial) force a secret, it was kept away from any contact with the traditional army. The Trained Soldiers were given their own administration, treasury and revenues, quite separate from the normal administration of war. The lucrative tax-leases that the sultan assigned to his new army provided money far in excess of immediate needs: the 'Supervisor of the Trained Soldiers' could afford to recruit officers in western Europe, and to replace the motley collection of uniforms and equipment with which they had begun. He also expanded his command to 200 men, once again drawn from the dispossessed of the Stamboul streets. For two years the little force developed in complete isolation, but by daily drilling and a rigorous code of discipline laid down by their French commander it developed a high degree of proficiency. By the autumn of 1794, when the existence of a full regiment of 1,600 men and officers was officially announced, it was confidently predicted that the Trained Soldiers would soon grow to an effective corps of about 12,000. Officially, they were designated as the 'Riflemen of the Corps of Gardeners', a masquerade that did nothing to disguise their novelty within the Ottoman host. But there were strong and accepted precedents for the creation of such special forces, and these showed the sultan's desire to avoid conflict with the traditionalists. In fact, at the time the new regiment was announced only 468 men and twenty officers had been installed at the new training-ground, and the elaborate barracks were only half-built: they still lived in a collection of tents and ramshackle huts. Nevertheless, their capacity to march, manœuvre and fire impressed all who saw them.

There were precedents in Ottoman history for the creation of the Trained Soldiers, but none that the sultan could publicly avow. They would in effect be the new janissaries. The many parallels were obvious. Just as the original fourteenth-century janissaries had been recruited among those with no roots in Ottoman society (through the *devşirme*), the Trained Soldiers were also from the margins of society – in their case, mostly the unemployed and the destitute of the Stamboul streets, or farm boys from rural Anatolia, sent by their beys or local potentates. And just as the first janissaries had developed their own unique style of war, so the Trained Soldiers were developing theirs. Because the well-paid ranks of the army of the New Order were open to the millions of village Turks, the pool of potential recruits was vast, and the regiment was quickly brought up to strength. A little colony was created at Levend Çiftlik, with three barracks, two mosques and a school. Tailors laboured to make uniforms, designed on French lines with soft, brimless blue hats like a Basque beret, red tunics and breeches. More French officers, sent from Paris by the new revolutionary government, taught a mixture of the old formal styles of European war and the newer patterns being developed in the armies of the Republic. In 1799 a second regiment was established at Üsküdar, once again at a discreet distance from the city. In the following year they moved into new barracks at Kadiköy, overlooking the Golden Horn. There, in their light-blue uniforms (to distinguish them from the first regiment at Levend Çiftlik), they could be seen drilling daily, both on the large parade-ground and on marches in the surrounding countryside. These new troops were drawn exclusively from the villages of Anatolia, and were carefully selected for health and strength; their families were paid a bounty for their enlistment. This, then, was the new *devşirme* advocated in the plans submitted to Selim, but, for the first time since the fourteenth century, it would be an army of free-born Turks.

The army of the New Order now grew rapidly. Four thousand three hundred men in 1799 had become 9,200 by 1801; by 1806, after massive recruitment in Anatolia, more than 22,500 men were under arms, either in barracks around the capital or posted to garrison towns in Europe and Anatolia. In combat, the 'toy army' had already shown its effectiveness at Acre and in blockading the French army at Rosetta, both in 1799. But the janissaries refused to have anything to do with the Trained Soldiers, neither fighting alongside them nor even sharing the same camp. Their hatred and suspicion grew as the red or blue uniforms became ever more visible in the Ottoman ranks. But, by growing so rapidly, the army of the New Order had departed from the plan for a well-trained and disciplined force. There had been twenty-seven officers commanding a little over 2,000 men in 1797, and there were still twenty-seven in charge of nearly four times that number four years later. By the time that the force had grown to its maximum size, it had more than 1,500 officers, but no army could increase its command so quickly without loss of quality. The new officers were not trained to the same standard as their predecessors, and certainly they had none of the close knowledge of their men which had formerly marked the regiments. The competition to enter the new army grew stronger, and influence was used to place the clients of influential Ottomans within its enlarged officer corps. Soon many of the same problems that had infected the janissaries – indiscipline, extortion and banditry – began to afflict the new army just as they had the old. The problem, as Bertrand had pointed out, lay in lack of adequate control.

Soon the new army began to follow the steeply downhill path taken by the janissaries. The daily drills began to fall into disuse, and indeed, with so many troops in the barracks, any effective manœuvres became impossible. But when they

were allowed out into the country they behaved so lawlessly –
raiding nearby villages on the route of march – that it was
necessary to confine them, idle, in barracks for ever longer
periods. So they were permitted to follow 'a trade in keeping
with the honour of the corps', just like the janissaries two
centuries before; and, although marriage was prohibited, many
contracted secret alliances with local women, often with the
tacit acceptance of their immediate superiors.

Much the same story – of high ambitions, substantial investment and, ultimately, limited results – could be told of the
Ottoman attempt to arm and equip the new force. The sultan's
aim was self-sufficiency, both in the creation of a modern
army and in all the material they needed for war. At first,
from 1792, finished arms and accoutrements were imported
from France, England and Scandinavia, but the large revenues
of the New Order were also used to buy the equipment which
would allow the Ottomans to make them for themselves. The
government of revolutionary France agreed to supply seventy
master craftsman and a full range of machines and equipment
from the arsenal at Valence to build a modern arms factory in
the old arsenal at Tophane, beside the Golden Horn. Rifle
works were set up at Levend Çiftlik and Dolmabahçe. Soon
each of the barracks had a gun factory attached to it, and
other countries vied to supply their own experts for this
lucrative potential market. Each gun works was equipped
with up-to-date machinery from the best European arsenals,
but the output was never up to the standard achieved in
similar factories in Europe. At every stage, officials made life
difficult for the foreign experts, refusing to admit all their
technicians to the country, obstructing access to supplies and
skilled Turkish labour, and even refusing to accept completed
arms for no reason other than whim. The resentment felt by
many Ottomans at the foreign intruders was incomprehensible
to most Europeans. By contrast, a huge new gunpowder
works, built in 1794 with all its machinery powered by water,

proved highly successful. But this was managed by a member of the Armenian community – an insider rather than an outsider – and, more important, was built under the active patronage of leading Ottomans. It soon supplied all the demands for gunpowder both from the Ottoman navy and from the janissaries and musketeer corps, as well as for civilian needs – hunting and the like. Since the great weakness of Ottoman artillery had always been the highly variable quality of the gunpowder, making accurate fire a matter of good luck rather than judgement, this was an advance of major importance.

The introduction of an arms industry to the empire was thus fraught with difficulty, and in Selim's reign achieved limited results: the Ottomans continued to depend on foreign suppliers for the most modern equipment. But, although some of the factories were destroyed when the janissaries later overthrew the hated Selim, others survived and formed the nucleus of an arms industry that lasted to the end of the empire, and indeed beyond.

By the spring of 1807, the sultan had – on paper – the military might to rout any opposing forces within the state. More than 20,000 Trained Soldiers were in barracks around the city, and, among the old corps, the 5,000 artillerymen at the arsenal were thought loyal to him. The Ottoman navy, enjoying new ships, better pay and pensions, had also benefited from the New Order. But at the same time it also seemed that good fortune – the essential quality of any successful Ottoman ruler – had deserted Selim. Deep in the heart of Arabia, the desert warriors of the Wahabi sect, fanatical in hatred for the wickedness of the world, had built a great army dedicated to purifying the Faith with fire and the sword. To many, they seemed reminiscent of the armies of the Prophet that had swept out of Arabia in the first century of the Muslim era. For the Wahabis, the luxury and good living in the holy cities of Medina and Mecca was an abomination, creating a new

Sodom and Gomorrah. In 1804 they captured Medina, the second city of Islam, and purged it of evil; then they rode north to take war to the gates of Baghdad. In the following year, the Wahabi leader Abdullah ibn Saud refused to allow the pilgrims on the *haj* – the pilgrimage to Mecca – to enter the holy city unless they accepted the principles of Wahabi puritanism. In 1806, the pilgrims humbled themselves before the Wahabis and were allowed entry.

The Ottoman sultan, protector of the pilgrims, whose personal presence on every pilgrimage was symbolized by his tabernacle, the *mahmal*, carried by a pure-bred camel at the head of the caravan all the way from Üsküdar to the doors of the Holy Kaaba in Mecca, could no longer ensure his people's safety. In February 1807 Abdullah entered the holy city of Mecca and loosed his warriors in an orgy of destruction and looting. They purged the city of anything which was not within the teachings of the Koran. Houses were stripped of jewels and finery of all sorts, and the Meccans (noted for their love of luxury) were reduced to the simple robes sanctioned by the Faith. Tombs and shrines which had become places of veneration were destroyed, and Abdullah ordered that his name should replace that of Selim in Friday prayers in the Great Mosque – a public humiliation in the most holy place of Islam.

The blow to Selim's prestige was incalculable. In his sonorous list of titles, he claimed to be 'Warrior for the Faith, Custodian of the Sacred Relics, Protector of the Pilgrimage, Servitor of the Two Holy Cities and [less certainly] Caliph'. For more than three centuries the Ottoman sultan had been honoured among pious Muslims as 'Defender of the Holy Places'. Over decades, the Ottomans had invested heavily in troops and fortresses to make the dangerous pilgrimage road as safe as possible. Now the sultan was unable to prevent a rebel turning back pilgrims from the holy cities of Islam, and each Friday his humiliation was made public. In Stamboul it was rumoured that the loss of the holy cities was a divine retribution for the 'infidel innovations' of the sultan. In the janissary barracks, and in the fortresses along the Bosporus, defended by the *yamaks*, it was whispered that the sultan had violated tradition and religion and would pay the price.

In the closed world of the Ottomans, violence often erupted from deeply laid conspiracies. The rumours grew fattest when they fed on fact, like the loss of the holy cities. But the reformers unwittingly provided their enemies with the material for their plots. It was mischance that, early in the morning of 25 May 1807, Raif Mahmud Pasha, the commander of the fortresses guarding the Sea of Marmara, set out in his official barge for the fort at Rumeli Hisarı, to pay the *yamaks* their wages, due each quarter. This was the first pay-day since the capture of the holy cities had become common knowledge in the capital. Earlier in the month it had been decreed that the *yamaks*, by origin mostly Albanian and Circassian mercenaries, would in future be incorporated within the army of the New Order and not attached to the corps of janissaries. Officers had already been sent to the forts, and experienced instructors were ready to train them in the new disciplines, while 3,000 uniforms were hastily made up in the factory at Üsküdar. The pasha did not know that he was entering a trap. Conservatives among the sultan's ministers had long planned to foment an uprising among the notoriously wild and temperamental auxiliaries, so they had encouraged Raif Mahmud to press ahead with the incorporation, while secretly sending messages to the *yamaks* warning them of the plan and saying it was yet another infernal scheme by 'renegades, infidels and bad Muslims'.

Raif Mahmud was escorted not by janissaries but by a detachment of Trained Soldiers, resplendent in their light-blue uniforms, and the pasha had taken with him some of the new uniforms, arms and accoutrements, in the hope of persuading the fortress troops to welcome the New Order. The little flotilla came to shore by the fortress walls, and the auxiliaries assembled in the courtyard to receive their pay, After the money had been distributed, and at a sign from Raif Mahmud, the commander of his small guard, named Halil Aga, addressed the sullen troops before him. He extolled the benefits of the New Order, and appealed to the *yamaks*' Islamic patriotism, calling on them to fight for the sultan and their faith. He appealed to them to join him among the Trained Soldiers. Cries of 'apostate' rose in the courtyard, and a large group of the auxiliaries pushed forward and, as the contemporary accounts describe it, 'tore him in pieces'.[18]

The pasha and most of his party escaped to their barges, and rowed at speed along the coast to a landing-place, hoping to hide until nightfall and then to escape over the hills to the barracks at Levend Çiftlik. But the mutineers had roused all the *yamaks* along the coast, and, when they landed, the pasha and his men were set upon and hacked apart. Messages were sent to all the other fortresses along the Bosporus, to kill all the New Order officers within their walls. Soon all the forts were in the hands of the mutineers. At nightfall, detachments of armed *yamaks* gathered at Büyükdere, where the mutilated bodies of the pasha and his guards were still lying unburied, and prepared to march on the capital. Their elected leader, Kabakji Mustafa Aga, sent messengers to the janissaries in the city, saying the time had come to restore Islam and end the hated foreign rule.

Faced with what was clearly a serious uprising, Selim summoned his ministers. While they were in session, they received a message brought by group of *yamaks*. Kabakji Mustafa declared that the revolt would be ended if the main body of the Trained Soldiers was confined to its barracks and the remaining detachments were withdrawn from their training-camps along the shore. Some of his officials, notably the arch-conservative head of the *ulema*, counselled the sultan to agree, and he acquiesced. But these were the very men who had secretly fanned the flames of the *yamak* outburst and were already conspiring with the janissaries against the sultan. When the rebels realized that the troops, who outnumbered them many times over, would not be used, they became much bolder. Now almost 1,000 strong and gathering adherents all the time, they marched on the city, while sending fresh demands to the palace. They now demanded that the sultan abolish the New Order and disperse the Trained Soldiers. Once again advised by his secret enemies at court, he agreed, in the belief that this would end the insurrection. Confident that the revolt would now peter out, he retired to the harem for the night.

During the hours of darkness, the other corps, supposedly loyal to the sultan – the bombardiers, the artillerymen – came over to the rebels. From dawn on 28 May, a fleet of small boats crossed and recrossed the Golden Horn, bearing heavily armed auxiliaries and artillerymen. The gates were opened by the janissaries of the guard, and the rebels swarmed up to the janissary quarter, all heading for Et Meydan. Soon the square was full of armed men, and there they were joined by all the janissary officers, who had resolved to overturn their cooking-pots and forswear their allegiance. Meanwhile, the Trained Soldiers mustered at their barracks and prepared to march on the city on the sultan's command. But instead they received his edict announcing their immediate dissolution. With the threat of intervention removed, the rebels' demands increased yet again: now, additionally, they required that the leaders of the reform should be sent to Et Meydan to answer for their crimes against Islam.

Selim temporized. Three of the rebels' intended victims were allowed to 'escape' through the palace park to safety, but three others were in attendance at court, and their fate was sealed. However, to spare them the humiliation of being dragged to Meat Square – and perhaps even dying under torture – he ordered them to be quickly strangled, and their heads were sent out to the rebels at the gates. One luckless official attempted to escape, but was captured by the *yamaks*. Once they found out who he was, they cut him in pieces with their long knives. Throughout the city, armed bands searched for anyone who had been associated with the New Order. After Friday prayers, the janissaries gathered at Et Meydan to hear a fiery speech from the *yamak* leader. Until the throne was free of Selim, he cried, Islam would not be safe. The only way to eradicate the evil for all time was to depose the sultan.

The janissaries acclaimed Kabakji Mustafa, and set out from their barracks to gather before the closed gates to the palace. They demanded a new sultan. In the mid-afternoon, the chief religious dignitary of the Ottoman empire, the *şeyh ül-islam* Attaulah Efendi, the hidden hand behind the revolt of the auxiliaries, read his fatwa to the massed janissaries. Selim, he declared, was no true sultan and should be deposed on the grounds of misrule and the violation both of tradition and of religion. Still the gates of the palace remained closed, but, shortly after the decree was read, Selim's secretary was discovered in the streets and was torn limb from limb by the angry mob. His head was hacked off and thrown into the palace as a warning to his master. Meanwhile the mob called loudly for 'Sultan Mustafa' – Selim's cousin, who was within the palace – to replace the infidel sultan. After a show of reluctance, Mustafa agreed, and, while Selim retired to imprisonment in the harem, the great gates were opened and the waiting janissaries were allowed to pour into the first court. In front of the Gate of Bliss, in the third court, eunuchs set up the imperial throne, and then the gates were opened to admit the mass of janissaries and the people of the city, to acclaim their new sultan.

The final act of the drama was to follow a year later. The short reign of Mustafa IV was inglorious, and the end of the reforms did not magically restore the health and fortune of the empire. The factions which had brought him to power dissolved and re-formed. The janissaries and *yamaks* monopolized the streets of the city, out of control, while the sultan, the grand vizier and the religious leaders who had unleashed the plot against Selim now looked on impotently. The real power now lay not in the capital but in the north, with the battle-hardened army of Bayrakdar Mustafa Pasha in the Bulgarian provinces. He had been a notable reformer within his own army, and his troops included many members of the former New Order, while many sympathizers with the reforms who had escaped from the capital had joined him in the north. Mustafa Pasha took upon himself the role of kingmaker, with the aim of restoring Selim. In July 1808, after endless and exasperating negotiations with the new authorities in the capital, he decided to settle matters by force. He marched his troops south, arriving at the Cyrpyci Meadow on 20 July. On the following day, the first detachments – mostly Albanians, the cream of the Ottoman forces – entered the city and began to arrest all those who had been involved in Selim's deposition. The northerners demanded the release of Selim from the palace, but the gates of the Yeni Saray were closed against them.

In anger, Mustafa Pasha marched back into the city with his full army of 15,000 men, heading for the palace, and for the Sublime Porte, to confront the grand vizier. The gates of the Porte were shut and barred, but the angry soldiers broke them down and forced the terrified grand vizier to hand over the seals of office. Then the army forced the religious authorities to reverse their earlier fatwa and restore Selim to the throne. A delegation of religious leaders, escorted by a band of Albanians, entered the palace and handed the sultan the decree deposing him. His fury sent them away in fear of their lives, and the gates of the inner courts of the palace closed firmly behind them. Immediately, he sent his executioners to kill not only Selim but the young Mahmud, the only other remaining member of the house of Osman. If both could be removed, then Sultan Mustafa IV, the last of the line, could not be deposed.

They found Selim in his rooms at prayer. When he saw the cords, he struggled violently, but in the end he was overpowered and the executioner completed his work. Then they began to hunt for Mahmud, who – forewarned – had left his rooms. The hunters moved systematically through all the innumerable passages, closets and rooms of the palace. The Albanians now demanded entry and, when the inner gates were opened, they saw the lifeless body of Selim, which had been thrown down in front of the Gate of Bliss. From behind the massive studded wooden doors someone shouted, 'Here is the sultan whom you seek,' and, in fury, the soldiers of Mustafa Pasha smashed their way through into the precincts of the third court and dragged Sultan Mustafa from his rooms, demanding to know the fate of Mahmud. Fortunately, the young man was soon found alive and acclaimed as the new sultan; Mustafa was allowed to retire to the rooms occupied only a few hours before by the unfortunate Selim.

The new sultan, Mahmud, was twenty-three years old. He had not suffered the complete isolation from reality which had reduced so many sultans to ciphers in the hands of their ministers: Selim had kept him well informed both about the progress of the reforms and about political and diplomatic matters in general. But Mahmud had also seen the disaster that had overcome Selim, and had known the terror of being hunted through the palace by Sultan Mustafa's executioners. What distinguished him, even in his first days on the throne, was a quality of determination coupled with patience – the very qualities that observers had once noted in his ancestor Mehmed the Conqueror. They did not know that he also shared his ancestor's capacity to bear a grievance over decades, until it could be expunged in blood.

In 1808 he had few assets at his disposal. Ottoman politics had become polarized around the issue of military reform and the whole notion of innovation. For a time, the reformers were once more in the ascendant. Appointed grand vizier, Mustafa Pasha reconstructed the army of the New Order, but now called it the New *Segbans*. The *Segbans*, the Masters of the Hounds, were one of the traditional corps attached to the janissaries. Selim had attempted to appease the sensibilities of traditionalists by pretending that his Trained Soldiers were part of the *bostancıs* (gardeners' corps); Mustafa's transparent device was no more successful.

The northern army treated the capital like a conquered city, and soon replaced the janissaries as the object for popular hatred. In their new European-style uniforms, the *Segbans* stood out in the city streets, and soon every crime, every breach with tradition, was attributed to their agency. The janissaries, by contrast, had remained in their barracks, with all their duties assumed by the grand vizier's troops. Early in November, a simmering revolt in the Bulgarian provinces – the basis of his power – forced Mustafa to send the bulk of his troops north to defend his interests, leaving only a skeleton force of *Segbans* and some untried Balkan highlanders, more bandits than soldiers, to guard the city. On the night of 14 November, the last day of the fast of Ramadan, the *Segbans* appeared at the great celebrations which traditionally ended the days of abstinence. Tempers were always short towards the end of the fast, and it was often a time when riots broke out in the city. Now, the appearance of *Segbans* on the most holy day of the year roused the janissaries to revolt.

The *yamaks* sent messages to Et Meydan that the time had come to rise up and destroy their enemies before they destroyed the whole janissary order and attacked Islam itself. The presence of the highlanders gave credence to these claims, for why else should these wild men be roaming the city streets? The *ortas* armed themselves and marched through the city to the Sublime Porte. They called for the grand vizier to show himself, which wisely he did not. In the early morning the janissaries burst in and found that he had taken refuge with his guards in a tower used as a powder-magazine. A furious fire-fight began, but, since they had no artillery, the janissaries could make little impression on the solid walls of the impromptu fortress. Plainly the grand vizier hoped to hold out until his supporters could be rallied; messages had been sent to the *Segbans* in camp at Levend Çiftlik, calling for them to march on the city. Some of the janissaries managed to clamber up on to the wooden roof of the magazine and set fire to it. As the beams and timbers burned through, they made ready to drop down on the defenders in the rooms below. But a spark from the burning roof ignited the powder and, in a vast explosion, the grand vizier, his guards and many of the besieging janissaries were killed. The body of Mustafa was found, taken to Et Meydan, and there impaled on a stout wooden stake set up in the centre of the parade-ground.[19]

Leaderless, the remaining *Segbans* in the city fell back on the sultan's palace, where they had their encampment in the first court. Soon the janissaries, roused to fury by the death of their comrades at the Sublime Porte, surged up the hill to the main gate of the palace and called for the restoration of their sultan Mustafa. Here, in reverse, was the same situation that had figured in the July rising: now it was Mahmud who determined to make himself the last of the heirs of Osman by killing his cousin. Accordingly, the stranglers were sent to the former sultan in his rooms in the harem; he submitted quietly to the silken cord.

When the janissaries were told of the death of Mustafa, and were ordered to return to their barracks, they responded by attacking the palace itself. Ladders were brought from the city, and they attempted to scale the high walls. They were beaten back by the *Segbans* whom Mahmud had stationed along the walls by the gates, but the vast perimeter of the palace made it almost impossible for it to be defended without an army, and the sultan's guards and the terrified *Segbans* could not hope to hold out for long against a serious assault. This, too, was just the situation in which the janissaries excelled: with their blood up, and the fortress walls before them, they were almost beyond control. Nothing seemed to shake their determination.

The sultan still had his lines of communication to the sea through the water gates of the palace, and he sent a message that the Ottoman warships at anchor in the Golden Horn should bombard the janissaries milling around the palace and then shell their barracks. Soon the city glowed with the light of many burning buildings, but, since the fire-fighters (all janissaries) were massed by the gates of the palace, the fires raged uncontrolled. The wooden houses of the city were dry after the summer and autumn, and the weather was fine: soon the areas close to the palace became an inferno:

the most popular quarter of Constantinople was covered in a sheet of flame. The cries, the groans of women and old men and children, attracted no attention, and excited no pity. In vain they raised their hands, in vain they pleaded for beams or planks to save themselves from their burning houses by the roofs ... they were seen with indifference to fall and disappear among the flames.

But still the janissaries persisted with their attacks, using the lights of the fires to mount assaults throughout the night. The senior janissary commanders, fearful that the sultan would rally all the troops outside the city to exterminate them, entered negotiations, and quickly agreed to a decree of obedience in exchange for a full amnesty for the rising. But the angry janissaries around the palace refused to accept the agreement, demanding instead the heads of the *Segbans* within the walls and suggesting that Mahmud was not worthy to sit on the throne.

Still the attacks continued, and janissary sappers managed to cut off the palace water supply, while others attempted to set fire to the buildings within the still-impenetrable walls.

A few janissary parties had succeeded in gaining entry from the palace park, but they were hunted down and killed by the sultan's bodyguards and the palace troops. Put to the test for the first time, the design of the courtyards, one within another, each protected by high walls and a single great gate, made them ideal for defence, and vulnerable only to artillery.

The janissary soldiers were now in a state of ecstatic rage at those within, all of whom they now declared, without discrimination, as worthy of death. This was the frenzy that Christians had faced so many times before, but now it was directed at the house of Osman itself. The *ulema* sought to mediate, calling on the janissaries' allegiance to the Faith. Finally, after two days of increasingly ferocious fighting, with bands of angry janissaries roaming throughout the city tracking down their supposed enemies, and fighting with parties of the sultan's loyal troops, an outline agreement was framed. While the negotiators talked, the artillerymen decided to join the rebels and prepared to cross the Golden Horn with their light guns. Faced with this new danger, Mahmud and the defenders resolved not to surrender but to fight on to the death. Finally, the religious leaders forced both sides to a compromise. The janissaries would lift their siege, and the *Segbans*, without their arms and no longer wearing their hated uniforms, would be allowed free passage to Levend Çiftlik, where they would be disbanded. In return, the sultan would grant amnesty to the janissaries, and no more would be heard of the projects for reform.

On the morning of 18 November the great gates of the palace opened, and a long line of *Segbans* marched out – no longer the trim disciplined force of a few days before and, in traditional trousers, turbans and coats, looking very like the janissaries who crowded and jostled them on every side. They marched in good order towards the city walls and the safety of their barracks, but, within a few hundred yards, taunted by the janissaries, the first of them were cut down by the yataghans of their enemies. Suddenly the janissaries closed on them and, in a frenzy of blood, most of the *Segbans* were butchered within sight of the palace walls. A few of the officers were more formally decapitated. The heads were cut from the mutilated bodies and piled outside the gate of the palace, as a taunt and a warning to the sultan within. Then the janissaries struck camp and returned to what was left of their barracks.

There had been many janissary revolts in the history of the house of Osman, but nothing to match the contest between Mahmud and those who now became his most hated enemies. Not since the capture of the Queen of Cities by Mehmed the Conqueror had war been waged on such a scale in the streets of the city, as ships rained down fire from the Golden Horn. Never before had a sultan been prepared to fight to the last and, if necessary, to die wrapped (metaphorically) in the sacred banner of Islam and armed with the sword of Omar. And, although the janissaries had many times broken their solemn oaths and killed the friends and advisers of a sultan or a grand vizier, never before had they breached an agreement negotiated under the sanctity of the Faith by the religious leaders of the empire.

The sultan's answer was to ignore their taunt and to uphold the peace. He had conceded nothing, except under the guarantee of the *ulema*. He had defended Islam within the sacred portals of his own palace. And, as one contemporary historian of the empire expressed it:

An imperial edict was issued in favour of the janissaries. All the customs of the Franks, and all the late innovations were solemnly cursed and renounced . . . But there were men of thought and action among the Turks, who had seen all these things and who saw in them only the sterner proof of the necessity of sweeping changes. They were obliged to think in silence . . . Above all, the Sultan himself watched from year to year for the hour and the means of ridding himself and his country from these worst, these home-oppressors of his race.[20]

Mahmud knew the history of his house and, above all, he knew the virtues of patience.

In the decade following the assault on the palace, Mahmud made few moves which would antagonize the janissaries, and none that was not, at the least, sanctioned by custom. He demanded routinely that they should be more attentive to their military duties, but he made no attempt to attack the huge overhang of corruption. Those who owned janissary paybooks were left in secure possession of their assets. He made efforts to improve the training and status of the artillery-men and the transport troops, increasing their numbers gradually from 6,000 to 14,000 by 1826. The fleet, which had loyally stood by him in 1808, was rewarded with new ships and better pay. He took advantage of the war between Russia and France to make peace with the Tsar in 1812 – advantageously, since the Russians were preoccupied with the Napoleonic threat. And, slowly, he began to extend his authority in the provinces, where the Ottoman writ had almost ceased to carry any weight. His method was always to seek allies rather than to make enemies. He provided the sons of the provincial notables with posts in the Ottoman administration, but far away from their families' source of power. Wherever possible, Mahmud bound the provincial warlords into the system.

His most notable overmighty subject was Mehmet Ali, the Ottoman governor of Egypt since 1805. Mehmet Ali had built the power of his office and the wealth of Egypt after destroying the Mamelukes, the Egyptian equivalents of the janissaries. The sultan knew how, in 1811, his governor had invited 300 of the leading Mamelukes to a feast at the palace in Cairo. An eyewitness described the events thus:

The Mamelukes had left the Divan and were arrived at one of the narrower passages on their way to the gates of the citadel, when a fire from 2,000 Albanians [Mehmet Ali's guards] was poured in on them from the tops of the walls, and in all directions. Unprepared for anything of the sort, and embarrassed for want of room ... those who were not killed by the fire were dragged from their horses, stripped naked, with a handkerchief bound about their heads, and another round their waists ... they were led before the Pasha and his sons, and by them ordered to immediate execution. Even there the suffering was aggravated, and instead of being instantly beheaded, many were at first wounded mortally. They were shot in different parts of their bodies with pistols or stuck with daggers ... the Pasha sternly refused them mercy ... impatient until he was assured the destruction was complete.[21]

The author, 'an English gentleman', used this as an example of Ottoman barbarity 'from a PASHA who piques himself upon his mercy'. There had been only one other such episode in recent memory:

The body of prisoners [2,000 of them] were marched out of Jaffa in the centre of a large square battalion. They foresaw their fate, but used neither complaints nor entreaties to avert it. They marched on silent and composed. They were escorted to the sand hills to the south-east of Jaffa, divided there into small bodies, and put to death by musketry. The execution lasted a considerable time, and the wounded were dispatched by the bayonet. The bodies were heaped together, and formed a pyramid, which is still visible, consisting now of human bones, as originally of bloody corpses.[22]

But these were not the victims of Ottoman brutality, but Turks (janissaries for the most part) who were massacred by the French army of Napoleon in 1799. The Ottomans had no monopoly on atrocity.

The immediate consequence of the extermination of the Mamelukes was the creation of the reformed Egyptian army – the *Nizamiye*, or Ordered Army – a lesson which cannot have been lost on the sultan. In 1813 these same troops slaughtered the Wahabi army and recovered the holy cities of Arabia. Mehmet Ali sent the keys of the cities to the sultan, and once again the sultan's name was honoured in the Friday prayers at the heart of Islam. There were great celebrations throughout Stamboul when the massive bronze ceremonial keys were received and carried in procession to the Treasury, where they were placed beside the sacred symbols of the Prophet.

In 1818 the triumph was completed when an Egyptian army led by Ibrahim Pasha captured the Wahabi leader, Abdullah ibn Saud, and sent him in chains to Constantinople. Mahmud handed the Saudi chief to the *ulema*, who questioned him closely and found him an incorrigible heretic. They returned him to the justice of the sultan. Abdullah was publicly beheaded, as an eyewitness observed, 'at the door of the gardens of the serail', and his head was displayed on a marble column. It had been open to the sultan simply to execute the Saudi leader as a rebel, but by handing him to the religious authorities he made clear his wish to cooperate with the *ulema* rather than oppose it. Similarly, he signalled his wish to collaborate with loyal janissaries, by promoting able officers, excusing them the normal *bahşiş* that was paid for advancement, and honouring courageous soldiers, often sending them his personal thanks in writing for acts of special bravery or obedience to orders. By slow stages he began to build a body of support within the two most powerful and conservative bodies of the state.

In 1822 the sultan began to cut himself off from the past, and to reveal his true intentions. He dismissed his long-serving grand vizier, Halet Efendi, who was one of the most rooted opponents of reform. But, unlike that of most Ottomans opposed to change, Halet's dislike was based on knowledge. As ambassador to Paris from 1802 to 1806, he had known the West at first hand and he had not liked what he had seen. 'I ask you to pray for my safe return from this land of infidels, for I have come as far as Paris but I have not seen this Frankland that some people speak of and praise ... In what Europe these wonderful things ... are to be found I do not know.'[23] The grand vizier's position was strong, because he had allies among the religious leaders, but the sultan used the perennial faction fighting within the Ottoman hierarchy to undermine Halet and replace him by a more pliable character.

Even out of office Halet posed a danger; he was too powerful and too well connected to be left alive. He had been retired temporarily to Konya, under the protection of an order signed by the sultan guaranteeing his safety and expressing his master's heartfelt esteem for his faithful servant. However, the former grand vizier had scarcely settled at his destination – a Mehlevi dervish lodge of which he was a lay member – when a messenger arrived with a personal order from the sultan requiring his execution. Halet was shown the cord, and he asked only to perform his ritual ablutions, say his prayers, and sip a final cup of coffee before submitting to the executioner, praising the sultan's mercy. Within a few days his head was on display atop a marble column in the outer court of the palace.

After Halet's fall, the sultan filled the two key posts – aga of the janissaries and grand vizier – with a bewildering succession of short-term appointments. No other official was allowed the long tenure of office that Halet had enjoyed; even the sultan's own supporters were rotated in and out of office. He installed a trustworthy cleric in the key position of chief of the religious directorate, but he also ensured the loyalty of the ordinary members of the *ulema* by increasing their pay and privileges. Mahmud laid great emphasis on his own piety, endowing scholarships, building mosques and paying for the publication of pious works. By slow and methodical stages, he broke the historic connection between the janissaries and the religious class, which had long given sanction to the janissaries' misuse of power. Meanwhile, he was also slowly amassing Western arms and equipment, stored secretly within the palace.

There is no doubt that Mahmud had prepared a plan not to reform the janissaries but to remove them entirely. Halet

Efendi, it was said, had once quoted a traditional Turkish saying that summed up Mahmud's method:

The mole works in silence and darkness but he makes his way as he purposes. The pace of the tortoise is slow; but if he make sure of every ascending step, he at last reaches the hilltop. The scorpion conceals his sting, and is a quiet and contemptible reptile, until he can dart it with death into his foe.[24]

The question was not *if*, but *when* and *how*.

Events presented Mahmud with an opportunity. The success achieved by Mehmet Ali after the destruction of the Mamelukes was never far from his mind, although the janissaries were too astute to fall for the ruse that had undone the Mamelukes. Since 1811, the triumphs of Egyptian arms had provided the few sparks of hope in an international scene far from favourable to the Ottoman and Islamic cause. In 1825 and 1826 Stamboul was full of news of the success of the Egyptian army which the sultan had invited to restore order in his rebellious Greek provinces. Years of janissary failures were followed by a string of successes for the skilled and disciplined Egyptians. These soldiers were portrayed as the warriors of Islam defeating the evil forces of Christendom. Stories of Greek atrocities were again circulated through the capital, and refugees from the Morea were encouraged to speak of their terror. In 1821, in the region north of the Mani peninsula in the Morea, 15,000 Muslim villagers had been massacred, and 40,000 fled to the towns and fortresses still in Ottoman hands.[25] Little was heard of this in the West, while much more was made of the Ottoman response. Mahmud executed prominent Greeks resident in the capital, and hanged the Greek patriarch from the gates of his episcopal palace on Easter Sunday, refusing all pleas for the body to be buried. After a few days it was flung into the sea.

On 23 April 1826, after a long siege, the Greek fortress town of Missolonghi was captured by Egyptian troops led by

Ibrahim Pasha, reconqueror of Crete and the Morea. With this example of a Muslim triumph before the people, Mahmud slowly revealed a plan to create a reformed army, not on any Western model but on that of Egypt. The proposals were framed within the language of Ottoman orthodoxy. The troops were to be called *eskenjis*, which was simply the traditional name given to the janissaries when on active service. Nor were these to be Anatolian peasant boys, foreign mercenaries or the riff-raff of the streets, like the Trained Soldiers or the *Segbans*: rather, selected janissaries would be chosen as a mark of honour from each of the messes in the capital.

The proposals were formally announced to a large gathering of Ottoman officials representing the civil, military and religious elements of the state, then the long and detailed decree was read, and the grand vizier asked *şeyh ül-islam* Kadi Zade Tahir to give his opinion. The cadi (the hand-picked choice of the sultan) announced the formal judgement of the *ulema* on the proposed decree, both to the janissaries present and to those in their barracks. His support was unequivocal – no previous plan for reform since the days of Suleiman had been so fully endorsed by the supreme judges of Islam:

Behold, O Janissaries, it has been demonstrated by the requirements of the laws of the book and the custom of the Prophet, and by the consensus of the *Ulema* of the people of religion, as well as the well known axiom of geometry that in order to kill the enemies of religion and successfully to resist the infidel, it is the religious duty of Muslims to learn military drill. Are you honestly resolved to assist in the attainment of the desires of His Highness to become organized and disciplined soldiers? Are you willing to accept the responsibility of persevering in this endeavour and do you swear to do so? [26]

'Yes, we swear to do this,' shouted all the janissaries who were present. When the documents were read again in the messes, officers marked the decree with their seals, signifying approval. It was said that so many wanted to sign that signet-makers were brought to the messes to make up seal rings so that the officers could affix their marks. In the end more than 150 janissary officers publicly declared their support and signed the document.

These deliberations occupied, in all, four days of open discussion, at each stage in the presence of the grand vizier. In the janissary messes, comment and advice was sought; but, unsurprisingly, no negative views were put forward. So much of Ottoman administration took place in private, concealed from all public knowledge, that these open debates had great symbolic importance – the sultan was seen publicly to consult with all his officials and with the janissaries themselves. But, unlike Selim's use of the *majlis* (see page 101), the officials were required not merely to advise and to submit written proposals in private but to declare their support openly for a decree which had been read to them clause by clause. It bound all the officials who signed, irrevocably, to support the sultan's firman sanctioned by the full authority of the *ulema*.

But, within a few days, many of the janissary officers who had signed the firman were saying that the reforms would never be accepted by their men, that their men would not serve in the *eskenjis*, nor would they serve alongside them. The sultan, however, had no intention of holding back the reforms: if anything, they were pressed ahead more firmly than ever. It was soon clear that the military revolution had been developed over many months. Within days of the decree being promulgated, the arms and uniforms for the new soldiers were ready for distribution: they had already been prepared, and were in store in the sultan's arsenal. The *eskenjis* would look very like the troops of Ibrahim Pasha, although they had knee-breeches, cloth leggings and a tall conical hat, not the trousers and tight coats of the European armies on which the Egyptians had modelled their uniforms. A similar sensitivity determined that long rifles and bayonets would not be issued, although these were used by the Egyptians; instead, each of the men would be provided with a carbine and a sabre. But the sabre was more symbolic than practical: these were to be riflemen relying on their fire-power, not the old style of janissary *gazi*.

Rather than delaying the implementation of the decree, the renewed janissary resistance seemed to hasten it. Having secured the approval of all the authorities in the state, the sultan was pressing forward with increased urgency. Small groups of volunteers had been quickly selected to form the first *eskenji* detachments and the first parade of the new troops had originally been scheduled to take place outside the city walls, on the Cyrpyci Meadow. But now Mahmud decreed that Et Meydan should be cleared and the ceremonial parade of the *eskenjis* should be held in the heart of the janissary quarter. Moreover, after the first parade was held, the leading religious and civil officials would speak publicly to the assembled janissaries, mustered to watch the drill, about the duty of all to accept reform.

The speed with which the sultan and his advisers moved dislocated janissary plans for resistance. Less than two weeks separated the promulgation of the reform decree and the first parade, which was to be held on Monday 12 June 1826. The mutineers' first plan had been to begin an insurrection at the first drilling of the new troops, but their preparations were incomplete. Also, many in the ranks began to question the likely success of a rising. While they hoped that their fellow janissaries who had become *eskenjis* would come over with their arms and equipment, some potential rebels realized that there were many in their ranks who now favoured reform. Moreover, they would gain many privileges within the ranks of the active troops, as well as the blessings of the Faith.

At first light on the day of the parade, orders were sent to each of the fifty-one designated *eskenji* detachments to muster between three and five men to Et Meydan, to parade after the noon prayers had ended. At the prayers, all were still wearing their old janissary uniforms, and were indistinguishable from the other janissaries at prayer. Then they gathered in line and were each handed the new uniform and arms. As they removed their turbans and their old uniforms, like so many snakes sloughing their skins, they were transformed into new soldiers. They had already learned the rudiments of the new drill, and quickly re-formed into companies, with fifty-eight of their officers standing in a long line before them.

The Ottoman officials, lead by the *ulema*, came forward on to the parade-ground, where they spoke at length about the need for the new organization and stressed that these were soldiers dressed and equipped like the ever-victorious Egyptians – good Muslims, not surrogates for infidel European soldiers as the janissaries had claimed. Then each of the officers was called forward and given a carbine which was then publicly blessed. When each of the officers had received his sanctified firearm, four drill instructors appeared – none of them European – and the officers went through the evolutions of the new drill. No ammunition had been sent, so there was no firing-practice, and the authorities had deliberately supplied three different patterns of carbine, of various calibres, lest the janissaries seize the weapons during the parade and turn them on the sultan's men.

The political meaning of the parade was not lost on those who were present. Holding it on Et Meydan, the centre of the janissary order, challenged the janissaries' credibility in the most dramatic fashion imaginable The *eskenjis*' casting off their old janissary uniforms, and donning the new, was another public affront to the janissaries. Finally, the blessing of the rifles negated in the most authoritative manner possible the janissary claim that rifles were not suitable for an Islamic soldier.

The private soldiers began their drills on the next two days, led by their officers, but on Wednesday 14 June they found janissaries from many different *ocaks* beginning to gather outside the square. After the sun set, the streets were filled with small groups of fully armed janissaries moving towards the square, carrying their copper soup-kettles. Their intention was obvious. At dawn on the following morning, surrounded by thousands of elated janissaries, the leaders of the revolt ordered the cooking-pots to be turned over, in a formal renunciation of the sultan's rations and thus his authority.

The mutiny had begun, but it had not started well. At midnight on the night before, they had planned to kill the janissary aga, but they failed to find him: he hid in a small privy while they ransacked his palace. Similar attempts to find the grand vizier and other notables were also unsuccessful: prudently, none of the leading Ottomans had remained within the city walls overnight. Mahmud was in his new palace at Beşiktaş, along the Bosporus, but, as soon as he heard that the long-expected uprising had started, he called for his barges and set out for the Cannon Gate of the palace. Janissaries could be heard in the streets close by the great mosque of Aya Sofya, shouting, 'Death to the givers of fetwa's, to the writers of judicial acts, to our opponents, to all who wear the *kayuk* [the huge turbans which marked the most senior Ottoman officials] . . . Death to Sultan Mahmud. Down with the *Nizam i-Jedid*. Long live the sons of Hajji Bektash [i.e. the janissaries].'[27] While they roamed the streets, all the leading religious and secular officials, plus many of the senior janissary officers loyal to the sultan, successfully eluded their enemies and gathered in the palace park. They were joined there by large numbers of soldiers from the professional corps – the engineers, marines, and bombardiers, as well as the horse artillery, complete with their guns. Surprisingly, the janissaries made no serious effort to halt the gathering.

By the time that the sultan's little flotilla was sighted, rowing briskly against the tide, more than 14,000 loyalists, many of them armed with muskets or rifles, had gathered at the palace. And the arsenal was still full with arms and ammunition gathered for the *eskenjis*. Opposing them were up to 20,000 janissaries, plus their allies and dependants within the city. Many of those loyal to the sultan remembered the terrifying events of 1808, and the enormous damage and bloodshed that had resulted. Some even suggested that they now should seek to reach agreement with the janissaries. But Mahmud's arrival stiffened the spirit of resistance. He summoned all the leaders to the great Hall of Circumcision, used for the ceremonies of state, and in a loud voice declared:

Since the day of my accession, I have taken great pains and care to serve the interests of religion and to do good unto the people delivered into my care by Allah. You all know that the Janissaries, whose rebellious acts have so frequently threatened my rule, have found me forgiving . . . In order to avoid bloodshed I have pardoned them. I have gone even further and have laden them with privileges. Finally, not being constrained in any other way than by kindness, they have sworn themselves to submit to the new reform law. What do you declare to be the appropriate measures to subdue these traitors and snuff out this insurrection?

He then asked the *ulema* present to decide what should be the fate of the rebels. They replied, so the history of these events records, in unison: 'The law declares that one should fight the rebellious. If violent and evil men attack their brethren, fight these men and send them back to their natural judge.' A sentence of death on the rebels was prepared and sealed by all the religious authorities. One of them cried, 'What are we delaying for? Let us all hasten against the enemy and crush them with cannon and sabres.' By now, all were in tears, including the sultan, who went to the Treasury and returned carrying the flag of the Prophet. He told them, 'I want to join you and fight in the midst of true Muslims, to punish the ingrates who offend me,' and the grand vizier had the greatest difficulty in persuading him to stay within the palace.

At morning prayers, a message was read in every mosque of the city, calling on all true Muslims to rally to the sultan at the palace. Within a few minutes, thousands began to gather in the square in front of the palace, although the janissaries now began to attack the mass of people gathering in ever greater numbers, and running battles broke out with some *softas* who were armed with knives and swords. Recognizing that the people had turned decisively against them, and seeing the loyal troops ready to march on the janissary quarter, the janissaries began to fall back, to the jeers of the crowd in front of the palace gate.

As the janissaries began to retreat, the sultan rode on his horse towards the great gate of the palace, and took up his position in the rooms above the gate, looking out over the city. Then he watched the huge mass of soldiers and citizens set off along the wide Street of the Divan. The artillerymen pulled their guns behind them, and the soldiers marched in ranks, in accordance with the new drill regulations, which they had begun to learn in earnest. When they reached the great square by the mosque of Beyazid, dominated by the forbidding walls of the Eski Saray, (now occupied only by the wives and concubines of former sultans), the vast mass, numbering 20,000 or more, divided into two huge columns. One, led by the artillerymen, set out directly towards the janissary quarter, which lay to the left of the main highway amid a tangle of smaller streets. The larger group – of students, tradesmen and the ordinary people of the city – set off towards the city walls, intending to swing to the west and to envelop Et Meydan from the north.

The rebel leaders, fearful about the outcome of their insurrection and the unparalleled popular revulsion against them, now sent emissaries to the grand vizier, saying that they were ignorant men and only a misunderstanding had prevented them from accepting the new drills. But by this time the first of the soldiers had come to within a few hundred yards of Et

Meydan. Before them the gates of the barracks were barred, and as they moved cautiously forward they were hit by a fusillade of shots from a group of janissaries hiding by a 'fountain' – the public water source from which the neighbour-hood drew its water. The assailants ran back to the barracks, while the artillerymen, incensed at the deaths of their comrades, loaded the two light cannon they had dragged with them up the hill. Inside the barracks, the doors and gates were blocked with large stones, making it impossible for anyone to get in – or out. The artillery commander shouted to the janissaries that they had one more chance to seek the sultan's 'magnanimous pardon', but the only response was cries of abuse and defiance from within the walls.

By now the square barracks block was surrounded on all sides, and the janissaries began firing from within. In response, soldiers were sent on to the roofs of nearby buildings and began to return fire. With the first shots from the cannon, half the barracks gate was blasted away by round shot, killing many of the janissaries who were massed behind it. Many more were hurt by the stone splinters from the mass of building stone they had piled up behind the gate. Chang-ing to grapeshot, the gunners scoured the entrance once more, and then an intrepid soldier ran forward and managed to pull open the undamaged gate, so that the troops and the cannon could enter the huge open square. Under a barrage of aimed fire from the soldiers, the janissaries, who numbered many thousands, retreated towards their large wooden bar-racks buildings, which filled part of the square; in front of them stood the butchers' stalls that gave Meat Square its name.

One of the gunners put a flaming torch to the stalls, and they began to burn furiously, with a smell of roasting meat filling the air. Some of the embers fell on the wooden barracks buildings, which began to smoulder. Soon they were ablaze, either from the volley after volley of musket fire which was poured into the cowering janissaries at close range, or deliberately fired by one of the soldiers. Now there were piles of dead or dying janissaries inside and outside the barracks buildings, but a desultory firing continued from within. More cannon were brought up close to the buildings and raked them again and again with grapeshot, which tore the barracks apart and scythed down the janissaries still resisting. By now the smell of roasting meat had a sweeter tinge and there was a crackling of burning fat as the charred bodies of the 'heaven-sent warriors' began to explode in the intense heat.

Even when the janissaries had ceased to return the soldiers' fire and merely cried for mercy, the firing increased rather than died away. A few janissaries had managed to escape into the range of buildings around the square, only to be hunted down and hacked to death by the exultant soldiers.

The fires had now spread uncontrollably to the wooden buildings in the streets around Et Meydan, and still more janissaries were forced out of hiding. They were taken prisoner and herded to the grand vizier, who was in the Sultan Ahmed mosque close to the palace. The Hippodrome nearby began to fill with janissary prisoners – some from the battle at Et Meydan, but many more taken from other janissary barracks around the city. As they were interrogated, those guilty of rebellion were strangled or beheaded, and their bodies were piled around a large plane-tree in the centre of the Hippodrome. It was a belated vengeance for the viziers whom rebellious janissaries had hanged from the same tree in 1648. Almost 200 bodies were soon piled up beneath its spreading branches.

Teams of soldiers now scoured the streets with lists of former janissaries who had been involved in the rebellion against Selim. More than 120 were executed in the cellars of the house of the janissary aga. In all, at least 6,000 died, either

in the assault at Et Meydan or in the subsequent vengeance.
(Some authorities put the figure as high as 20,000, but this
seems improbable.)

The news of the victory and the purge was relayed to
Mahmud, who came to see the consequences of his work in
the Hippodrome. He called his council to him in the palace,
and it was decreed that the name of 'janissary' should be
banned, and the order should be disbanded throughout the
empire. But those janissaries who had remained loyal were to
be rewarded, and the paybooks would continue to be
honoured.

A long decree, outlining the long and evil history of the
janissaries was prepared, and a catalogue of their crimes was
read to an excited throng of officials from the pulpit of the
Sultan Ahmed mosque, to cries of 'let us obey our ruler's
command' from every part of the mosque. Teams of scribes
began to copy the decree, and a hundred copies were circulated
to every mosque in and around the capital, to be read from
the pulpit after prayers, and many more to the provinces.
Special instructions were sent by Tartar messengers to the
governors of provinces and cities where the local janissaries
were especially strong, so that they could make a pre-emptive
attack on them before they heard the news from the capital
and rose in rebellion. Meanwhile all the gates of the city were
sealed. The British ambassador, Stratford Canning, who
watched the events from the heights of Pera across the Golden
Horn, described how, as the days passed:

The mere name of janissary, compromised or not by an overt act,
operated like a sentence of death. A special commission sat for the
trial, or rather for the condemnation of crowds. Every victim passed
at once from the tribunal into the hands of the executioner. The
bowstring and the scimitar were constantly in play ... The sea of
Marmora was mottled with dead bodies.[28]

Over a space of a few days, janissaries in provincial cities who had become little more than local traders were suddenly attacked and massacred without warning. Away from the capital, guilt went with the name 'janissary', and the killings were often accompanied by great atrocities, as those who had envied the janissaries' privileged status took out their spite on the bodies of those who had, until only a few days before, lorded it over their neighbours. One pasha told how:

Not many of these dogs of janissaries have taken refuge in my pashalik, for they fear me; but, Allah be praised, one did fall into my hands. I had known his fine deeds at Stamboul . . . so I had him come and see me. When he arrived, we chatted for a moment . . . then I had him imprisoned in a door and had the door walled up. It will please Allah to have him die of hunger.[29]

In the space of a few days, Mahmud signalled that the transformation of Ottoman society had begun. He appeared at Friday prayers on the day of the victory, 16 June 1826, and instead of the traditional guard of janissaries and halbardiers he was surrounded by artillerymen and bombardiers. Within a week the first of the new soldiers to replace the janissaries – now called the 'Triumphant Soldiers of Allah' – were ready for inspection by the sultan. A visitor to the first court of the palace on that historic day, 'was suddenly caught by the sound of fifes and drums, and to his astonishment, [there appeared] a body of Turks in various dresses but armed with muskets and bayonets, arranged in European order, and going through new form of exercise . . . the men acted by word of command both in marching and handling their arms.'[30] Then the sultan appeared to inspect them. He was wearing not the traditional imperial robes – no caftan, nor a turban – but a new style of dress: 'His Highness was dressed in Egyptian fashion, armed with pistols and sabre, and on his head, in place of the Imperial Turban was a sort of Egyptian bonnet.'[31] This was the measure of the Auspicious Event,[32] as the destruction of the janissaries was now officially termed. Cast out with them were all the trappings of the old Ottomanism, while Mahmud – more secure on his throne than any sultan since Suleiman – was free to build anew.

CHAPTER 5

Stamboul, The City

WESTERN IMAGES OF THE OTTOMANS

European travellers found Stamboul irresistible. From about 1800 onwards, a stream of visitors braved the dangers of travel by sea or the discomfort of the journey overland to visit the fabled city. They felt that they 'knew' the Queen of Cities long before they saw its mosques and palaces. They had bought paintings and engravings of its exotic 'Oriental' splendours. They had fantasized over its mysterious veiled women, and seen the inner life of the harem laid bare on stage. They had agonized vicariously over brutal Turkish punishments – the hooks, the impalings, the discarded harem women drowned by cruel eunuchs in the sea off Seraglio Point. They came expecting the city of their imagination, and found reality an anticlimax.

The city had many names. Europeans called it Stamboul or Constantinople. The Turks called it Constantinople as well, but in conversation would also use its Turkish name, Istanbul. The unwary visitor quickly discovered a minefield of ambiguities. Only the old Byzantine city within the walls could properly be called Stamboul. The city across the Golden Horn was Pera, which the Turks also called Beyoğlu. 'Istanbul', the name given to the city by Mehmed the Conqueror, embraced them all – Stamboul, Pera and later the suburbs which grew up along the Golden Horn and the Bosporus. So it was in theory, but a Turk might use 'Stamboul' in its narrow sense to mean the old city, or 'Istanbul' to include the whole of the capital. The potential for confusion typified a city which used to operate four different calendars (two Christian and two Muslim), and where every clock or watch showed two separate systems for telling the time of day.[1]

Stamboul (meaning the old town within the walls) was like most capital cities of the early nineteenth century: often squalid and sometimes sublime. But many European visitors, inflamed with Romantic notions, came expecting to discover their imaginary Orient. A young Londoner, Albert Smith, revealed his dismay when he arrived from Malta aboard the French steamship *Scamandre* in September 1850:

I must confess that the first view of Stamboul as we neared that part of the city certainly disappointed me. I had heard and read such extraordinary accounts of the *coup d'œil* that my expectations had been raised to such an absurd height, that although I knew I was staring hard at the Mosque of St Sophia, and that the dark cypress grove coming down to the blue water before us surrounded the Sultan's Hareem and this blue water was the Bosphorus, my first exclamation to myself was 'And is this all?'[2]

The artists and engravers had quickly discovered which images of the city sold best. Many illustrators conjured up fantasies which they knew would satisfy their audience; the subjects and the content of the images were conventional rather than true to life. The artist John Frederick Lewis had no difficulty in preparing a highly successful set of *Illustrations of Constantinople* fully three years before he first set eyes on The City in 1837. One of the most popular views was *Stamboul as Seen from the Golden Horn*, which was the vista travellers first encountered as they sailed up the Bosporus from the Mediterranean. Julia Pardoe was transfixed by her vision of the East: 'The great charm of Constantinople to a European eye exists in the extreme novelty, which is in itself a spell; for not only the whole locality but all its accessories, are so unlike what the traveller has left behind him in the West, that every group is a study and every incident a lesson.'[3] Until a ship reached Seraglio Point, the succession of domes and minarets seemed a confused jumble:

But when we rounded the Seraglio Point, and slowly glided into the Golden Horn, where the whole gorgeous panorama opened . . . in its unequalled loveliness, the feeling of wonder and admiration became absolutely oppressive . . . the magnificent domes and lofty minarets that detached themselves from the amphitheatres of buildings as we proceeded, and stood in clear white relief against the bright blue sky.[4]

To the traveller, it seemed that the city itself was in motion, as new buildings were disclosed and new relationships were struck between the slender verticals of the towers and the endless recession of domed roofs. Stamboul's allure lay in this distant prospect. The Revd Robert Walsh, newly appointed as the embassy chaplain, was enraptured as he looked across the Golden Horn from the secure comfort of the British embassy:

On the other side of this living lake rises the city of Constantinople. It displays a mountain of houses extending both ways, as far as the eye can reach; the seven hills form an undulating line across the horizon, crowned with imperial mosques . . . they are altogether disproportionate to everything about them, and the contrast gives them an apparent size, almost as great as the hills on which they stand . . . The whole of this view as I gazed on it from the palace windows, was singularly lovely, and I never contemplated one which seemed more to invite a visit.[5]

There was another side to Stamboul. This reverend Scots gentleman had come overland in December, and his first encounter had been with an unattractive aspect of The City. The cold of a Thracian winter was 'more intolerable' than any he had experienced in his native land far away to the north, and Walsh was consequently in no mood to appreciate the city as an aesthetic experience. His first impression was decidedly un-Romantic:

As I approached the capital [along the coast road] there was no cheering appearance of a dense population, no increase of houses and villages, to intimate the vicinity of a large city. For the last ten miles we did not pass a house nor meet a man; and we suddenly found ourselves under the walls, before I was aware I was approaching the town. We passed through the Silyvria Gate, and the desolation within was worse, because less expected, than that without. As our horses' hoofs clattered over the rugged pavement, the noise was startling, so desolate and silent were the streets. The only other noise we heard was that of some savage dog, who had buried himself in a hole under the foundation of the house, and howled dismally at us as we passed.[6]

But this was an accurate view of the city and its life. The illusion was the picturesque vista which Walsh saw the following day across the waters of the Golden Horn.

When Walsh came to know (and dislike) The City, he compared it with the less salubrious parts of his native Edinburgh. There too the former houses of the nobility and merchants had been abandoned by their owners, long departed for more genteel neighbourhoods, and the narrow lanes or wynds of the Old Town were piled high with filth and refuse. In London and other great European cities, many fine buildings were also embedded in slums, and few thought it worthy of comment, but travellers found the decay of Stamboul disturbing. Like Walsh, they came expecting the sublime and found the reality rank and offensive to the senses. Most foreigners, like Walsh, blamed all these failings on the 'Oriental' lassitude of the Turks; very few visitors looked for other causes. But there were reasons for the stark contrast between the impression of The City at a distance and that close to.

The broad Thracian plain, which Walsh had noted on his map as 'naked country covered with tumuli', extends past the walls into Stamboul in a narrow finger of low hills, roughly from the north-west to the south-east. This line of six hills runs to the tip of the triangular promontory on which The

City was built. On either side of this high ground, the land falls steeply away down to the shoreline, with the Sea of Marmara on one side and the long harbour of the Golden Horn on the other. Close to the point where the great land walls meet the sea, the ground rises again to form a seventh hill; and the river Lycus flows down into the heart of The City along the valley cleft between the seventh hill and the other six.

Stamboul gained and lost from its unique situation. The geology of the peninsula predetermined how both Byzantines and Ottomans would use this incomparable site. The best land for building was along the line of the hills. The low ground towards the sea was unhealthy and more often enveloped by the winter fogs and the summer heat than the land above. But much of the unhealthiness also had a human cause. The rich and powerful occupied the high ground, and for centuries their houses and palaces discharged their sewage and foul wastes downhill. The liquids in this putrid mess trickled down the slope to the shore. 'There are no sewers in Constantinople, and the offals are thrown in heaps to accumulate in different places.'⁷ Stambouli society was graded vertically: the worst place to live was in the filth at the bottom of the hill. Such a pattern was not unique to The City. Other cities which were built on a ridge of high land, like Edinburgh, also created a moat of foul-smelling effluent outside their walls. But Stamboul was partially cleansed by the scouring sea, which carried the streams of filth from The City out into the deeper waters of the Bosporus. Without the swift-flowing waters, the Golden Horn would have become a midden.

The Ottomans built where their predecessors had built. The high road of The City ran along the backbone of the hills, dipping down into the valleys between them. It started from the Milion, a triumphal Byzantine archway in the great open space before the imperial palace, the Yeni Saray of the Ottoman sultans, built on the site where the acropolis of the

Byzantines had once stood. On the seaward side of the square stood the mosque of Aya Sofya, the symbol of Ottoman victory, and behind it the Blue Mosque of Ahmed III, set against the shimmering azure of the Sea of Marmara.

The great state buildings to either side of the highway that led from the Yeni Saray to the Edirne Gate were all Ottoman. Only the Aqueduct of Valens, carrying water into The City from reservoirs in the hills outside, gave a clue to Stamboul's Christian history. The other visible remains of Byzantium were little more than a few columns and some standing stones. In the heyday of Byzantium, the main highway – the Mese – had been flanked by a marble portico and a succession of triumphal columns; by the time of the conquest, only the paved highway remained. The road climbed up to the crest of the second hill, which the Forum of Constantine had once occupied, and then down across the valley between the second and the third hill to the Eski Saray built by Mehmed the Conqueror on the site of the Forum of Theodosius. The traces of Byzantium were eclipsed by a succession of mosques which proclaimed the glory of Islam and the line of Osman. Both the son and the great grandson of the Conqueror placed their monuments on the third hill. Beyazid II built his mosque complex between 1501 and 1506, but it was overshadowed by the Suleimaniye, designed and erected by Sinan, the greatest of Ottoman architects, between 1550 and 1556.

This mosque of Suleiman the Lawgiver, with its four minarets and a vast dome like the boss on a Turk's shield, was the crown of Stamboul. It astounded the sultan's near contemporary, the English traveller John Sanderson:

the marvellous church and sepulchre of the triumphant and invincible Sultan Suleiman; a building worthy of such a monarch, in the best and most frequented place of the city, which passeth in greatness, workmanship, marble pillars, and riches more kingly, all the other churches of the emperors his predecessors, a work which meriteth to be matched with the 7 Wonders of the World.[8]

'The emperors his predecessors' had built their monuments on the summits of the fourth, fifth and sixth hills. The Conqueror's 'town of lead-covered domes' on the fourth hill, as the seventeenth-century Stamboul historian Evliya Çelebi described it, comprised a huge mosque, the Fatih Mehmet Camii, and the twin *türbes* (tombs) of Mehmed and Gülbahar, the mother of his son and successor Beyazid II. Its *medresse* (school) had space for about a thousand students of the Koran, and the *tabhane* (hospice) provided travellers visiting the mosque with free lodgings. The mosque also provided the surrounding community with an *imaret* (a soup-kitchen for the poor), a hospital, a caravanserai (hostel) for traders, with safe storage for their goods, a school for local children, a library full of fine books and manuscripts, and a *hamam* (public bath). It extended, in all, over an area of four acres, the 'greatest social complex in the Islamic world'.⁹

The mosque atop the fifth hill bears the name of Selim the Grim, conqueror of the East. It was built in his memory by his son Suleiman and stands, austere and beautiful, on a high plateau above the Golden Horn. The imperial mosque upon the sixth hill lies just inside the Edirne Gate at the end of the highway which began in the courtyard of Aya Sofya. This too was closely associated with Suleiman, for it was commissioned by his daughter Mihrimah from Sinan, the creator of the Suleimaniye, and built between 1560 and 1565. The mosque's slender minaret, visible from every part of the city, marked the end of the long procession of monuments to Ottoman glory.

The sultans' officers and officials were also great builders, following the example of their imperial masters. By the nineteenth century there were more than 500 mosques and shrines in the capital. To endow a mosque was an act of pious ostentation. It provided a burial place for its founder, as his *türbe* usually formed part of the mosque complex, and the building carried his name into perpetuity. Many mosques

were the sole memorial to officials who fell from favour and were later executed. While their estates were confiscated, the endowment (*vakf*) given to the mosques remained untouched. Such a gift could also have direct financial benefits for the donor and his family, because the religious charitable funds were empowered to lend money at interest – a practice otherwise prohibited by Islam. Many donors were able to provide security for their families by giving money for religious purposes, with the proviso that the endowment then paid a pension to their descendants for ever. Nor were these pious acts the province of men alone: the women of the imperial family and the wives of Ottoman officials were also noted for their good works, and many mosques bear their names.

Piety and prudence worked in harmony, and The City acquired a huge stock of religious buildings, schools, fountains, markets, public baths and libraries, all endowed by the Faithful. The imperial mosques were filled for Friday prayers and the great religious festivals. The hundreds of small mosques and shrines were used for daily prayers and served local needs. They were the focal point of their communities, as the Byzantine churches had been in earlier centuries. Indeed, a building which had been used for Christian worship often continued in use as a mosque with only the most minimal alterations.

The City had been, through all the Christian centuries, a jumble of small communities existing uneasily side by side. In Byzantine times, many of these villages had built walls to keep their neighbours out. The walls disappeared after the conquest, but the spirit of closed communities was carried over into the Ottoman city. Fresh 'quarters' or ghettos were created as Stamboul became a magnet drawing the ambitious and the rootless from every part of the empire. One writer in 1873 observed the crowds in the commercial heart of The City:

Constantinople is a city not of one nation but of many, and hardly more one than another ... Eight or nine languages are constantly spoken in the streets and five or six appear on the shop fronts. The races have nothing to unite them; no relations, except those of trade, with one another; everybody lives in a perpetual dread of everybody else.[10]

Each community, whether Muslim, Christian, or Jewish, was governed by its own leaders, and centred around its mosque, church or synagogue. Its boundaries were invisible but real. Racial or regional groups clustered together for mutual protection. New arrivals from the provinces would join families already settled in the capital to form a new hamlet of, say, Anatolians or Albanians. But there were few outward signs to distinguish one community from another. The dilapidated wooden houses looked the same whether inhabited by Muslims, Christians or Jews. Only the few palaces of the very rich were built of brick or stone, and most of the better houses were made of wood, lath and plaster like those of the poor.

Rambling Ottoman mansions covered the hills of central Stamboul, while the Greek merchant families lived in great style in the Fener quarter along the Golden Horn. From the street, these houses looked shabby and dilapidated, but inside they were comfortable – even luxurious. Mrs Harvey, 'of Ickwell Bury', described her visit to a well-to-do traditional Ottoman household in the summer of 1871. She remarked on passing a small door, barely visible in the front of the building, into a small shady court, surrounded by arcades, 'up the columns of which climbing plants were trained. In the centre, was a fountain with orange trees and masses of flowers arranged around its basin'. A broad flight of steps at the end of the court led to the principal apartments. At the head of the stairs was a large saloon:

quite magnificent, so richly was it painted and gilt. There was the usual divan, and the floor was covered with delicate matting, but there was no other furniture of any sort ... The walls were exceedingly pretty, being painted a cream colour and bordered with Turkish sentences, laid on in matt or dead gold, a mode of decoration both novel and graceful ... many of the phrases were extracts from the Koran; others set forth the names and titles of the *hanoum*'s [lady's] father, who had been a minister of much influence and importance.[11]

In an adjoining room she observed 'a console table, with the usual clock, a piano and some stiff hard chairs ranged against the walls.'

Few Ottoman houses presented much more than a blank, dusty façade to the world. Even the imperial palaces were hidden away behind high walls. Life in Stamboul was lived indoors, with the outside world excluded. The life of the street was ugly and distasteful, for reasons that the Revd

Robert Walsh soon discovered when he penetrated into the heart of old Stamboul:

The interior of the town presents a melancholy contrast to its very inviting aspect at a distance. The whole area is intersected by crooked narrow lanes, not one of which deserves the name of street. They run either up or down hills or wind along the sides of them ... The streets are laid down with misshapen blocks, presenting all manner of sharp angles above and void spaces between. In some places narrow trottoirs, about a foot wide, run along the houses, but they are so rugged and intercepted by steps and other impediments, that it is always easier to keep in the middle of the street ... mules and horses, with long boards and beams trailing after them, constantly obstruct the crowded passages ...

In any other town in Europe you expect some better built or more open space, and you come to it; but here all is the same, and the first narrow dirty lane you enter presents you with a specimen of the whole city, thirteen miles in circumference. The trees and edifices which looked so beautifully interspersed on the face of the hill before you, you never see. Mean, ragged-looking houses, with projecting windows of wood, nearly meeting at the top, and obscuring the light, obstruct every other view.[12]

By the middle of the nineteenth century almost 400,000 people lived in The City. Most of their houses were shabby and flimsy, quickly built and easily destroyed by the fires and earthquakes which plagued The City. The French novelist Theophile Gautier remarked in 1854 that a house over sixty years old was a rarity.[13] But these natural perils afflicted the houses of the rich as well as the hovels of the poor. Even stone buildings were not immune. There was a disastrous earthquake in 1766 that destroyed most of the mosque complex erected by Mehmed the Conqueror; the mosque was restored in a florid style quite unlike its original austere form. Another earthquake, in 1894, caused even more widespread devastation. Fires were an almost daily occurence and, if not quickly extinguished, could sweep through great tracts of the city, burning for weeks on end. The Sublime Porte was burned and rebuilt three times in the first thirty years of the nineteenth century. A great fire of August 1826 also gutted much of the first court and part of the second court of the Yeni Saray. More than thirty years after this holocaust, maps of the city still showed vast blank tracts marked 'Destroyed by fire'. Great efforts were made by the authorities to establish a fire-warning system and teams of fire-fighters, but they were never sufficient for a city built of old, dry timber.

The Christian city of Pera (centred around the old Genoese watchtower at Galata) on the other side of the Golden Horn was even more at risk. Built on the side of a steep hill with a jumble of tiny lanes, fires spread even faster than in Stamboul: a fire in 1870 destroyed or gutted 3,000 houses, even though many of them were built in stone rather than wood. Both Muslim Stamboul and Christian Pera were part of the same city, subject to the laws of Islam, but in practice they were two separate entities. The difference was given legal status in 1858, when Pera was the first part of the capital to be given a town council with authority over the local communities. Although there were endless quarrels between the many racial and social groups which made up the 'Giaour City' ('Giaour' being a contemptuous term for 'Christian'), the council succeeded. The face of Pera was transformed. As the century progressed, the contrast between Stamboul and Pera grew more evident. In 1895 an American visitor wrote, 'In Galata, the East seems transformed as if by a magician's wand. Jealous latticed windows are almost nowhere seen. The furtive minarets are few and humble ... Galata/Pera is sneered at as the Giaour City ... And so it is: a Western city stranded in the East.'[14]

No effort was spared to create the illusion of European civilization in an alien environment. The main street of the town had a French name – the Grand Rue de Pera. There were newspapers imitating those of Paris and London, daily dances, and soirées. There was a Perote beau monde, mostly consisting of Greeks and Armenians who had adopted fashionable Western habits of speech and dress. They looked down on the 'uncouth' Ottomans, and were despised in their turn by European visitors for their airs and pretensions. The tone of society was set by the embassies, whose magnificent palaces dominated Pera. All of them spied and conspired against the Ottoman government and against each other, and it was the European governments rather than the Ottomans who were the real power in the Christian city. Concessions granted by the sultans – the infamous 'capitulations' – allowed the embassies almost sovereign privileges over anyone they claimed as one of their nationals. All of them had lists of protected persons, who were given immunity from Ottoman law and fell under the jurisdiction of their own governments. There was a lively trade in forged or altered papers, and Pera was full of 'Frenchmen' who had been no closer to France than the bottom of a brandy bottle, or 'Ingleesh' who spoke barely a dozen words of the language. The American economist Nassau Senior was told in 1857 that, 'There is not a worse set of ruffians than the Ionians and Maltese who wander all over the East and bully and defraud and assassinate under British protection.'[15]

Where Stamboul brimmed with mosques, Pera had a profusion of churches and chapels of every conceivable sect: Roman Catholics, Armenians, Chaldeans, Nestorians, Syrians, Presbyterians, Russian Orthodox, Anglicans and Uniates. The streets were 'bordered with shops kept by Italians, Greeks, and Frenchmen'.[16] Albert Smith noticed that there were 'many English articles for sale – stockings, cotton prints, cutlery and blacking. In one window was a number of *Punch* . . . at the corner was a sign with "Furnished Apartments to Let" painted on it; and on the wall of the small burial ground a Turk sat with a tray of Birmingham steel pens on cards.'[17] Europeans stayed in Pera and never on the Stamboul side; Murray's

Handbook for Travellers in Turkey did not even list a hotel where they might reside in The City. Their view of Stamboul was coloured by the relative freedoms of the European city. Drink flowed freely in Pera, whereas it was officially prohibited in Stamboul. Until the 1830s there was not even a proper bridge between the two cities, and all communication between them was by boat – usually the slender caiques which Europeans found so quaint.

The bridges were not universally welcomed. The first spanned the Golden Horn at its narrowest point, roughly where the Byzantines had hung the chain to close the harbour in 1453, and was opened in 1838. It floated on a set of wooden pontoons, so it rose and fell with the gentle movement of the waves. A second bridge was opened in 1850, further down the Golden Horn. The floating bridge was replaced in 1878 by a new construction, with 'a broad carriageway and spacious footpaths',[18] which remained in use until the 1890s, when a German company spanned the Golden Horn with a massive cast-iron structure.

The sense of separation between Pera and Stamboul was diminished by improved access, but never abolished. Both communities wished to maintain their distance. Pera would be visited by Ottoman women, 'whom it allures through its windows of plated glass', but they would 'hurriedly complete the purchases and hasten home'.[19] Ottoman men who could not observe the Koranic prohibition on intoxicants would obtain their supplies of wine and spirits in the 'Giaour City', but they looked on it with a mixture of envy and disgust.

Halil Halit came to the capital to study in one of the many *medresses*, under the care and supervision of his uncle. One evening, shortly after his arrival, he visited Pera and was amazed by the 'evident signs of prosperity and richness of its population'. But, as the evening drew on, he descended into its old core, Galata, and saw sights which appalled him:

Here may be seen dirty cut-throats with crime written large on their faces, and above all, many a habitual drunkard ... Here too we saw disreputable houses, with painted half-naked creatures sitting on their balconies or standing on the thresholds of their doors, and calling out invitations to all who passed by ... We were disgusted with such an exhibition of what most Moslems believe to be a 'Christian' life. After this excursion I was not permitted to revisit the European quarter for a considerable time.[20]

Many enlightened Ottomans, who rejected the old hatreds for the Giaours, still had no desire to become Westernized and live the life of a Perote. After the 'new' bridge was built in 1850 and access was improved between the two cities, rents increased dramatically on the Stamboul waterfront, and street crimes, mostly committed by Greeks and Armenians, rose alarmingly. It was not a good advertisment for European civilization.

Most Europeans were glad to be separated from Muslim Stamboul. They appreciated the relative convenience and civilization of the Christian city and disliked what they saw as its 'Turkish' qualities – dirt and decay – although some honest observers, like Charles White, an English visitor, noted, 'It is but justice, however, to the Turks to observe that the streets of Pera and Galata are infinitely more filthy than those of Constantinople, especially in the quarters inhabited exclusively by Greeks and Armenians.'[21] Travellers were content to spend a day seeing the sights of old Stamboul, before returning to Pera and the comforts of the West.

By mid-century, Pera was growing at a great pace. Stone and brick houses in the Western style were spreading up the hillside, and by 1844 the European population was estimated at about 25,000.[22] By contrast, the British consul was noting that 'The Musselman population of the Osmanli race in Constantinople is known to be decreasing ... while the Osmanli are decreasing in number yearly, the Christian and Jewish populations tend to increase in rapid ratio.'[23] By 1878, the European population stood at more than 120,000.[24]

The 'Giaour City' had become a boom town. Ottoman demand for European goods surged ahead after the Crimean War of 1853–6. Opportunists, confidence tricksters, financiers, pimps and prostitutes, shopkeepers and traders flooded into the city. The statistics are erratic, but it has been estimated that the trade in imports (mostly from Britain and France) doubled between the early 1840s and the late 1850s, and increased fourfold up to the end of the century. The first steam ship, the *Swift*, arrived in 1828; by the late 1840s, the Austrians, French, British and Russians were all running regular steamship services to Pera, speeding the passage of both goods and travellers. The flood of imports was matched by a torrent of exports, much of it channelled through the merchant houses of Pera. Until the 1880s,

Constantinople was the emporium for all the produce that found its way from the interior to the Black Sea and the Marmara shores. Small native coasting craft used to collect it and bring it to Constantinople, and in the Golden Horn there was a large and active market not only for Turkish produce, but for the grain, oil seeds, wool, hides, and tallow of Southern Russia and the Danube.[25]

The first photographs of the Golden Horn in the late 1840s show it crammed with merchant shipping.

Most of the imports from Britain and France were consumed not by Europeans but by Ottomans. Walsh was gleeful at the transformation sustained by commerce:

Constantinople having for centuries exhibited a singular and extraordinary spectacle of a Mahometan town in a Christian region, and
stood still while all about were advancing, has at length, as suddenly
as unexpectedly, been roused from its slumbering stupidity; the city
and its inhabitants are daily undergoing a change as extraordinary
as unhoped for; and the present generation will see with astonishment that revolution of usages and opinions during a single life,
which has not happened in any other country in revolving centuries
. . . The traveller who visited Constantinople ten years ago saw [the
sultan] in kiosks, with wooden projecting balconies having dismal
windows and jalousies (closed up from all spectators); he now sees
him in a noble palace . . . as beautiful and commodious as that of
any European monarch.[26]

By the 1840s the leaders of Ottoman society had left the old
city, with its stifling summer heat, for the cleaner and more
comfortable life along the Bosporus and on the Asian shore at
Üsküdar. Sultan Mahmud II (1808–39) had used the excuse of
the fire of 1826 to move his official residence from the Yeni
Saray to a new palace at Beşiktaş on the Bosporus; in practice,
he had rarely used the Yeni Saray after 1815. Over the next
forty years, new imperial palaces were built at Beylerbey on
the Asian shore of the Bosporus, at Çirağan on the European
shore, and at Dolmabahçe, where a vast building linked up
with the much smaller palace at Beşiktaş. The sultans delighted
in creating fanciful palaces in a strangely Ottomanized Western
style. Theophile Gautier was shown round Dolmabahçe by its
architect, Nikogos Balian. The French man of letters was at
something of a loss to describe it: 'It is not Greek, nor Roman,
not Gothic, nor Saracen, nor Arab, nor yet Turkish.' To his
eye the main façade resembled 'a giant piece of goldsmith's
work, in respect of the complicated luxury of its ornaments
and the exaggerated minuteness of its detail'. He described
its 'wreathed pilasters and festooned [window] frames', and
how 'the intermediate spaces were crammed with sculptures
and arabesques between them'. But if it conformed to no

classic style, of East or West, it was magnificent in its setting
on the shores of the Bosporus: 'The enormous structure of
the marble of Marmora of a bluish white, which the gloss
of novelty makes look somewhat cold, produced a superb
effect, standing between the azure of the sky and the azure
of the sea'.[27]

By 1878, Mahmud II and his successors Abdul Meçid
(1839–61) and Abdul Aziz (1861–76) had built or refurbished
no less than ten further residences strung out along the
Bosporus. The cost was prodigious. In 1856 the sultan's civil
list, much of which was spent on new building and purchasing
furniture in Europe, amounted to more than 14.5 per cent of
state revenues, but at the height of the palace building boom,
in the 1860s and 1870s, Abdul Aziz was spending more than
double that amount.[28] It was an insupportable drain on
national resources.

The sultans' senior officials, who had always preferred their
yalıs (houses along the water's edge where they spent the
summer) to their homes in The City, also fuelled the building
boom. By the late 1850s the city was sprawling out beyond the
walls. The rich were moving to houses along the Bosporus;
the poor were creating shanty towns outside the land walls
and along both sides of the Golden Horn. In 1888 the arrival
of the railway linking Stamboul directly with Paris symbolized
the destruction of the old city by the new. The line curled
around the foot of Seraglio Point over ground where once the
ancient Byzantine sea walls and latterly the sultan's kiosks and
summer palace had stood. All had been destroyed in the name
of change and progress, to make way for the iron wheels of
commerce.

In 1878 John Murray announced a new edition of his
famous *Handbook for Travellers in Turkey*:

The Great Changes which have taken place in TURKEY within
the last few years have rendered necessary a new edition of the

Handbook. Wars and revolutions have removed old national landmarks; roads, railways and steamboats have opened up large sections of the country before scarcely accessible; and tramways and carriageways have made it easy to visit the most famous monuments . . .'[29]

A new Stamboul grew out of the old, as streets were cut through areas of ramshackle housing and a new commercial centre developed around the new bridge and the railway station.

The focus of the city remained the great harbour, 'accommodating 1200 sail at the same time . . . deep enough to float men of war of the largest size, which can moor close to the shore'.[30] By the 1870s the deep-water harbour (more than eighteen fathoms) was regularly occupied by ships of all types and sizes, from the traditional feluccas and sailing dhows of the eastern Mediterannean, through coastal steamers of many different nations, up to the warships of the Ottoman navy which anchored in the Golden Horn each winter and in the Bosporus during the summer. A steamship line was established in 1851 with regular services to the villages along the Bosporus. The bridge which linked Pera and Stamboul was 'so constructed as to form a swing bridge, to allow vessels of the largest class to pass to and fro. By means of massive iron hinges, affixed to one angle, it can be drawn back and replaced in a few minutes.'[31]

The Pera bridge was the focal point for the modern systems of transport which came with the rebuilding of Stamboul, the expansion of Pera, and the creation of new Ottoman suburbs along the Bosporus. A tramway ran up the hill from the Stamboul end of the bridge to the old Hippodrome by Aya Sofya, and then through the narrow streets of the old city to the point close to the Castle of the Seven Towers where the walls came down to the Sea of Marmara. On the Pera side another tramline ran along the shore of the Bosporus past the sultans' new palaces at Dolmabahçe and Çirağan, through the new suburbs to the village of Ortaköy. Horse-drawn omnibuses, 'clean and comfortable' in the opinion of Murray's *Handbook*, connected with the tramways and provided a public-transport system to other parts of the city. The new streets were wider and straighter than the old, but, with the profusion of trams, buses, private carriages and horses, they soon became as crowded and dirty as the old narrow streets and alleyways.

But in the roadways leading off the newly paved streets, and in the ramshackle townships far from the great buildings on the six hills, old Stamboul continued apparently unchanged. Its persistence was a challenge and a reproach to reforming sultans like Mahmud II and Abdul Meçid, and their ministers; they intended to make Stamboul into a modern city, an Islamic Paris with wide boulevards, squares and efficient public services.

The first tangible reform concerned the enforcement of the law. (It is revealing of Ottoman priorities that the principal task for local officials was the enforcement of the strict dress laws, first those established by the Conqueror and then those 'reformed' codes ordered by his descendant Mahmud II.) A regular police force was created, at first based on the old palace gardeners (*bostancıs*) who had functioned as policemen inside the Yeni Saray, and then, after 1845, a regular force controlled by a police council. In 1853 the old city was surveyed street by street and the ownership of all landed property was established. The survey revealed that, after centuries of pious bequests, virtually all the principal areas of the city were owned by the charitable endowments of the mosques. The religious authorities were the strongest of the vested interests which had dominated Stamboul for centuries and had strongly resisted any change which they believed would diminish its Islamic purity. They united with the trade guilds to resist the pressure for change.

The resistance to 'improvement' was slowly worn away,

and by the 1880s the power had been stripped from the guilds and the mosque authorities. Stamboul was provided (like the 'Giaour City') with a district council, and a substantial bureaucracy. Building inspectors, school inspectors, a board of trade assessors, sanitary inspectors and city policemen enforced the torrent of local ordinances which poured forth from the City Hall.

Perhaps the most striking change concerned the packs of dogs which had since Byzantine times roamed the streets. Europeans regarded them with either terror or fascination, and asserted that they were allowed to wander freely because of an Islamic love of noble animals. This love of animals they contrasted with Ottoman callousness towards fellow humans. The reality was more prosaic: the dogs had ruled the city at night because no one had had much interest in stopping them. They also performed a useful function by acting as a primitive system of waste disposal. Charles White observed that much of the city would 'become intolerable from dead horses and agglomerations of filth, were it not for the multitude of dogs. At present nothing escapes their voracity. In less than twelve hours after a horse has fallen, not a vestige remains of its carcase.'[32] But wild dogs were not consistent with the image of a modern city, and the city council ordered that all the strays should be rounded up and shipped to an isolated, waterless island in the Sea of Marmara to die. A 'picturesque' old Oriental feature of the city was abolished at the stroke of a pen.

The 'dog problem' revealed both the strengths and the weaknesses of Ottoman administration. Specific abuses could be righted, but the long, patient process of 'improvement' was against the social ethos. There was little enthusiasm for the creation of the invisible infrastructure of a modern city – sewers, water, gas supply. Why, Ottoman critics of 'progress' argued, spend a decade and a fortune on maintenance and improvements when a single earthquake or a major fire would destroy all the work? The dogs could be disposed of by a single ruthless act, but the promised drains to remove the filth of the city involved long-term planning. Consequently they were not built for another thirty years, and Stamboul just got dirtier.

Many of these failings could legitimately be explained by financial stringency. The Ottoman state squandered its resources, and, when its revenues were insufficient, raised loans at high rates of interest. The inevitable consequence followed in 1875, when the empire was forced to admit bankruptcy, and the European governments imposed a settlement which guaranteed their own investments. Years of financial restraint followed, and the support for invisible and intangible benefits like drains wasted away. What money remained was used where it could be seen: the building boom continued.

Nineteenth-century sultans, like their ancestors, left mosques and palaces as their gift to posterity, but the buildings themselves embodied the principles of change and progress. Mahmud II built the Nusretiye ('Divine Victory') mosque to celebrate his triumph over the janissaries. He chose for its site not a location within the old city but the shore of the Bosporus on the road to Beşiktaş, where he had built his new palace. In style it was quite unlike any other mosque in the city. Designed by Kirkor Balian, it owed more to the European view of what an 'Oriental' building should look like than to its Islamic antecedents. It was intended to mark a new direction in the Ottoman empire, away from the past, as typified by the buildings of Stamboul, towards a new Ottomanism which would incorporate the best qualities of the West. It was designed as the landmark of a new age.

But the principal monuments of the 'new' Ottoman sultans were secular and military. The most dramatic, a building visible across the Bosporus above the Asian shore at Haydarpaşa, was the barracks first erected by Selim I in 1808 in wood, rebuilt in stone by Mahmud II in 1828, and extended by his son Abdul Meçid between 1842 and 1853. Built around three sides of a vast parade-ground, the barracks stood three storeys high with a slender tower at each corner and more than 1,100 windows on the side facing towards Stamboul. Florence Nightingale, who used part of it for the famous British Military Hospital during the Crimean War, described the filth inside its cavernous rooms, but Julia Pardoe, who had an eye for fine buildings, said it had the appearance of a palace.[33] Whitewashed and gleaming in the sunlight, it seemed to have more in common with the new palaces along the Bosporus than with the older buildings of The City. A string of other barracks was erected just outside the walls and on the Pera side of the Golden Horn, enabling the sultan to keep loyal troops close at hand.

If the confident (and financially expansive) spirit of Mahmud and his successors was expressed in their new buildings, old palaces and mosques were also made to serve the principles of the new age. In 1828 the Eski Saray ('Old Palace') was cleared of its remaining female inhabitants, the relicts of former sultans, who were transferred to the abandoned and fire-damaged Yeni Saray ('New Palace') on Seraglio Point. This latter now became (confusingly) the 'Old Palace', or more colloquially the Topkapı (Cannon Gate) Saray. In the women's place came soldiers – the harbingers of the new age. The Ministry of War occupied the old palace buildings until 1865. When fire devastated the old wooden palace buildings, a new and more grandiose Ministry of War was erected on the same site. Even the mosque of Aya Sofya was not immune to change: two Swiss architects, the Fossati brothers, were commissioned by Abdul Meçid to 'restore and improve' the mosque and its approaches. Their main work had previously consisted of embassies and churches in Pera; let loose on an Islamic building, they allowed their inspiration full rein. As a result, Aya Sofya (and the Suleimaniye mosque on which they worked subsequently) were made to conform more exactly to a European imagination. If these benefits were questionable, the other consequences of their work were entirely good. The great cathedral-mosque which had been falling into ruin was stabilized and made secure for future generations.

Vast sums were spent on new buildings. 'Paper' reforms covered every aspect of life. Some areas of the city were modernized; old wooden houses were rebuilt in more durable materials in accordance with the new regulations. Attempts were made to reorganize the warren of small streets which had grown up around the *bedestens* (markets) and along the shore of the Golden Horn. But there was no money for more radical alterations, and the impact of any change was localized to the immediate area around a new building. Only in districts where fire had cleared a large area was more comprehensive redevelopment attempted.

The closed ethnic neighbourhoods of The City remained impervious to change and continued to provide the human material for riot and violence, which was an ever-present danger in Stamboul. The British diplomat Sir Charles Eliot, writing under the pseudonym Odysseus, observed in 1900:

Every Turk is born a soldier, and adopts other pursuits chiefly because the times are bad. When there is a question of fighting, if only in a riot, the stolid peasant wakes up and shows a surprising power of organization and finding expedients, and, alas, a surprising ferocity. The ordinary Turk is an honest, good-humoured soul, kind to children and animals, and very patient; but when the fighting spirit comes on him, he ... slays, burns and ravages without mercy or discrimination.[34]

The back streets of Stamboul and the derelict hovels of the poor were filled with 'ordinary Turks', and the sultans had reason to be wary of their people. On several occasions, rioters had broken into the Yeni Saray itself. Mahmud's own kinsman,

Selim III, had been deposed by just such a riot. Mahmud and his successors had encircled the city with barracks as a precaution against the people; security from the menace of the Stamboul mob was a strong motive for the sultans to move out of the city.

The corps of janissaries had once been the cutting edge of any popular revolt, leading the poor and the *softas* from the mosque schools. After the janissaries' dispersal in 1826, the students became the disciplined and organized leaders of any uprising. Halil Halit, himself a student, described how 'roused and egged on by politicians, they would assemble in the courtyards of the great mosques, bearing yataghans and heavy clubs under their long cloaks, and numberless common people would follow them.'[35] The *medresses* could marshal as many as 20,000–30,000 fit and fanatical young men who would respond instinctively to any threat to the purity of Islam.

The *softas* were unpredictable and, once roused, were difficult to control. They hated Christians, Jews and Muslim heretics, but for a brief period during the 1870s they became ardent in support of social change, declaring that reform was a truly Islamic path. In May 1876 the students of the Suleimaniye, Beyazid and Fatih Mehmed *medresses* rioted before the Sublime Porte. They demanded the resignation of the grand vizier and the introduction of a programme of change, and they ostentatiously measured the railings outside the building to see if they were high enough to hang the grand vizier from them. The government crumbled and the *softas* were heroes. Their zeal for reform was shortlived, however: by August they were writing to attack the whole concept of a progressive constitution and threatening the new grand vizier, Midhat Pasha, with assassination if he persisted in his reforms.[36]

In the last quarter of the nineteenth century, the *softas* of Stamboul came to see themselves as the spearhead of militant

24. *Interior of an Ottoman House, Cairo*, Frank Dillon RI (1823–1909)
This interior of the Cairene house of a senior Ottoman official bears all the marks of
a wealthy Ottoman home before the intrusion of Western styles.

25. (Above) *Women and Children around a* Sebil *or Street Fountain, c. 1845*
Amadeo, Count Preziosi (1816–82)
Ottomans lavished care and attention on their children, as can be seen by the fine
garments worn by the girl and boy in this image.

27. (Opposite below) *Street Scene in Pera, c. 1810*, Anon.
The clean and orderly streets of Pera seen here are something of a fiction: the 'European'
city (where all the embassies and Western business were located) was said to be
more disreputable than Stamboul across the Golden Horn.

26. (Above) *The Fountain at Tophane, 1829*, William Page (1794–1872)
The water for the city was brought by aqueduct from great reservoirs in the heights
above Constantinople. Running water was essential for the ritual ablutions required
of all Muslims before prayer.

28. (Above) *The Sultan in Procession Leaving the Great Gate of the Yeni Saray,*
c. *1810,* Anon.
The ceremonial procession of the sultan from the palace to Friday prayers or to the war
camp at Davut Paşa was a timeless feature. Depictions of sixteenth-century processions
differ little from this observation of Mahmud II on his horse.

29. (Opposite left) *Janissaries with their Cooking-Pots,* Anon.
These are small cooking-vessels; the regiments possessed larger pots as well, from which
the whole detachment would take their soup or stews, and it was these which were
ceremoniously overturned to symbolize that the janissaries would no longer eat the
sultan's rations and were in rebellion.

30. *The Entrance to the Golden Horn, 1852,* Amadeo, Count Preziosi (1816–82)
The Golden Horn and the Bosporus were the highways of Constantinople, linking
the Asian and European shores, and Stamboul and Pera.

31. (Opposite) *An Arab from Iraq,* Amadeo, Count Preziosi (1816–82)
Preziosi sought out exotic types at the point when they were becoming a rarity in
the Ottoman capital. Many of those he depicted were recently arrived in the city,
or travellers, like this Arab from Iraq. But, as always, his depiction is accurate, and
may be compared with the photograph of the Syrian in plate 44.

Fethosar -
Wled Gabdullab

Babilonia
1854.

32. (Above) *Massacre in a Balkan Village, 1876*
Orlando Norie (1832–1901)
The image of the 'Terrible Turk' was heightened by pictures such as this.

33. (Left) *Kurdish Warrior from the Region of Lake Van, c. 1843*
Amadeo, Count Preziosi (1816–82)
The 'irregulars' who flocked to the sultan's standard were responsible for much of the savagery that attached to the name of Ottoman.

Islam. Their hatred of foreign innovations gave their narrow, fundamentalist protest a wide appeal. By 1900 fear of European domination had become universal among Ottoman Muslims. The students were bigoted but not stupid, and they sought to gain support from all levels of Muslim society. They supported political reform when it was for the benefit of Muslims, but when it included Christians and Jews they declared it was against Islam. They put forward economic and social reasons for their xenophobia, as in 1895 when the *softas* of Stamboul asked, 'Why do hundreds of Europeans daily come here and enrich themselves at our expense? For public works construction they send us workers as if we don't have any of our own.'[37]

The students gained the tacit support of civilized and educated Muslims who deplored sectarian violence but saw Christians as dangerous enemies. Sir Charles Eliot described a common Ottoman attitude to the Christian world. His Turkish narrator was a man of great eminence: 'all that a Turk should be. He had an ample beard, his figure was like a haystack and his nose like a potato. He was a Field Marshal . . . He had been successively Minister of War, Finance and Foreign Affairs and for a few months, Grand Vizier.' This imposing figure told a story of how once, when:

I was a very young man and went for a ride with my old father. I was very foolish then and my head was stuffed with silly notions and liberal ideas. I told my father we ought to reform our constitution, systematise our administration, purify our family life, educate our women, introduce liberal ideas and imitate Europeans. And my father answered not a word.

So we rode along the banks of the Bosphorus. At last we came to a Christian village and round the Christian village were many pigs. Then my father said to me, 'My son, what seest thou?' I replied, 'Pigs, Father.' 'My son,' he said, 'are they all similar in size and colour, or do they differ?' 'They differ, Father.' 'But all of them are swine, my son?' 'All, Father.' 'My son,' he said, 'it is with the

Christians even as with the pigs. There are big Christians and little Christians, Russian Christians, English Christians, French Christians and German Christians; but they are all of them swine, and he who wishes to imitate the Christians, wishes to wallow with the swine in the mire.'[38]

The equation between Christians and unclean beasts (pigs) would have surprised most foreign visitors, who remarked on the kindness and civility they always received from Muslim Turks. Yet even the most liberal Ottomans, 'once roused', would echo the attitudes of the fundamentalists. Halil Halit, an educated and liberal man, made the direct connection between the restiveness of non-Muslim minorities and European commercial domination of the empire:

Foreign Powers ... take up, some of them, the cause of those eastern Christians who are under Ottoman rule, alleging they are acting in the name of 'humanity'. Their real motive, however, is that they may use them as a *point d'appui* for their political schemes and designs ... each native Christian community entertains, nowadays more or less without disguise, sentiments of animosity towards the Osmanlis, and even sympathizes with the enemies of the Turkish empire in times of international trouble or war.[39]

He continued to suggest that the attacks on Christian minorities, 'which would be represented in Europe as an outburst of Musselman fanaticism', were an understandable response to provocation: 'The Turk's patience is almost inexhaustible, but when you attack his women and children, his anger is roused, and nothing on earth can control it.'

The Turks were portrayed as savages and barbarians in the West; they saw themselves as slow to anger but implacable once roused. Europeans looked down on the Turks with disdain, and the Turks returned the compliment. Educated Ottomans accused Westerners of ignorance and insensitivity. A leading reformer, Çevdet Pasha, told the French ambassador, 'You have been living in Beyoğlu [Pera]. You have not learned properly the spirit of the Ottoman state or even the circumstances of Istanbul. Beyoğlu is an isthmus between Europe and the Islamic world. From there you see Istanbul through a telescope.'[40] Westerners, as Halit suggested, always reacted with fury at the ill-treatment of Christians by Muslims. The Turks were condemned as the enemies of humanity for their treatment of the Greeks during the Greek War of Independence (1821–9). But the 15,000 Turkish men, women and children slaughtered in southern Greece in 1821 were ignored: the Greek slogan 'Not a Turk shall remain in the Morea' was a prescription for genocide. During the 'Bulgarian atrocities' of 1875, the atrocities committed against the Christians were widely publicized in Europe and the United States, but the equally atrocious murders of Muslims were ignored. In the 1890s, when Armenians used violence to secure an independent Armenia, the killings of Turks were ignored by the Western states, while the Ottoman response was condemned as mindless racial murder. Sir Charles Eliot wrote of the chain of massacre and reprisal during the Greek war 'not from a desire to prove that Turks and Greeks are all much of a muchness, but that it is important to realise that the Turks really have cause to fear Christians. Otherwise such events as the recent Armenian massacres (1896) would be inexplicable.'[41]

The occasions on which the streets of Stamboul actually did run red with Christian blood were few. The different ethnic communities coexisted, perhaps because no one group predominated. In Anatolia, where the Muslims massively outnumbered the Christians, and in the Balkans, where the Christians were the minority, there was far more racial violence. For all the great Islamic monuments, and the fervour of the *softas*, Constantinople (including Stamboul, Pera and the outlying suburbs) was not a Muslim city: it actually had fewer Muslims than Christians (384,836 Muslims to 444,294 Christians, plus 22,394 Jews[42]).

But the statistics do not adequately measure the changing

nature of The City's population. Between 1876 and 1896, more than 1 million Muslim refugees fled to the Ottoman empire from the Balkan regions and from southern Russia. Many of them had a deep personal hatred for all Christians, and a large number of these Balkan Muslims made their homes in Stamboul and in the shanty towns around the walls. Other poor migrants to the capital included many Kurds, whose hatred for the enterprising, energetic Armenians was notorious. Most of the 6,000 Armenians murdered in August 1896 were clubbed to death by Kurds with a score to settle. The Christian population was also in flux. Most of the Christian communities – the Greeks, for example – had been established in Stamboul for centuries. But their numbers were swollen by many who had suffered at the hands of the Muslim majority in Anatolia and the eastern provinces of the empire. These refugees had gravitated towards the capital in search of greater security and to find work, and they brought their fears and hostilities with them into Constantinople, heightening its tension and social hatreds. In the last years of the Ottoman empire, with growing economic pressures and ethnic/religious hostility, Constantinople became what it had never been before: a microcosm of the empire.

CHAPTER 6

Dreams from the Rose Pavilion

THE MEANDERING PATH OF REFORM

On 3 November 1839, within a few months of the death of Mahmud II (now proclaimed to his people as 'Mahmud the Just), an elaborate ceremony was held at the northern end of the pleasure grounds between the Topkapı Saray and the sea walls along the Golden Horn. In the gardens were numerous small kiosks, described by an English traveller of the seventeenth century as being 'a core of three or four rooms with chimneys, whose mantel trees are of silver, the windows curiously glazed and besides protected with an iron grill all gilt over most gloriously: the whole frame so set with opals, rubies, emeralds, burnished with gold, painted with flowers, and graced with inlaid works of porphyry, marble, jet, jasper and delicate stones'.[1] Subsequently the kiosks had many uses, and one of the larger ones had been used by the chief confectioner of the palace to soak and distill rose petals into an essence used for making the sweetmeat known to the West as 'Turkish delight'. The Rose Pavilion, as it was colloquially known, was consequently in a good state of repair, and it was here that all the leading Ottoman dignitaries and, for the first time in the history of the empire, the representatives of foreign nations assembled to hear the reading of an Illustrious Rescript (*Hatt ı-şerif*), an expression of the personal wishes of the sultan. The foreign minister, Mustafa Reşid Pasha, read the document – appropriately enough, since he had drafted it in the name of the new sultan. Its spirit was of restoration, not change; a re-ordering (*Tanzimat*), not a radical transformation of Ottoman society. Reşid began:

It is well known that during the early ages of the Ottoman monarchy, the glorious precepts of the Koran and the laws of the empire were ever held in honour ... For 150 years a succession of incidents and various causes has checked this obedience to the sacred code of the law ... and the previous strength and prosperity have been converted into weakness and poverty ... supported by the intercession of our Prophet, we consider it advisable to attempt by new institutions to obtain for the provinces comprising the Ottoman empire the benefits of a good administration.[2]

In an Ottoman decree, written in the script and language of the Koran, every word was precious and pregnant with meaning. Yet the deeper meaning of the *Hatt* was not readily comprehensible to the men of the West who had gathered to hear the future. There was a French text and an Ottoman text, and they varied both in style and their implicit message. For each part of his audience, Reşid provided the message they wanted to hear. The guarantee of 'perfect security for their lives, honour and property' and the declaration that the 'property of the innocent heirs of a criminal will not be confiscated' addressed a long-standing grievance within the Ottoman official class, who craved security and a status independent of the will of the sultan. The foreign representatives heard that for the first time the Christians within the empire would be treated equally with Muslims: 'All the subjects of our illustrious sultanate, both Muslims and the members of other *millets* [religious groups] shall benefit from these concessions without exception.' But the religious and conservative *ulema* (and there were many among the gathering) were reassured that 'As these present institutions are solely intended for the regeneration of religion, Government, the nation and the empire, we engage to do nothing which may be opposed to them.' From the outset, therefore, the Ottoman reform was a charter of ambiguity, such that the West eventually came to assume that it was merely an attempt to deceive it. The Westerners' mistake, honestly made, was to seek an analogue in terms they could understand. Many Westerners later compared the *Hatt* (falsely) to Magna Carta or the Bill of Rights, and it is true that the French text amplified the rights of non-Muslims in a way that the Turkish text did not.[3] Much more, it was an attempt to balance ambiguities by refusing to recognize their existence.

An Ottoman and a western European would look at the same events and see things differently. One would see a slow and deliberate advance on the path of progress; the other would recognize only a failure, a promise dishonoured. And, even as the Ottomans and the West came closer together in economic and political terms during the nineteenth century, the gulf of misunderstanding broadened. While the Ottomans were still obviously alien, with their flowing robes and barbaric customs, they were outside the civilized world and were not to be judged by its standards. Once they had welcomed Western civilization, travelled abroad, learned to speak French and English, sat on chairs and eaten at tables, then any alien tendency was regarded as some form of apostasy, a reverting to their former, unenlightened selves. As a French colonel said to Charles Macfarlane, a British officer, on his second visit to Constantinople in 1847, 'Reschid Pascha has lived a good deal in Paris and in London. He knows the usages of civilized society. He knows perfectly well what an incongruous and monstrous thing it would be thought if the domestics of the Prime Minister of France or Britain were to run downstairs after every visitor clamouring for baksheesh.'[4] (Yet were not visitors to the great houses of Britain assailed by just such demands – the expectation of 'vails' (tips) that generated so much irritation against the avarice of the servant class?) Moreover, the colonel continued:

[Reschid and Ali Efendi, the minister for foreign affairs,] the leaders, par excellence, of civilisation and reform; the men who have most loudly proclaimed in France and in England that the manners and the customs of the Turks were changed, and that were they not changed they would soon change them . . . You cannot go to their houses without being robbed. And see how they live at home! Their wives and women separated, and shut up, and caged just as they were when the Turks first came to Constantinople.

Macfarlane was 'somewhat amazed', but thought the Frenchman must be prejudiced. But many in Europe had the same expectations: reform had only one course and one end – the path of Westernization in all its aspects. It was useless for Ottomans like the writer and political thinker Namik Kemal, writing in 1872, to note that 'It took Europe two centuries to reach this condition and while they were the inventors in the paths of progress, we find all the means ready to hand . . . can there be any doubt that we, too, even if it takes us two centuries, can reach a stage where we would be counted as one of the most civilized countries?'[5] Westerners were impatient or suspicious of Ottoman intentions, and demanded results not in two centuries but in as little as twenty years.

Gauging the erratic progress of economic, social or political reform within the Ottoman empire is difficult, for what is true of one region does not necessarily apply in another. Nor is it easy to follow through the other consequences, political and financial, that resulted from the process. But in one sector – military reform – our evidence is better, and the tangled skein of consequences that followed from it is a little easier to untangle. Securing an up-to-date and efficient army had been a priority for Selim II and for Mahmud II. The creation of a new army was one of the positive and most visible achievements of Mahmud's long reign; yet, on closer examination, the extent and effectiveness of the changes diminish. The small return for all the efforts put into military reform points to the realistic limits on any programme of change within the empire. Often the alterations were symbolic rather than real, and it was characteristic that Ottomans read the intentions rather than looked to the fact. Much of what passed for radical innovation was not progressive in European terms.

Reform, driven from above by the sultan, followed an erratic path: for Mahmud, war was an aspect of heroism just as much as it had been for the janissaries. He loved leading his three new household cavalry squadrons into the charge at full gallop, and, as one observer noted, 'Mahmood is undoubtedly the best horseman *à la Européene* in his army; and this acquirement together with another proficiency ... that of commanding and manœuvring a squadron of horse, formed his pride and glory.'[6] His cavalry drill commander, the renegade Piedmontese Calosso, said that the sultan commanded his squadrons as well as any European major or captain of long standing. His approach and attitudes were those of a regimental officer; he had an obsessive interest in all the minutiae of harness, arms, accoutrements and uniforms, and he learned to ride in the European style – not easy for someone accustomed to the very different Turkish saddle, and the sultan fell off more than once while learning. His military horizon was his cavalry and the thrill of the pursuit. But this was a model army, a miniature of the whole, rather as the grand vizier's toy soldiers formed the basis for the New Order.

The sultan had a fixity of purpose, but no breadth of vision, and an impatience to achieve results. The most pressing need was to give the Ottoman state an army on modern (Egyptian) lines, for, useless though the janissaries had been, they had at least maintained a semblance of order; without an army, the Ottomans were defenceless against the ambitions either of Mehmed Ali or of the equally predatory Russians. The issues were more complex than simply recruiting and equipping new regiments, but the long, patient preparation which had built up the new Egyptian force to a formidable degree of efficiency seemed unnecessary;[7] all that was required, in the sultan's eyes, was some new equipment and a few drill instructors.

He first asked Mehmed Ali for the loan of a dozen Egyptian officers, but the pasha respectfully declined, saying that his men were not 'sufficiently prepared' for such an important task.[8] As a consequence, the sultan simply assembled a collection of instructors from a variety of European nations – some of them competent, like Calosso (who had never risen above the rank of captain in the army of Piedmont); others not, like the chief infantry instructor, a Frenchman named Gaillard, who had once been a sergeant in Napoleon's invasion of Egypt and was an unimaginative martinet. Mahmud was also sent a few expert young officers – one or two from Austria and more from Prussia, like the young Helmut von Moltke, whose years in Turkey were a searing experience. His later dictum that a plan never survives the first minutes of battle very much embodied his education in the Ottoman way of war.

Apart from the Austrian and Prussian professionals, these instructors were drawn from half a dozen different military backgrounds, with divergent systems of drill and training. Inevitably, they taught a rag-bag of the tactics that they themselves had learned, and then, to justify their employment as experts, developed others. 'Each instructor, in order to please his Pasha, invented new manœuvres, ridiculous as well as useless. In 1828, a former corporal, in order to satisfy the desire for novelty of the Kapitan Pasha, had even invented a triangular or a semi-circular deployment of his platoons and made them march in this formation.'[9] But in the eyes of the sultan they all taught that desirable skill, the Western way of war. He recognized the special quality of someone like Moltke, but he chose most of his instructors indiscriminately, on the basis of chance meeting, or mere availability in the capital. Even the most rudimentary experience was a sufficient qualification.

This undifferentiated sense of 'the West' diminished as more Ottomans had direct experience of a variety of European societies, but ignorance continued to sap the potential effectiveness of the new army. Its judgement of what change was appropriate, or what model should be followed, was invariably erratic. In the 1830s, officials recognized the need for a new manual of fortification; in their ignorance they chose a work by Vauban more than a century old – a classic of military science, but not what they needed as a simple guide to current developments. And it was only at Moltke's insistence that they agreed to settle on a single drill manual for the army, although the proposal to translate the current Prussian regulations never became a reality, for the project lapsed after his departure. Not much had changed since the days of Baron de Tott with his complaints about the Ottoman pashas. A reader senses Moltke's rising incredulity as in his letters he describes 'The most unfortunate creation . . . an army on the European model with Russian jackets, French regulations, Belgian weapons, Turkish caps, Hungarian saddles, English swords, and instructors from all nations'.[10]

A new army (the 'Triumphant Soldiers of Allah') was, however, created with amazing speed, and when in 1828 it gathered at Davut Paşa to march north against a Russian invasion, to the practised eye of Macfarlane the soldiers seemed:

extremely quick in all their movements. I several times saw them perform evolutions with a rapidity that astonished me, even with . . . some fine European regiments fresh in my memory. These, it is true, were not done neatly or symmetrically, but the result was obtained   the lines were changed, squares, solid or hollow, formed and the troops again deployed with celerity . . . there was nothing to be said against the promptness and regularity of their fire.[11]

However, as he also pointed out, only two or three thousand men had reached that stage, and the rest were 'bad indeed'. As with the janissaries before them, the quality of the new troops was variable, in part due, no doubt, to the way in which they had been taught the new arts of soldiering. But, as Moltke shrewdly observed, 'this new army had one quality which placed it above the numerous host which in former times the Porte could summon to the field: it obeyed.'

When war came in the 1830s, the troops fought bravely, especially in defence, but the quality of their commanders was as inadequate as it had been before the destruction of the janissaries. Indeed, in many cases they were either the same commanders or drawn from the same social milieu. The senior officers had little grasp of the art of war, and no capacity to use even the limited skills which their soldiers had so painstakingly acquired. After the end of the war, renewed efforts were made to improve the quality of the officers, and by the end of 1831 promotions were to be made only on the basis of an oral examination. All appointments to senior ranks required the personal approval of the sultan. However, he would not be bound by his own regulations, and in 1833 he made one of his own attendants a brigadier general of cavalry; by 1838 this man had become commander-in-chief of the army. (However, Mahmud's practice was not so very different from that of the British army, where purchase of command, favouritism and rank incompetence also flourished.)

By the late 1840s there had been little improvement. English officers still complained about the slovenliness of the troops and 'the canker of Turkish indolence: half the officers instead of marching at double quick time over the hills with their men, remained behind on the drill ground to gossip and smoke pipes with the officers there'.[12] And a French officer 'who had studied them well' and 'who had lived long in the East', commented, 'They have hardly any competent officers': the old system still persisted where the great pasha

placed by Court intrigue at the head of an army, has never been a soldier and is in military affairs about the most ignorant man in the army. He takes some officer into his favour and relies for some time on his judgement and advice; then he changes and takes another advisor, or if his difficulties become at all complicated he will seek the advice of a dozen men, who may very probably entertain twelve different opinions and plans.[13]

It took almost fifty years to create a more competent officer corps.

The Triumphant Soldiers of Allah were utterly routed in their first encounter. In 1832 the long expected falling-out between the sultan and the pasha of Egypt had resulted in war. Mehmed Ali asked for the pashalik of Syria to add to his already large domain. Mahmud refused, and the Egyptian army under the pasha's son Ibrahim invaded the province, occupied Acre, and, in a series of battles, utterly defeated the Triumphant Soldiers, capturing their commander, who promptly went over to the Egyptian side. By October, Ibrahim had advanced from Syria north into Anatolia, taking the old city of Konya, and the road to Constantinople lay open. The sultan was forced into the humiliating position of summoning Russian aid to prevent his own vassals, the Egyptians, marching on his capital. Fighting against the battle-hardened veterans of the Greek campaigns, the Triumphant Soldiers showed themselves to be the half-trained farm-boys that Macfarlane had observed. Asked to what he attributed the failure of Turkish arms, after six years' effort in retraining and re-equipment, Ibrahim Pasha, victor in Syria, Crete and Greece, remarked, 'the Porte has taken civilisation by the wrong side; it is not by giving epaulettes and tight trousers to a nation that you begin the task of regeneration ... instead of beginning with their dress ... they should endeavour to enlighten the minds of the people'.[14]

Mahmud had indeed concentrated on the externals. He abolished the traditional dress worn by all Ottoman officials; just as the Triumphant Soldiers had new uniforms, so too did the civil officials. Gone were all the elaborate gradations of

rank noted by Luigi Marsigli, a Habsburg subject taken prisoner by the Turks in the eighteenth century: 'There is a custom of the Turks to distinguish ranks by different turbans, as well as by fashion of dress, by the way of wearing sashes, and by the colour of shoes, in public and private use.'[15] Gone was the role of the aga of the turbans (*tülbend ağasi*) – a court official whose sole responsibility was to answer questions of protocol concerned with headgear. His, with many other offices, was abolished. All functionaries were now to wear a long, black, straight-cut coat replacing the caftan, modelled on Western dress but still with an indefinably 'Eastern' quality to it. So typical was it of the Ottoman official that it came to be called a 'stambouline'. Sandals or slippers gave way to short black boots (Muslims had normally worn only red or yellow); black or dark-grey trousers were cut tight in the European style. And to complete the ensemble there was a conical red felt hat, which was called the 'fez' after the city in Morocco where it was first made. The resulting form of dress was neither traditional nor truly Western, but a hybrid, and in that sense it was a suitable emblem for the transformation wrought by Mahmud. Only the *ulema* were left with their full panoply of turbans and flowing robes.

The force for reform came from the sultan, which perhaps explains the haphazard and incoherent way in which it moved forward. Progress was possible only because there were an increasing number of Ottomans with experience of the West. In the eighteenth and early nineteenth centuries the number of Ottoman missions in Europe had grown considerably, but they were always regarded as having a strictly limited duration, even when, like the first embassy to Paris, they lasted over two years. Nor would the Ottomans recognize the permanent status of European embassies in Constantinople. Foreign diplomats were regarded as guests of the sultan, and most of their costs in the Ottoman domains were borne by the Ottoman state. When, as frequently happened, relationships worsened between the two countries, the unfortunate diplomats had no immunity and would be imprisoned for flouting the laws of hospitality. Indeed the attitude of regarding diplomats as guests was one obstacle to establishing a mutual exchange of representatives, because the Ottomans expected the foreign governments to reciprocate by bearing the cost of the sultan's legations. Under Mahmud's reform, the Ottomans began to accredit and receive embassies in the European manner, and the demands on the office of the chief scribe (*reis ul-küttab*), which functioned as the Ministry of Foreign Affairs, grew dramatically. Similarly the Translation Bureau, a small and peripheral office of the state whose duties had largely been confined to interpreting and providing elegant Persian or Arabic embellishments to rather rough-hewn documents in Ottoman Turkish, suddenly became more significant: a tiny staff in the 1820s grew to more than forty by 1841.[16] Three of those who later became the leading statesmen of the empire (Ali Pasha, Fuad Pasha and Mustafa Reşid Pasha) spent their early careers there, acquiring familiarity with the world outside the empire, and then serving in posts and embassies abroad. From being a minor element of the structure of government, the 'foreign service', as it effectively became, was the path to rapid advancement within the Ottoman bureaucracy. Those officials with experience of the outside world, with skills in French, English and, sometimes, German, were at a premium.

Westerners approved of those Ottomans who seemed progressive in their outlook, had some experience of the outside world, and spoke a language other than Ottoman Turkish. Most of the rest were damned as a species of Asiatic recidivist. Mahmud II had been immediately classified as a reformer in the Western sense despite speaking only limited French, and his occasional lapses into 'barbarism' were deemed to be justified by circumstance. Some writers even identified with the brutal directness of his methods, and accounts of the end of the janissaries often mix a salacious glee with only a mild hint of censure, justifying the massacre as an exercise of the popular will:

The vein of kindred blood [of the janissaries] once opened flowed like a torrent without exciting sympathy ... the hearts of the gathered thousands were animated with one aim – the annihilation of the Janissaries. Even those who, in the natural state of their minds, would have retired ... were now carried on by the general stream; and from the same feeling which throws a pack of whelps on a dog beaten by his antagonist, the mob mechanically added its weight to crush the falling Janissaries.[17]

Creasy, more distant from the events in time and place, merely suggests that Mahmud 'swept away the military tyranny under which the Empire had groaned for centuries'.[18] But, plainly in his view, the sultan aimed to institute the values and practices of the Western world within an Eastern context. Moltke, whose experience was at first hand, suggested that but for the opposition of Russia 'the sultan might have carried out the needful reforms in the administration of his country, have infused new life into the dead branches of the Ottoman Empire.'[19]

Europeans considered the Ottomans backward and corrupt in exactly the measure that they did not measure up to the standards of Western civilization. Those standards were applied flexibly, as in the case of Mahmud, but usually to the disadvantage of the Ottomans. There is often an incongruity between the changes expected in the sultan's domains and those which had been accomplished in the West. Social and political reform was long in coming in even the most advanced western-European countries, and then only sporadically applied. The reforms to the British Parliament freeing it from the 'Old Corruption' of rigged voting and purchase of seats were accomplished only in 1832, and the path of further improvement and extension of the franchise was long and bitterly opposed over the succeeding decades. Charles Macfarlane was complaining about the inferior status of the Christians in Anatolia and the Balkan provinces at a time when Catholics in Britain were still prevented from holding office or attending university. But there is rarely any recognition in Western accounts of the empire that reform in the Ottoman lands might be equally incremental, and by slow stages, as at home.

It is rare, for example, to find a Western writer who suggests that bribery was as common in the Western world as it was in the East.[20] Edmund Hornby, for ten years a British consular judge in Constantinople in the mid nineteenth century, and later serving in Canada, was one of the few who made the comparison, remarking that Canadians were just as avid for bribes as the Turks. And some visitors to Ireland during the famines of the 1840s said that conditions there would not even have been tolerated by the Turks. In general, however, the Ottomans were judged and found wanting.

The Ottomans who had travelled and served abroad were

thought to have become 'Westernized'. In a sense they had. For them, the West meant the end to arbitrary rule and insecurity of life, and, from their experience of London, Paris or Vienna, the taste of a quality of life far superior to anything they could expect within the confines of the empire. They stood uneasily between the world of traditional values and the Western world where, by mid-century, the cardinal virtues were utility, industry and thrift. At home they were assailed by conservatives: an anathema pronounced by Asim Efendi, the imperial historiographer under Selim III, still represented a powerful strain of Ottoman official opinion, jealous at the advancement being given to the Westernizers.

Certain sensualists, naked of the garment of loyalty . . . [who had] from time to time learned politics from them [the French]; some desirous of learning their language, took French teachers, acquired their idiom and prided themselves . . . on their uncouth talk. In this way they were able to insinuate Frankish customs in the hearts and endear their modes of thought to the minds of some people of weak mind and shallow faith.[21]

However, after an initial honeymoon with the reformers, the West eventually saw only their faults and accused them of duplicity. Ali Pasha, confronted with evidence of corruption and maladministration in his government, 'listened with an appearance of attention and made some remarks which induced me to believe that he was sincere and earnest. He rather frequently exclaimed *"That is bad"* and *"that is very unjust"*, *"that is contrary to our Tanzimat and our existing laws"*, *"that must be remedied"*.' But he added that the pasha in question though 'a man of very limited intellect and far in the rear of his epoch, but he was *strongly supported* [italics in the original]; and though he had no genius he had so much talent for intrigue that it was much better for the present government that he should [not] . . . be near the court.' His English visitor surmised that this meant that there was 'but the slightest chance of getting redress.' In his leave-taking, Ali Pasha 'showed no lack of courtesy, inviting me to return to his house whenever I chose. I never saw the little man's face again: he had seen quite enough of me! The next time I called he was engaged – was very busy – was just going to the Porte; and as I had the means of knowing to a *certainty* that all of this was untrue, I never returned.'[22] This encounter might stand as a synecdoche for the whole troubled relationship between the West and the Ottoman reformers.

The question is often asked whether the Ottomans were 'sincere' in their espousal of Western values, for some of the leaders of reform seemed as much given to bribery and peculation as their opponents. The story was told that the great reform vizier, Ali Pasha, gratefully accepted a bribe from the khedive of Egypt which a less reform-minded colleague had refused. Ottomans saw not hypocrisy so much as pragmatism, the force that governed all the Ottoman reforms. Ali remarked later, 'Our speed is limited by the fear of making the boilers burst . . . our metamorphosis must be cautious, gradual, internal and not accomplished by flashes of lightning.'[23] For most Westerners this smacked not of realism but of insincerity. They were in a sense misled by the apparent promise contained in the *Hatt* from the Rose Pavilion and its amplification in the *Hatt* of 1856 that marked the advance of the Ottomans towards Enlightenment.

Reform in an Ottoman context did not have the same meanings that attached to the concept in the West. It was driven by different motives, and 'Westernization' was a means and not an end. It has been described as a 'defensive modernization'[24] against the Western world; but within the empire it was used as a weapon by competing groups to enhance or defend their position. First, 'modernization' was used by some sultans, Mahmud II and his grandson Abdul Hamid II, to reclaim the power of the centre, meaning the sultan personally, which had been eroded over the centuries. Second, 'reform' was adopted by part of the Ottoman ruling class to secure its position: extending the Ottoman way (*Osmanlılık*) to the disenfranchised elements of the empire in a way which would still leave the present rulers in control, at the pinnacle of society. Thus the sultan and the ruling class were in competition for power. On one side the 'modernizers', Mahmud II and Abdul Hamid II, struggled for centralized autocracy; on the other, the 'reformers' pressed for a more parliamentary system, dominated (of course) by them.

The third, and increasingly intrusive, element in the equation was the interest of the Western countries. Every nation wanted to influence the Ottoman government in the direction that best suited that nation's strategic and political purposes. Each European power had its own specific agenda, but its concern invariably found expression as a defence of the Christian minorities. The concentration on the plight of the Christians simply ignored the way in which Muslims and Jews were treated in similar circumstances. Sometimes it was Christians who were the agents of oppression. Mary Eliza Rogers remarked how 'A gentle-looking little girl, of about six years of age, whose father was a much respected European, and mother an Arab, surprised me very much one day, by saying in Arabic, without any provocation, and with a gesture of scorn, to a Jewish workman "*Go thou Jew, and be crucified.*"' When she was told what the words meant, she 'by her own impulse, and to his great wonder, kissed his hands, while tears stood in her eyes'.[25] Whether her guileless words were heard from her Christian father or her Arab mother cannot be known, but the incident suggests a gloss on the simplistic presentation of Christian-as-victim which dominates most European accounts of the empire. Even in the Balkans, where Europeans were committed to the idea of genocide by the Ottomans, the atavistic hatreds of village life could often be more significant than a straightforward division between

Christian and Muslim. However, this was not the simple message of Turkish 'barbarity' that the West required.

After the death of Mahmud in 1839, his sons Abdul Meçid (1839–61) and Abdul Aziz (1861–76) successively yielded to their ministers' concept of 'reform'. Abdul Meçid, aged only sixteen, had no alternative, but it seems clear that he believed sincerely in reform, and his reign produced the two great totems of the Ottoman *Tanzimat*, the Rose Pavilion decree of 1839 and the Imperial Rescript (the *Hatt ı-Hümayun*) of February 1856. The latter aimed, as the preamble declares, to 'renew and enlarge yet more . . . the dignity of my empire and the place which it occupies among civilized nations'.[26] The sultan stressed that he did not speak merely about his Muslim subjects, but talked of his 'desire to increase the well-being, and prosperity, to obtain the happiness of all my subjects, who in my eyes are all equal and equally dear to me, and who are united among themselves by the cordial bonds of patriotism'. And Abdul Meçid also sought 'to assure the means of making the prosperity of the empire grow from day to day'. The words were those of the grand vizier, Ali Pasha, but there is no doubt that they represented the wishes and sentiments of the sultan. They also gratified the empire's allies, France and Britain, for the decree was invoked in the ninth clause of the agreement that ended the Crimean War as 'of high value'; the same Treaty of Paris marked the admission of the Ottoman empire to the group of civilized European nations. Or, as William Ewart Gladstone, four times Britain's prime minister, later described it, 'Britain and France determined to try a great experiment in remodelling the administrative system of Turkey, with the hope of curing its intolerable vices, and of making good its not less intolerable vices'.[27] It was a dramatic fulfilment of the promise of the reform programme; but also a false dawn.

The failure was prefigured in a bizarre incident at the great reception given by the sultan to celebrate the signing of the treaty. His new palace at Dolmabahçe on the Bosporus had replaced a more modest building used by his father. The vast new palace, a flamboyant building by the leading family of Ottoman architects, had taken eleven years to complete, at a cost of 5 million gold crowns. To Stamboulis it seemed the embodiment of the new Westward vision for the empire; to European visitors it appeared a curious mixture of East and West. A crystal staircase led up to the 'hall of the ambassadors', gilded from floor to ceiling, with four huge open fires, all lit and making the room stiflingly hot. The banquet celebrating the treaty was held below, in the throne room, with its huge dome, encrusted with layer upon layer of frieze and ornament. From a clerestory running around the dome, the women of the sultan's numerous harem could look down on the celebrations below. It was the first building in the capital to be lit by gas, and British engineers had built a substantial gasworks to serve the palace and its grounds. Edmund Hornby attended together with a large British delegation, military and civil, and,

a minute or two after the sultan had retired we were startled by two frightful claps of thunder followed by a storm of wind and hail. The whole building seemed to shake, and in a moment the gas went out and we were in total darkness. The band dropped their instruments with a clash and fled. For some moments no one spoke. And then a thin, shrill voice was heard in French, saying 'It wants but the handwriting on the wall, and the words, "Mene, Mene, Tekel, Upharsin," to make this a second feast of Belshazzar.'[28]

The empire was indeed weighed in the balance and found lacking by the nations of Europe.

The interests of the Western nations were precise. They were genuinely concerned to protect the interest of the Christian minorities, but also they had growing commercial interests at stake within the empire. Creasy, writing the *History of the Ottoman Turks* in the last days of the Crimean War (1853–6), laid out the implicit European plan for the empire:

With improved internal government, and with increased security for person and property, European capital will be poured into Turkey, and will enrich the land where it is employed, even more than the hands by which it is invested. The soldiers and the standards of France and England may disappear from the Sultan's dominions, but not their artificers, their navigators, their miners; nor will the flags of their merchant ships cease to thicken over the ports of the Levant. The sounds of Frankish warfare may be heard there no more, but the busy hum of European industry, will increase and find innumerable echoes.'[29]

By these means, the Ottoman empire would be 'taught how to strengthen and how to elevate herself'. 'Elevation' was a moral concept entirely familiar to his readers: the entry of British commerce would provide both an example and the means to further advance.

The West began as investors and traders within the empire, but eventually the main European governments moved to a much more active and central role. They did so to protect their investments from the failure of the Ottoman economic system, which culminated in a national bankruptcy in 1875. In 1851 the grand vizier and leading reformer Mustafa Reşid secured the offer of a loan of 50 million francs from a British and a French bank. At that point a prescient Ottoman prince remarked. 'If this state borrows five piasters it will sink. For once a loan is taken, there will be no end to it . . . It [the state] will sink overwhelmed with debt.'[30] Although that offer was not taken up, many others were, and with the predicted results. There was almost a financial collapse in 1861, staved off more by good fortune than by financial skill.

The Ottomans were justly accused of waste and extravagance. After the end of the Crimean War the Ottoman state had continued to spend money lavishly, far in excess of tax receipts. The empire found no difficulty in continuing to raise money on the European market, and entry into the 'concert of Europe' bolstered financial confidence abroad. Within the empire, however, prices were rising by more than 100 per cent annually, and there was growing discontent amongst Muslims at the benefits given to the religious minorities under the 1856 decree. Abdul Meçid's sudden death in 1861, aged only thirty-eight, raised fears of instability and fuelled a crisis of confidence; a financial crash was avoided only by good luck. Abdul Aziz, who succeeded him, was seven years younger than his brother, and a contradictory figure. Massive where the remainder of his family had been slight, he initially seemed a 'simple Turk', not so given over to the delights of the harem, and not so anxious to follow the path to the West. Once on the throne, he reversed most of the anticipations.

The new sultan, far from shunning foreigners, became the first Ottoman ruler to travel to Europe. He visited Paris for the Exhibition of 1867 at the invitation of Napoleon III, and spent eleven days in the French capital. He went on to London, as the guest of Queen Victoria. The British were anxious at least to equal France's hospitality, and they were aware of his passion for ships, so visits were arranged to naval dockyards and he watched the evolutions of the fleet in the English Channel. The result was orders for warships, which the British yards were happy to fulfil, and the British government was delighted at the additional influence it might legitimately expect in Constantinople. The ships would be paid for by further loans to be raised in London. So seriously were Turkish interests regarded that the Queen agreed to make Abdul Aziz a Knight of the Garter, an honour on which, according to her diaries, 'he had set his heart'.[31] His homeward journey was equally crowded with incident, honours and decorations. Leaving for Constantinople via Brussels, where he was received by King Leopold, he continued his travels, down the Rhine, to meet Kaiser Wilhelm I at Koblenz in the

Prussian Rhineland, where he reviewed the Prussian army, which impressed him deeply. His last engagements were in Vienna, where the days were spent at military manœuvres and the evenings as the guest of honour at numerous receptions. Contacts were made with the Austrian gun-makers, who presented samples of their wares.[32]

This journey to the West marked Ottoman acceptance in Europe, and produced reciprocal visits to Constantinople. Abdul Aziz was the first Ottoman ruler to receive Christian monarchs: the Emperor Franz Joseph of Austria, Empress Eugénie of France, and the Prince of Wales, representing Queen Victoria. All this was seen as evidence that the process of 'civilization' continued. He, like his brother, became a great builder, with two palaces – Beylerbey on the Asian shore and Çirağan on the European shore – being built on the Bosporus. But, as the sultan and his government moved towards the West, hostility to the reform process (in all its aspects) was rising thoughout the 1870s. An American writing from Syria early in 1874 noted, 'Hostility to foreigners, and jealousy of their presence and operations of every description, commercial, educational and religious, are on the evident increase.'[33] Nor was that the only problem. Harvests were disastrous for several years in a row. In 1873 the winter was the worst for seventy years, and wolves prowled in the suburbs of the capital. In the Balkans and Anatolia, villagers starved.

The financial consequences of Westernization were both direct and indirect. The import of Western military equipment and luxury goods rose steadily, while domestic industries were destroyed by foreign competition. In many textile-producing areas of the empire, local cloth had been virtually superseded by imports from Manchester, while the introduction of European styles of fashion in the court harem created a wave of emulation among Ottoman women. The visit of the Empress Eugénie hastened the process, and couturiers from Paris established contacts with the dressmakers of Pera to emulate

European styles. All these were made of European rather than local fabrics, and the trade in fine silks was ruined. Even outdoor dress, although more traditional, began to show strong foreign influences.[34] With fashion in dress came a new taste in Western-style furniture, which had begun under Mahmud II but rose to new heights of extravagance under Abdul Meçid and Abdul Aziz. The furnishings of the Ottoman palaces, which can still be seen today, show the extent and the self-evident cost of the *stylistic* transformation of the empire.

Both the sons of Mahmud II spent money on a prodigious scale. Abdul Meçid built palaces, bought warships and armaments, and financed a harem on a remarkable scale, while Abdul Aziz, who began with protestations of economy, soon discovered equally expensive tastes. The civil lists and special payments to members of the imperial house grew uncontrollably, because no official dared to make any serious efforts to restrain them. Growing expenditure was coupled with an ineffective and uncertain means of revenue-collection. The promise to abandon 'tax farming', a licence for speculators to exploit taxpayers, was contained in both the 1839 decree and its more ambitious counterpart in 1856; it was never fulfilled. This made the Western nations doubt the sincerity of the Ottomans in other parts of those decrees.

Progress, as all the reformers reiterated, could not be achieved quickly. But it seemed that steady progress was being made, and it is paradoxical that hatred of the West and national bankruptcy (1875) came together just at the point when the Westernizing process reached a peak.

The Ottoman constitution of 1876 extended the rights of full citizenship to virtually all who lived within the 'great heaven-protected domains'. It should have crowned the achievement of the reformers, now a new generation – 'Young Ottomans' – led by Midhat Pasha, a man of great competence and domineering personality. His credentials were impressive. During his years first in Bulgaria and latterly in Baghdad he had established strong but fair government and gained a huge popular following.[35] His implacable determination and administrative skill had made him seem the right man to restore Ottoman fortunes; his weakness was that he lacked the tact and diplomatic sense of Ali Pasha or Fuad Pasha. He served briefly as grand vizier, but Abdul Aziz feared and distrusted him. In part, this was a consequence of the sultan's increasing mental instability. He demanded that all ministers should prostrate themselves before him, and prohibited the use of the name Aziz except to refer to him alone. Ministers who were unfortunate enough to bear this common name were forced to use another before they could be admitted to his presence or before their names could appear on a document. (Midhat offended him by wearing spectacles without first seeking the sultan's approval.) However, the sultan was right to fear the former governor's obvious ambition and desire for power.

The old conflict with the Ottoman ruling class re-emerged after an abeyance of more than thirty years. From the financial and political chaos of 1875, Midhat emerged in alliance with the army and the religious authorities to depose the sultan, establish a constitution, and place Murad (Abdul Aziz's nephew and the heir apparent) on the throne as a constitutional monarch. By the night of 29 May 1876, all the plans for a *coup d'état* were complete. Before dawn on the morning of 30 May, two battalions of troops quietly took up positions which blocked all access to the Dolmabahçe palace, while ships of the Ottoman navy were stationed to prevent any escape by sea. Midhat and his co-conspirators met at the Ministry of War, and the *şeyh ül-islam* read the decree of deposition. The grounds were the sultan's mental state, his ignorance of political affairs, diversion of public revenues for private matters, and conduct injurious 'to the state and community'. The conspirators then acclaimed Murad V, who had been brought in secret from his private apartments. When his deposition was announced to Abdul Aziz, he accepted without comment in a spirit of resignation, and was removed to a comfortable confinement in the Topkapı Saray (the former Yeni Saray). The 101-gun salute announcing Murad's accession seemed to promise a new beginning, and the end of Abdul Aziz's reign was described in the same words as the destruction of the janissaries fifty years before – as the Auspicious Event (*Vakayı Hayriye*).

The official announcement of Murad's accession declared that he had become sultan 'by the will of God', which was the usual formula, and, uniquely, by 'the will of the people'. However, the transfer of power to a constitutional government under Murad, guided by Midhat and the leaders of the Ottoman official class, was unhinged by events. The ex-sultan, who disliked Topkapı, had asked to be transferred to the Çirağan palace that he had built on the Bosporus. But there, on the morning of Sunday 4 June, his body was discovered. He had apparently slashed his veins and opened an artery using the small pair of scissors he had asked for to trim his beard and, nineteen of the leading doctors in the city, including some prominent Europeans, concluded that he had committed suicide. But within hours rumours were circulating that the plotters had murdered him: lurid tales were passed that Midhat had used a knife personally to dispatch his former master.

The news of his uncle's death pushed Murad into a state of nervous collapse. With all his plans in disarray, Midhat asked the sultan's younger brother, Abdul Hamid, if he would act as regent until Murad recovered. But Abdul Hamid replied that he would, reluctantly, accept the throne, but not the position of regent, which was an un-Ottoman concept. Another coup was engineered to depose Murad, and on 7 September Abdul Hamid, mounted on a white horse, rode to the mosque of Eyüp to buckle on the sword of Omar and thus symbolically assume the rights and burdens of sultan. So, the empire had its third sultan within the space of six months – one who was to reign for the next three decades.

Abdul Hamid ascended, at the age of thirty-four, to the throne of a state that was officially bankrupt and about to go to war with Russia. These two elements – financial catastrophe and war – were to be the leitmotifs of his long reign. His achievements in both respects were substantial. The bubble of Ottoman credit had burst in 1875, when the Treasury defaulted on interest payments due on Ottoman loans. For Western speculators, Ottoman bonds had offered a high rate of return – up to 12 per cent – and for Western bankers the risk was set against the prospect of a substantial killing. For the Ottomans, the cost of borrowing became insupportable. By 1874, servicing foreign debt occupied up to 60 per cent of Ottoman state revenues.[36] Abdul Hamid refused to yield to the more savage plans of the state's creditors, and waited for a compromise. Eventually, protracted negotiations culminated in 1881 when a Public Debt Commission, made up of representatives from all the main creditor nations (Britain, the Netherlands, France, Germany, Italy, Austria-Hungary), was established as a bureau of the Ottoman state. This commission was empowered by the sultan to collect certain revenues, notably the tribute paid by the newly independent Bulgarian province and excise duties from salt and the new tobacco monopoly. These revenues would be applied directly to the reduction of the debt, rather than disappearing into the national budget. By 1900 this bureau had a staff of more than 5,000, with 720 separate tax-collecting centres scattered throughout the empire. It was increasingly resented as an alien intrusion at the heart of the nation. The tobacco tax was seen as a Christian plot, although it was an Ottoman government that had introduced the tax in the 1870s. The commission levied taxes equitably, but tax-collectors are never popular, and it became a consistent focus for anti-Western agitation.

The bankruptcy was a humiliating reverse,[37] and the creation of the Commission was a hurtful loss of sovereignty. Nevertheless, the agreement created a solid basis for the future. It capped a deficit which could never have been repaid by normal means. In 1881 the amount outstanding was reduced to half the full debt, and the rate of interest was fixed at less than 5 per cent. Stabilization was allied with drastic internal economies, and, by this means, the percentage of national revenue allocated to debt redemption fell from just under 60 per cent to just over 32 per cent between 1877–8 and 1905–6. And, once the deficit was under control, Ottoman credit recovered: Abdul Hamid was able to raise nineteen large loans in Western financial markets after 1881.

As his grip on government and administration strengthened, Abdul Hamid found other ingenious ways of raising money. Among the most remarkable was the expedient of funding the Islamic Railway through the Hejaz, linking Damascus to the pilgrimage centres of Arabia, by donations (not always voluntary). Three million Turkish pounds were raised by this device, which meant that it could be built without an excessive drain on the Treasury and without handing the concession to any foreign company, as had happened with all the other railway lines within the empire.[38] Since the pilgrimage was a major source of revenue, and the railway also generated income from passengers, it was a successful investment.

The other fundamental weakness of the state was the near-constant state of war. As a proportion of national resources, the scale of the empire's military involvement, and consequent financial drain, was much greater than for any of her neighbours or competitors. The Ottoman empire was at war in every decade up to 1914. Half a century of conflict began with the 1853–6 war with Russia which developed into the Crimean War, involving Britain and France as the empire's allies. There was a bitter guerrilla war in Crete, ended only with much loss of life and at a huge cost, from 1866 to 1868. The resistance of the empire's Balkan provinces and neighbours led to a major conflict, which drew in Russia, between 1876 and 1878. There was endemic strife with tribesmen in Syria and Arabia throughout the 1880s,[39] and in 1896 a fresh Cretan insurrection developed into full-scale war with Greece which lasted into the following year. In the twentieth century the scale of conflict increased, with the empire battling with Italy in Libya and, much more dangerously, with all her Balkan neighbours from 1912 to 1913. This catalogue does not express the full drain on Ottoman resources – human and financial – but the monetary cost is the most easily measured. In 1880–1, the military budget was 52 per cent of all state expenditure; by 1907, it amounted to 63 per cent, and that was without the enormous cost of the Balkan wars, still to come.

Confronted at his accession with the present crisis of the Ottoman bankruptcy and the impending crisis of a major war with Russia in the Balkans, Abdul Hamid seemed an unlikely candidate for a successful autocrat. Slight in stature, almost to the point of frailty, dour and quietly spoken, excessively mild in manner, he seemed a typical product of the harem system. He was quickly nicknamed 'the Armenian', because, it was said, those dark, doleful features must have come from his Armenian mother, although she was in fact a Circassian. Others more crudely questioned his paternity, by suggesting that it was his father from whom he inherited an Armenian cast. Both suggestions are ironic given his later reputation as an oppressor of the Armenian people.

Since his brother had been the heir apparent, Abdul Hamid had been able to spend much of his youth out of the palace hothouse. He had accompanied his uncle on his visit to the Paris Exhibition, and he later developed many contacts with the Europeans in Constantinople as well as with members of the Jewish and Armenian communities; he had learned much about finance from the Armenian banker who handled his personal fortune. He was aware of the ruinous cost of his father's and his uncle's courts, and lived in a much simpler – almost austere – style. His ministers were impressed by his interest in the creation of the first Ottoman constitution. But he also showed a political astuteness which belied his seeming innocence. Midhat Pasha, now the most prominent leader of the reform movement, tried to have men personally loyal to him within the palace administration placed close to the new sultan. Abdul Hamid declined the suggestions, and appointed his own men. This was the first hint of an independent spirit, and one which Midhat unwisely ignored. An American met the sultan shortly before the ceremony of girding at Eyüp, and noted their conversation. Asked what his policy would be, the young sultan answered, 'Now, my policy is to obey the ministry. After I have learned what is needed, I shall change my policy and make the ministry obey me.'[40]

The new Ottoman constitution was promulgated on 23 December 1876, in the middle of a violent storm – an ill omen for the future. Large crowds gathered in the early afternoon in the large open square by the Sublime Porte, to hear the reading of the sultan's decree. Abdul Hamid was not present – he was said to be 'indisposed'. Like its precursors in 1839 and 1856, the decree advanced the Western idea of reform – as was pointed out by the Ottoman envoy to the Constantinople Conference of European Ministers, at that moment sitting in judgement on the empire in the Admiralty building less than a mile away. The reform charter, like its predecessors, was an ambiguous document. It granted new rights to the subject peoples of the empire while at the same time enhancing rather than reducing the power of the sultan. For the first time he was declared caliph of Islam, with wide if indeterminate powers over all Muslims; his person was inviolable, and he alone was responsible for all his acts. The sultan was to appoint all his ministers, without reference to Parliament or the grand vizier, and was declared the supreme authority in secular legal matters, and responsible for enforcing the decisions of the *şeriat* courts. Only the sultan could order elections or convene Parliament, and all parliamentary legislation required his signature before it became law, but he could make decrees without reference to Parliament. And, most significant of all, in Article 113, which was inserted at his personal insistence, he retained full residual power: Abdul Hamid could suspend the constitution or banish anyone with only the flimsy cover that it was 'in the interests of the state', based on information provided by the police.[41]

These clauses largely reiterated the traditional powers of the sultan, but they weakened the position of the grand vizier, who now had no real power over ministers who owed their appointment directly to the sultan. There was no restriction on the sultan exercising his own authority – in effect governing personally – as he had been constrained from doing by the traditional system. Even Parliament could be manipulated: part elected (the Chamber of Deputies) and part appointed by the sultan (the Chamber of Notables), its role was tightly circumscribed. Even its powers to supervise the annual budget were undermined by a provision that 'in urgent cases, arising from extraordinary circumstances, the ministers may . . . by Imperial decree . . . cause an unforeseen outlay on the budget.'

The constitution seemed, in Western eyes, to be a successful culmination to the reform process, and gave the empire a much more liberal structure than her mortal enemy, Russia. The constitution guaranteed that 'All subjects of the empire are . . . called Ottomans whatever religion they profess . . . All Ottomans are equal in the eyes of the law. They have the same rights and duties towards the country without prejudice regarding religion.' And it was also declared that 'All Ottomans enjoy individual liberty on the condition that they do not interfere with the liberty of others.'[42] But the reserve powers allowed the sultan enormous latitude if he cared to exercise his full potential authority. In Austria-Hungary, the governments of Emperor Franz Joseph would also use emergency clauses to dispense with the restrictions of parliamentary rule.

Abdul Hamid moved quickly to reclaim power: Midhat Pasha was dismissed after only forty-nine days as grand vizier, and was sent into exile under cover of Article 113. The Parliament survived its principal architect by little more than a year; allowed a few sittings until February 1878, it was then formally prorogued by the sultan, who failed to summon it again as required by the constitution – a lapse which lasted for almost three decades. The settlement of 1876 was never withdrawn or formally abrogated, however, and for the remainder of his reign Abdul Hamid continued to describe himself as a constitutional monarch, and the Ottoman constitution was printed annually at the beginning of the official government yearbook.

The sultan had decided to follow a traditional path. In one of the final sessions of the parliamentary committee of senators and deputies, Abdul Hamid declared, 'I made a mistake when

I wished to imitate my father Abdul Meçid, who sought reform by permission and by liberal institutions. I shall follow in the footsteps of my grandfather, Sultan Mahmud. Like him I now understand that it is only by force that one can move the people with whose protection God has entrusted me.'[43] Unlike his grandfather, however, Abdul Hamid had an excellent sense of what the West had to offer a modernizer, and over the space of three decades he created a centralized system of social and political intelligence unsurpassed in Europe. The skill with which he neutralized all potential forces of opposition, mostly within the letter if not the spirit of the new constitution, was assured and astute. He exiled Midhat and the other leading reformers so swiftly and so effectively that there was soon virtually an Ottoman reform movement in exile in Paris. Later, recognizing that the exiles could be more dangerous abroad than at home, he allowed some of them to return, promising that they would not be persecuted for their political opinions. But soon after Midhat returned he was placed on trial for complicity in the murder of Abdul Aziz – the old canard which had been circulating since the sultan's untimely death. A compliant judge and jury duly found him guilty, and he was sentenced not to death but to perpetual imprisonment. The humanitarian gesture was for public consumption only: the former grand vizier ended his days in the grim fortress of Taif in Arabia, strangled by the executioners sent by the sultan. But officially he died after a long illness. His head was sent to the capital, it was rumoured, in a box labelled 'Japanese Ivories'.

The treatment of Midhat was an extreme action because he would not succumb to pressure and was too dangerous to leave alive. Enemies were usually neutralized by more subtle means.[44] Abdul Hamid could not forget that Midhat had already deposed two sultans and might well unseat a third. Indeed, much of the extreme anxiety undoubtedly displayed by the sultan had a firm basis in fact. There was indeed a conspiracy to restore Murad, who was living quietly in the Çirağan palace, and it was only because his brother was plainly in no state to be even a figurehead for a revolt that the attempt failed. But, despite the danger posed by his brother as a focus for future coups, Abdul Hamid simply had him moved to the greater security of a new compound he was building in the Yıldız Park, on the hills above the Beşiktaş district, and he continued to live untroubled until his natural death in 1904. The sultan's daughter related her father's own description of these events:

After the Ali Suavi affair [the attempt to reinstate Murad on the throne], I had to be very careful. My eyes were opened, and if I allowed my brother to remain free, neither of us would have any peace ... For both our sakes I took very strict measures. If not neither he nor I would have died in our beds of natural causes.[45]

The more usual impression of Abdul Hamid is not as a man of decision but as one racked by fear and uncertainty. The British ambassador Sir Henry Layard (better known to history as the excavator of Nineveh) reported that the sultan was convinced that the British intended to kidnap him on a warship and to restore Murad. Layard described this as an absurd delusion; yet it was precisely the firm, high-handed action that the British adopted when dealing with intractable officials in Egypt. Perhaps Abdul Hamid's sense of prudence did become excessive, however: it is frequently suggested that he was paranoid.

It is not uncommon for political adversaries to describe an opponent as 'evil' or 'mad'. The enemies of Abdul Hamid, both inside and outside the empire, considered him both mad and bad. His 'madness' lay in not following the approved path of Westernization. For a generation it had been believed that the appropriate model for the empire's development was provided by the enlightened European nations: the French and the British especially demanded a Western style of polity, with responsible ministers, operating within a parliamentary context, accountable to the people. In reality, no major European power quite lived up to the ideal. The franchise in Britain was restricted; politics in Germany and Austria were strongly influenced by the monarch; while Russia had no effective constitution at all. Spain was highly unstable, subject to civil war and military coup; and Italy was riven by the dispute between Church and State. Nevertheless, Westernization had been the programme advanced by the Ottoman 'reformers' for over thirty years. But by the accession of Abdul Hamid their energy and popular support had reached its limit: the 1876 constitution was the zenith of their achievement. Reform had disappointed not only the Western sponsors of change but also those patriotic Ottomans who accepted the need for modernization but not necessarily in a Western context. Meanwhile they had watched the country decay into defeat and financial chaos. There was support for turning in a new direction that owed nothing to any of the European states.

Abdul Hamid offered them, by slow stages, a different programme. It was based on the values of Islam, and built on the title of caliph secured for him by the constitution of 1876. The Russians justified their intrusions into the Balkans as support for their Slav brothers – a pan-Slav crusade. The pan-Islamic concept was developed slowly by Abdul Hamid, who neatly elided an Islamic ideology with the most modern instruments of power. This was a *gazi* creed recreated for a new context. As caliph, Abdul Hamid claimed the loyalty and the service of all true Muslims, from the East Indies to the shores of the Atlantic. For the West, this retreat into Islam meant that the sultan 'wrapped himself more and more deeply in unreal daydreams, laying continually greater emphasis on his religious dignity as caliph, by means of which he hoped to achieve dominion over all Muslims'[46] The Ottoman sultans had never made formal claim to the title of caliph, except in some general, honorific sense. Abdul Hamid transformed the claim into a statement of temporal power. At its apogee, the empire had never needed to claim the vague caliphal authority, and the attempt to create this new house of Islam late in the nineteenth century was, of itself, an admission of Ottoman weakness. Pan-Islam emerged after the Ottomans had been effectively expelled from the whole of the European mainland, except for a patch of land up as far as Adrianapole. But this was also the point at which Abdul Hamid came to the throne, and there seems to be no doubt that he believed sincerely in his role as caliph. In political terms it had the effect of uniting all the forces in traditional Ottoman society behind him. If his rhetoric was of the past, the sultan was also the most effective modernizer of Ottoman society.

Many of the promises embodied in the constitution were fulfilled. He provided the empire with a basic structure of secondary education, with a network of railways and, late in his reign, with plans to improve the network of roads. The telegraph soon extended over the entire country, down to the level of the small town.[47] He ran the bureaucracy through the huge staff (almost 12,000 in the palace complex) that he had gathered in the Yıldız palace. Yıldız and the sultan's household virtually superseded both the traditional vizieral structure and the new ministerial system set up under the constitution. But this too was in the Ottoman tradition, back to the days when Mehmed the Conqueror first laid down the structure of the Yeni Saray. Abdul Hamid created a system which made the centralized exercise of power a possibility.[48] He could rule the state from his rooms in the palace, because his eyes and ears were everywhere. Reports ('journals') were sent to him weekly or even daily by informers who reported on conditions in every part of the empire. He frequently knew more about events in a distant rural locality than the official in charge of the region, sitting in the provincial capital. Sir Charles Eliot, writing as 'Odysseus', remarked that:

it [the telegraph] is the most powerful instrument for a despot who wishes to control his own officials. It is no longer necessary to leave a province to the discretion of a governor ... with the telegraph one can order him about, find out what he is doing, reprimand him, recall him, instruct his subordinates to report against him, and generally deprive him of all real power.[49]

The old provincial overlord, like the pasha whom the English gentleman and diplomat Robert Curzon met at Trebizond ('he smoked the pipe of tranquillity on the carpet of prudence and the pashalik of Trebizond slumbered in the sun'[50]) had gone; he was, as Eliot noted, 'a centrifugal force', whereas his modern counterpart was entirely centripetal.

Abdul Hamid was one of the first to recognize the informational value of the photograph, made possible by the roll-film camera. With a photograph, the sultan could judge for himself the validity of the information he received. Alongside the volumes of reports and texts submitted were ranked volume after volume of photographs. These are not works of art or reportage in the Western photographic tradition, but documents of social or political intelligence.[51] They show a bridge half-built (when the provincial governor, or *vali*, had assured him it was complete), an empty market (when he had been told there was food in plenty) or a deserted school that should have been full of children. Sometimes the images are of individuals, and from the accompanying notes we can deduce that these are potential 'subversives'. The consequences of failure could be exile, a worse posting or demotion. Although there was considerable brutality – particularly in the capital, with the sultan's secret police – fear rather than brutality was the controlling ethic of the system. No one knew how much the sultan knew, but, because Abdul Hamid was both hard-working and obsessive, he knew a great deal. Individuals were encouraged to inform on their neighbours, and complaints would be investigated and were frequently acted upon.

The sultan was not an 'innovator', in the way that his father and grandfather had relished novelty for its own sake: he was a creator of systems. Thus, Abdul Hamid was a great user of the telegraph, but the bulk of the network had been created by the time that he came to the throne. There were 25,000 km of telegraph line in 1869, but by 1904 this had only increased to 36,000 km – a slow and cautious advance. In the army, in contrast to his predecessors, Abdul Hamid rationalized rather than innovated. It had suffered from an excess of new ideas and ill-coordinated weapons-buying. When its troops faced the Russians in 1877, they carried a bizarre assembly of equipment. William Herbert, who served in the war on the Ottoman side and was captured at the fall of Plevna, admired the Turkish army; yet he was amazed when ammunition arrived one day that would fit *none* of the various patterns of rifle carried by his troops.[52] The troops fought well, with a dogged determination that amazed Europe (and most of all the Russians), but their military system had failed them. Although under Abdul Hamid there was little innovation (partly because he feared giving the army too independent a role), much improvement was made to the system. Long-term contracts were made with the German and Austrian arms-makers, who produced standardized equipment for the Turkish market. One type of ammunition then fitted all the rifles used by the front-line troops; the artillery all came from the same source.[53] The military are a clear example of the Hamidian approach to change. His political programme was in the tradition of his grandfather, but, unlike Mahmud II, he applied a ruthless organizational and bureaucratic logic to accomplishing his ends. Mahmud the Just wheeling with his cavalry is one characteristic image; of Abdul Hamid the Damned, the equivalent would be of a man sifting through papers, rarely stirring into the open air and even more rarely leaving the confines of his Yıldız palace.

This Hamidian system outlasted its creator, and formed the

substructure for the modern Turkish state. When in 1908 an army coup forced him to become a constitutional monarch in practice as well as in theory (he was eventually turned off the throne in 1909, after the failure of a counter-coup), the 'Young Turks' (whose name and nationalist aspirations set them apart from the Young *Ottomans* of the earlier generation) took over a modernized efficient bureaucracy – one which could continue to operate under the most rigorous wartime conditions, and survive invasion and civil war. When in 1923 Mustafa Kemal (the later Kemal Atatürk – 'Father of the Turks') finally swept away the residue of the old order, the Ottoman dynasty and the last vestiges of former imperial power, the caliphate, his inheritance was the structure and system built by Abdul Hamid during thirty years. In the hands of its new masters it worked better than it had done before.

The Hamidian system was flexible and responsive to the guiding hand of whoever operated its mechanism: Atatürk drove it better than his predecessors. Abdul Hamid failed not because he was brutal or cruel but because he lacked the will to control his own creation. The flood of information from the periphery to the centre provided an enlarged sense of power, but also a ramifying impression of subversion and threat. Informers were valued by the plots they uncovered, the incompetence they unearthed, the dangers which their efforts averted. In consequence, they developed skills at reporting the embers of dissent as a raging conflagration. A chance remark in a coffee-house grew into a network of revolutionaries. As the sultan himself believed that his throne was in danger, he was susceptible to every wild suggestion of conspiracy or sedition. And at the hands of his investigators, skilled in all the techniques of torture, his worst fears were confirmed.

As the secret Hamidian state became more powerful and more secretive, its need for enemies – real or imaginary – grew ever greater. The most notable focus for these obsessive fears was the Armenians. There is no doubt that during the 1880s and 1890s the traditionally quiescent Armenians became more and more determined to enhance their position within the state. As a group, they were not popular, given their traditional role as moneylenders and bankers. Many of the Western reports by journalists and missionaries supported the Armenians' cause; others condemned them. The bloody events under both Abdul Hamid and his successors are read differently by each side,[54] but for the Ottomans the Armenians represented a threat to their control of the state. Abdul Hamid was himself a target for assassination, and the occupation of the Ottoman Bank in Constantinople by Armenian nationalists in 1895 was a mortal affront. The degree of the sultan's responsibility for the killings that followed is uncertain: he assuredly cannot have been unaware of what was going on, both from the reports of his own informers and from the bombardment of complaints from Western governments, supplied with details by their consuls and missionaries. There was a pattern both in the events and in the Western response. There was a marked similarity in practice to the sanguine inter-communal conflicts in Bulgaria, Bosnia and Herzegovina (1875–7), where the Ottoman authorities simply encouraged long-standing hatreds to spill over into massacre. The role of the state was one of 'restoring order'. A not-dissimilar practice was followed by the Russian government when instituting pogroms against its Jewish citizens. In the Armenian case the Western outrage followed on very much the same lines.[55]

No Ottoman sultan has ever been more universally execrated than Abdul Hamid. On the one side he was condemned as 'Abdul the Damned', or 'the Red Sultan', whose hands were awash with blood. On the other he was derided as a man so ruled by cowardice and terror that he would not sleep more than one night in the same room, and who would not stir from his palace for fear of assassination. In Western eyes, by 1907 he had come to embody all the worst features attributed to the Ottomans – cruelty, cowardice and, less plausibly, lust. He was an appropriate leader for a diseased and sickened monarchy. He was 'the sick man of Europe'. The origin of this phrase is well known. In January 1853, Tsar Nicholas I, 'sweating violently' from a high fever and in agony from gout, had risen from his sickbed to meet Sir Hamilton Seymour, the British minister in St Petersburg. Their conversations turned inevitably to the Tsar's main preoccupation. Nicholas was convinced that the Ottoman empire was on the point of imminent collapse. He told Seymour, 'we have a sick man on our hands, a man who is seriously ill; it will ... be a great misfortune if he escapes us one of these days, especially before all the arrangements are made'.[56] The 'arrangements' he had in mind were for the dismemberment of the Ottoman empire by the European powers.

Thereafter, Turkey was 'the sick man of Europe': cartoonists, notably in the British comic journals *Punch* and, its imitator, *Judy*, invariably depicted the sultan, representing the Ottomans, as either a decrepit figure in a fez or an unhealthy fat Oriental; the sick man soon became a political and visual cliché. But this image of an enfeebled, decaying, moribund empire did not begin with the Tsar, for it had been common for centuries. Long before Nicholas produced his phrase (for the Ottomans' tombstone?) Europeans had predicted the imminent collapse of the empire. In 1622, Sir Thomas Roe, ambassador to the Sublime Porte, had written of the 'fatal sign ... of their declination'. He described the empire as being 'like an old body, crazed through many vices, which remain when the youth and strength is decayed'. Other Christian writers confirmed his observations. The Venetian envoy to Constantinople, Lorenzo Bernardo, suggested in 1595 that 'it [the Ottoman empire] rose to great strength very rapidly, in the same way that plants which quickly mature and produce fruit are also quick to wither'.[57] These critics, whose views were echoed by Ottoman reformers,[58] drew a stark comparison between the virtues of the great sultans like Mehmed the Conqueror or Suleiman the Lawgiver and the vices of their successors. They suggested that the empire was being poisoned by the corruption at its heart. And that corruption, like a pustule, came to its head in the person of Abdul Hamid. A shabby little figure in his fez and stambouline, he embodied both visually and symbolically the decline from the great sultans of the past, with their turbans, furs and egret feathers.

The forces that swept away the sultan in 1909 – the army, the politicians and the influence of the Western powers – restored the Ottoman ruling class to power, together with the dreams embodied in the Rose Pavilion decree. The constitution of 1876 was revived, and the Young Turks now exercised all the power that Abdul Hamid had gathered for himself. The new sultan, Mehmed V, was a ceremonial figure, without political influence. In government the Young Turks were little more successful than Abdul Hamid had been. Asked what the difference was between the old and the new regimes, a German arms salesman confided that nothing had changed, except the bribes required were larger.

War undermined the fragile new stability of the Ottoman state in what was to be its last phase. The Balkan wars showed the formidable power of the new Slav nations, while in Libya the Ottomans were forced to defend their last territory in North Africa against an Italy hungry for new colonies. The entry of Turkey into the world war in 1914 on the side of Germany and Austria was a calculation of advantage, but one made under the guns of two large German warships which had evaded the Allied blockade and sailed into the Bosporus. And although the Turkish army performed well throughout the war – defeating the British, Australians and New Zealanders on the beaches at Gallipoli; forcing the surrender of the invading British force at Kut al-Amara in Iraq; and, holding the invading Russians and the Balkans nations at bay

– by 1918 all the Ottoman armies were starved of resources and in retreat. The Allies assumed the empire was ready for dismemberment: the sick man was finally on the deathbed.[59] Yet this was not the final turn of the wheel. The Turkish army in Anatolia found a new spirit under Mustafa Kemal, the victorious commander at Gallipoli, and fought back. Eventually all the occupiers – French, British, Italian, Greek and Russian – were expelled from Turkish soil. The war against the Greeks saw more savage fighting than any in the world war, and the burning city of Smyrna (İzmir) became both a beacon for Turkish resurgence and the beginning of a new narrative of atrocity.

The final ruler of the Osmanli dynasty, Mehmed VI, who had been placed on the throne in 1918, was seen as a pawn of the Allies; under the victorious nationalists he was shorn of his powers as sultan but was allowed to continue as caliph until that title was also abolished in 1923. Thereafter, the Turkish Republic, born out of the First World War, abandoned the dreams of the ruling class and vested sovereignty in 'the people' of a national-state. Mustafa Kemal (Kemal Atatürk) destroyed the transnational Ottoman state and created a new Turkish nation, once more rooted in the Anatolian heartland whence the Ottomans had come centuries before. As the Turkish Republic developed, power again centred on a single individual – Atatürk himself. The old Ottoman order had been destroyed, but its lineaments refused to disappear. The Ottoman way was reborn as Turkish nationhood,[60] and Atatürk rejected the path of mimicking Europe, taking only what he wanted from the West.

CHAPTER 7

'The Lustful Turk'

In the space of four centuries, it seemed, nothing changed, and yet, on the surface, everything had changed. The outward alterations – caftan to stambouline, turban to fez – had marked a dramatic shift from tradition towards reform; when Mustafa Kemal, leader of the new Turkish Republic, wore a Panama hat for the first time, in 1925, at Kastamonu, in the heartland of Islamic conservatism, the shock was as great as when Mahmud II abandoned the caftan and the turban. Kemal stressed the importance of his symbolic gesture. He declared to a large crowd:

The Turkish people, who founded the Turkish Republic are civilized; they are civilized in history and reality. But I tell you that . . . the people of the Turkish republic, who claim to be civilized, must prove themselves to be civilized, by their ideas and mentality, by their family life and their way of living . . . They must prove in fact that they are civilized and advanced persons in their outward aspect also. I shall put my explanation to you in the form of a question:

Is our dress national? (cries of no)

Is it civilized and international . . . (cries of no, no)

I agree with you. This grotesque mixture of styles is neither national nor international. A civilized international dress is worthy and appropriate for our nation, and we will wear it. Boots and shoes on our feet, trousers on our legs, shirt and tie, jacket and waistcoat – and of course, to complete these, a cover with a brim on our heads. I want to make this clear. This head covering is called a HAT.[1]

For women there was an even more dramatic shift, for 'civilization' meant the abolition of seclusion and the veil, and legal equality with men.

Yet the West remained preoccupied with the entrenched images from the past. 'Civilization' did not bring acceptance, merely a greater fear of the alien qualities of the Turk. Most Westerners could not understand the transformations that were so clear to all Turks, whether Ottomans from the days of the empire or nationalists in the new republic after 1923. They fixed instead on the superficial, the exotic and mysterious images from the distant past.[2] These attitudes had deep roots in the earliest days of Christian–Muslim contact, but from the early eighteenth century there had been a shift in emphasis from fear and hostility to patronage and admiration. It has been pointed out that this was the point at which the Ottomans ceased to be a military threat, but that is *post hoc propter hoc*, too simple a conclusion. The nature of the contact certainly changed, for, instead of the West seeing the Turks only on the battlefield or as captives, they began to appear as emissaries in the courts of the West. This new vision of the Ottoman was fanned into fire as a fashionable 'Turcomania' which swept through all the countries of western Europe in the first half of the eighteenth century. The preoccupation with all things Turkish began with the embassy of Mehmed Efendi to France in 1720–1. The French courtiers were intrigued by the furs, the rich caftans and the thrilling exoticism which the ambassador and his retinue exuded. Their responses to these alien creatures was predictable. Diarists remarked censoriously that, while the ambassador would refuse alcohol in public, he was evidently entranced by the newly invented concoction champagne, and consumed large quantities in his private rooms. Similarly, the presence of women at public events apparently caused the Ottomans some discomfort, but, noted the diarists, it was quite the reverse in private. But in the years after the embassy, for no reason which is particularly attributable to Mehmed Efendi, the French shifted from seeing the Turks predominantly as figures of terror to seeing them as a focus of exotic pleasure, lust and duplicity. And where France led, Europe followed.[3]

Soon mendacity, dissimulation and rapacity were also being presented as characteristically *Ottoman* vices. Add to these the all-too-easily imagined scarlet lusts and violent passions of the harem, and the old stereotypes of the Lusty Moor and the Ensanguined Turks were reinforced, not displaced, by the contact with reality. As the Ottomans ceased to be feared for their warlike and manly virtues, they were half-envied, half-despised for their assumed athleticism and subtle cruelties in the bedchamber. Depravities inflamed the imaginations of European men when they conjectured about the East. How appropriate that in the apartments where de Sade's *The One Hundred and Twenty Days of Sodom* was enacted 'splendid Turkish beds canopied in three-coloured damask with matching furniture adorned these suites whose boudoirs offered everything and more for most sensual that lubricity might fancy'.[4] Or that some of the victims were described as '*sultanas*' or '*bardashes*' – catamites.

The misapprehensions were not only from the Western direction: Ottomans coming to the West suffered a profound shock and conjured up their own fantasies. Sheikh Rifaa noted of the French: 'Men among them are the slaves of women whether they be beautiful or not. One of them said . . . women among the people of the East are like household possessions while among the Franks they are like spoiled children.'[5] A Moroccan ambassador, visiting Spain in 1766, was shocked by the way in which

The women are very much addicted to conversation and conviviality with men other than their husbands, in company or in private . . . It often happens that a Christian returns home and finds his wife or his daughter or his sister in the company of another Christian, a stranger, drinking together and leaning against one another. He is delighted with this . . . and esteems it as favour from the Christian who is in company of his wife or whichever other women of his household it may be.[6]

The horrified reaction of the ambassador, al-Ghazal, probably echoed that of many Muslims of his day: 'we returned to our lodgings and we prayed to God to save us from the wretched state of these infidels.' Yet this mutual incomprehension, cloaked in a sense of self-satisfaction, blinded both parties to the realities of their own societies. Men from Britain and France despised the closeting of women in the Ottoman lands, and congratulated themselves on the open freedom enjoyed by women in the West. The enforced silence of women in their own nations passed without remark.

Before the eighteenth century, admission to the Ottoman empire was a rare privilege, and very few Ottomans made the reverse journey. From the beginning of the eighteenth century, the pattern of mutual exchange grew year by year. Constantinople became a port of call on the grand tour, and an increasing number of Ottomans came to the West. A number of parallel attitudes emerged, from both sides of the exchange. First, and the fewest in number, were the enthusiasts, who found fulfilment in the contact. At the other extreme were those who abominated every aspect of the alien world – a large assembly. Both these groups, passionate in their advocacy for or against, were not so much experiencing the alien – the 'other' – as finding reinforcement for their own hopes and fears. Much the largest group were simply inquisitive, and in their often naïve and ill-informed curiosity lie the unconscious attitudes with which their own cultures had infused them. Finally there was the largest category of all: those who passed judgement on the Ottomans without the benefit of seeing for themselves. Indeed, as the means of printed communication improved, and most substantially with the growth of the illustrated press in the nineteenth century,[7] the 'matter of the East' became the property of anyone who could read a newspaper or a pamphlet, or who listened to opinions expressed in the alehouse or at the dinner table. At certain points, after the 'Bulgarian atrocities' of the 1870s or the 'Armenian massacres' of the 1890s, the issue of the Ottomans was at the heart of politics, most dramatically in Britain, but throughout Europe and the United States. In Britain, certainly, the distinction between those who had been east and those who had not was often marked. Benjamin Disraeli, entranced by the romance of the Orient, had spent many months in Greece, Constantinople and Egypt, living 'indolently *à la Turque*'. For Disraeli, 'the meanest merchant in the Bazaar looks like a Sultan in an Eastern fairy tale,'[8] and the East was to be enjoyed and understood. For William Ewart Gladstone, who had been no further east than Italy and treasured Western Christian civilization, the Turk was to be abominated.

The atavistic preoccupation of the West with the Ottomans falls under three broad headings: lust, cruelty and filth. The last overarches the first two. Virtually every traveller felt compelled to comment on some or all of them; in none of very many texts that I have read have the topics been ignored entirely. For most, the experience of the East brought an inner personal struggle to a head; and for women travellers the issues were more complex and subtle than they appeared to men.[9] Because they could, if they were persistent, be admitted to the harem world, about which men could only mutter and conjecture, women confronted a particular conflict between the stereotype and the perceived reality. They were also aware of constraints they suffered in their own societies: for every Madame de Sévigné, honoured and applauded as a savante, there were many more women of spirit and accomplishment who were stifled by their lack of fulfilment. And for even a woman of accepted quality and intellectual stature, there was a division of spheres. As Pope put it, in his *Epistle to a Lady*:

> But grant, in Public Men sometimes are shown,
> As Woman's seen in Private life alone:
> Our bolder Talents in full light display'd,
> Your Virtues open fairest in the shade.[10]

Alain Corbin has pointed out the connection of darkness and disease: cut off from the light and the open air, it was thought, women deteriorated physically and psychologically.[11] The harem, with its blank windowless walls, remote from the outside world, seemed to men an inevitable breeding-ground for vice and moral decay. Yet were not European women cast by men into 'the shade', and suffering from being cloistered? Did they not feel a kinship with those secluded behind the walls of the harem? The first European woman to visit the inner world was Lady Mary Wortley Montagu, and it need not be added that Lady Mary was one of a most privileged élite, with an independence far beyond that of most women. But Pope's cruel lines could have been addressed to her predicament: a clever woman chained to a dull man. She was transformed by her experience of the Ottoman world, and began her life anew.

During the first days of 1717 she travelled to Constantinople with her husband, the new English ambassador to the court of Ahmed III. She took with her all the prejudices of her class and race, topped up with a surfeit of literary imaginings about the mysterious East. Her mind was open, however, and contact produced profound changes in her attitudes from the first days of her entry into the Ottoman-occupied Balkans.

She noted of her host at the town of Peterwaradin:

Achmet-Beg ... has had the good sense to prefer an easy, quiet, secure life to all the dangerous Honnours of the Port[e]. He sups with us every night and drinks wine very freely. You cannot imagine how much he is delighted with the Liberty of converseing with me ... I have frequent disputes with him concerning the difference of our Customs, particularly the confinements of Women.

He assures me there is nothing at all in it; only, says he, we [that is the Turks] have the advantage that when our Wives cheat us, no body knows it.[12]

Featured in this letter to Alexander Pope (whose appetite for the bizarre and the grotesque she knew well) are three stereotypes of the Ottomans, bundled together: dissimulation (the wine), lust (intimate proximity to a European woman) and cruelty (the confinement of women). Yet Achmet-Beg's behaviour and responses undermined each of the prejudices in turn. Hospitality demanded that he entertain his guests, and, anyway, the prohibition against wine was observed only by the pious. Drunkenness, on the other hand, was to be shunned. And, plainly, it was the conversation not the unveiled face of Lady Mary that roused him. Indeed, her fine, bright eyes could only have been diminished by the sadly pockmarked face below. And his remark about cheating wives had perhaps a particular resonance for her, who had married her husband after clandestine meetings and endless intrigue, because her father was negotiating to sell her more advantageously to a vapid but rich young Irish peer. Her alternative had been not the violent death that disobedient daughters were (wrongly) believed to suffer in the Ottoman lands, but a prolonged social death. Indeed, said her father, she could refuse to marry Viscount Massarene, but on condition that she never married *anyone* else, with the consequent effective exile from society into country living. And she would be allowed only £400 a year for the rest of her life to cover all her needs. His implication was clear: she could choose freely, but only between his choice for her husband and the end of the life she desired.

For Lady Mary, therefore, the Ottomans were alien but not unappealing. Add to that the bitter fact that her husband, Edward Wortley Montagu, with whom she had eloped to escape the viscount or a life of maidenly penury, turned out to be a dullard, immune to romance, and her sense of identity with Ottoman women grew ever stronger. When she first went to the baths, in Adrianapole, she was 'in my travelling Habit, which is a rideing dress, and certainly appear'd very extraordinary to them, yet there was not one of 'em that showed the least surprize or impertinent Curiosity, but receiv'd me with all the obliging civility possible.'[13] Nor did she ignore their common fate as victims of male proclivities:

The Lady that seem'd the most considerable amongst them entreated me to sit by her and would fain have undress'd me for the bath. I excus'd my selfe with some difficulty, they being all so earnest in perswading me. I was at last forc'd to open my skirt and shew them my stays, which satisfy'd 'em very well, for I saw they beleiv'd I was so lock'd up in that machine that it was not in my power to open it, which contrivance they attributed to my Husband.

She concluded the thought with an aside: 'I was charm'd with their Civility and Beauty and should have been very glad to pass more time with them, but Mr. W[ortley] resolving to pursue his Journey the next morning early, I was in haste to see the ruins of Justinian's Church . . .' No doubt the female friend to whom she addressed the letter would have recognized the implicit complaint.

One of her first acts on arriving in the Ottoman domains was to equip herself with a full set of clothes suitable for an Ottoman lady of quality, which she described to her sister as 'admirably becoming'. Once within the enveloping muslins and silks, she discovered the benefits of invisibility, for no Ottoman would dare to intrude upon a woman's inviolability. Like the blank external walls of the harem, the utter anonymity of the Ottoman dress repelled intruders more than it restrained the woman within. Indeed, abandoning the armour of her stays, Lady Mary found other elements to the liberation within the veil: 'Now I am a little acquainted with their ways, I cannot forbear admiring either the exemplary discretion or extreme Stupidity of all the writers that have given accounts of 'em.'[14] The (male) gender of the writers was unspecified. The truth, as she had discovered, was:

'Tis very easy to see they have more Liberty than we have, no Woman of what rank so ever being permitted to go in the streets without 2 muslins, one that covers her face all but her Eyes and another that hides the whole dress of her head and hangs halfe way down her back; and their Shapes are wholly conceal'd by a thing they call a Ferigée [ferace], which no Woman of any sort appears without . . . You may guess how effectually this disguises them, that there is no distinguishing the great Lady from her Slave, and 'tis impossible for the most jealous Husband to know his Wife when he meets her, and no Man dares either touch or follow a Woman in the Street.

This, then, was the meaning of Achmet-Beg's amused aside over dinner, as he thought of how 'This perpetual Masquerade gives them entire Liberty of following their Inclinations without danger of Discovery.'[15] But presumably, if he was aware, then so too were other Ottoman men; yet the traditions

that permitted women to leave the walls of the harem, accompanied by eunuchs and dressed in the prescribed clothing,
could not be undermined. The only constraints were the
savage penalties if caught *in flagrante*. Much of Pierre Loti's
1879 novel *Aziyadé*, in which effective liberty was balanced by
death or worse if discovered with a lover, was dominated by
this theme. But Lady Mary, remembering those fearful and
uncomfortable assignations with Wortley, in terror of being
seen by her father's spies, must have understood better than
most the benefits of the Ottoman way.

Other advantages for a woman soon became clear to her.
She found that married women could inherit property, and
control their estate, regardless of their husband's wishes. And
while the life of an Ottoman official could hang by a hair, she
noted that women were

the only free people in the Empire. The very Divan pays a respect to
'em and the Grand Signor himselfe, when a Bassa [pasha] is executed,
never violates the priveleges of the Haram (or Women's apartment)
which remains unsearch'd entire to the Widow. They are Queens of
their slaves, which the Husband has no permission so much as to
look upon . . . except that his Lady chuses.[16]

As time went on, however, she discovered that the practice
did not quite match the theory, and that women were forced
into marriage, cheated or dispossessed just as they were in
England.

These views from within the hidden world of women
deserve discussion at some length because they not only allow
a unique insight across the gender barrier which kept out all
men, they also obliquely allow a clearer vision of the male
Ottoman world. The latter is possible because of Lady Mary's
extravagant sympathy for all things Turkish, which extended
even to the point of absurdity. The English criminal code was
harsh and often unjust, but to suggest that Turkish law was
'better designed and better executed than ours'[17] seemed to

suggest that she thought the executions enacted on the shores of the Golden Horn were less barbaric than civilized English justice. Yet perhaps she did, for, barely two years before she left on her voyage to the East, the leaders of the failed Jacobite rebellion suffered the disgusting rending and dismembering rituals of the English law of treason, while their followers were sold into slavery. One who could easily have met his end on the scaffold at Tower Hill was her own brother-in-law, the earl of Mar, who had escaped to exile in Paris. Or perhaps she had in mind French justice, where criminals were 'broken on the wheel' before expiring. A woman of learning, sharp sensibility and acute powers of observation, her letters bear the marks of careful thought and should not be lightly dismissed.

Her narratives[18] go to the heart of Ottoman ambiguities. The letters to male correspondents, to Pope and the Abbé Conti, differ in tone from those to her female acquaintances, who were able to decipher her half-hidden meaning. And so too were her female readers, when these 'letters' were published. She wrote to her sister in exile with her husband in Paris, 'I went to see the Sultana Hafife [Hafise], favourite of the last Emperour Mustapha, who . . . was deposed . . . This Lady was immediately after his death saluted with an Absolute order to leave the Seraglio and chuse her selfe a Husband from the great Men at the Port[e].'[19] This was only partly true, for the custom was for former wives to be required to live in the Eski Saray built by Mehmed the Conqueror and colloquially known as 'the house of sorrows'. So the sultana 'threw her selfe at the Sultan's feet and begg'd him to poniard her rather than use his brother's Widow with that contempt.'

The sultana demanded an independent life, but the suspicious Ahmed was not willing to go so far. He was well aware of the power of women in the Ottoman court. But since it was a free choice of a husband:

She chose Bekir Effendi, then Secretary of State, and above fourscore years old, to convince the World that she firmly intended to keep the vow she had made of never suffering a 2nd Husband to approach her bed, and since she must honnour some subject so far as to be call'd his Wife she would chuse him as a mark of her Gratitude, since it was he that had presented her at the Age of 10 year old to her lost Lord.[20]

For someone who since childhood had known only the life of the imperial harem, she had a strong political sense and, plainly, a will of steel.

Sultana Hafise married as required, but

she has never permitted him to pay her one visit, thô it is now 15 year she has been in his house, where she passes her time in unintterupted Mourning with a constancy very little known in Christendom, especially in a widow of 21, for she is now but 36 [a very few years older, indeed, than Lady Mary and her sister]. She has no black Eunuchs for her Guard [and thus provided no means for her husband to exercise any control over her], her Husband being oblig'd to respect her as a Queen and not enquire at all into what is done in her apartment.[21]

Lady Mary, locked into a sour marriage, and her sister, carried by her husband's failure into a half-life of exile, might have envied Hafise's independence. Perhaps there is some clue to the deeper meaning of her letter when it concludes, 'It may be, our Proverb that knowledge is no burden, may be true to one's selfe, but knowing too much is very apt to make us troublesome to other people.'[22]

The Ottomans whom Lady Mary met represented a society already changing, and one about to undergo even greater transformations. She largely ignored the manifest cruelties and injustice implicit in the system, but, as a corrective to the highly coloured or ill-willed imaginings of most male commentators, her testimony is unequalled. She wrote as the narrow opening-up to the Western world was beginning under

Ahmed III – a policy which continued under his successors. Many of her observations were coloured by her own needs and interests, as were those of male travellers to the empire, but there is a strength of analysis in the women writers, like Lady Hester Stanhope, that is more evidently lacking in the men.

Many male visitors were preoccupied with the rampant sexuality of the Ottoman empire which they were so certain they would find. They echoed the attitudes towards Islam that had their origin in the medieval writers surveyed by Norman Daniel. He writes that 'The special lubricity of Muslims was everywhere believed to be a fact and this, of course came from the teaching and example of the Prophet, which the Qur'ān preserved.'[23] It was asserted that Muslims were given to sodomy, and introduced foul vices into 'the garden of nature'. Daniel describes the 'fascinated horror' with which Christendom devoured stories of Muslim carnality: 'The Christian criticism and exaggeration of the licence attributed to Muslims was often excessive; *there was great unanimity*' (my emphasis).[24] Thus, William of Adam, titular bishop of Sultaniyah, was certain that 'In the Muslim sect any sexual act at all is not only not forbidden but allowed and praised.'[25] Centuries later these same canards were presented as fact to Halet Efendi in Paris, and he responded angrily, and with some justice. 'They say: know that as a general rule ... the Muslims are homosexuals ... listening, one would think that all of us are of that persuasion, as if we had no other concerns.'[26] He also pointed out:

In Paris there is a kind of market place called Palais Royal where there are shops of various kinds of goods on all four sides, and above them rooms containing 1500 women and 1500 boys exclusively occupied in sodomy. To go to that place by night is shameful, but since there is no harm in going there by day, I went to see this special spectacle. As one enters, from all sides males and females hand out printed cards to anyone who comes, inscribed: '*I*

*have so many women, my room is in such and such place, the price
is so much*' or '*I have so many boys, their ages are such and such,
the official price is so much*' all on specially printed cards ... the
women and boys surround a man on every side, parade around and
ask, '*Which of us do you like?*' What is more great people here ask
proudly, '*Have you visited our Palais Royal. And did you like the
women and the boys?*'

He concluded piously, thanking God that 'in the lands of
Islam there are not many boys and catamites.' What impressed
him most was the vast scale of the enterprise, and the use of
printed cards. No doubt, also, the 'great people' thought that
these were the aspects of the city most interesting to an
Ottoman, given Ottomans' well-known proclivities.

The expectations of Lord Charlemont, a young Irish peer
on the grand tour in Constantinople, were not very different
from the Parisians'. He too was convinced 'that there is too
much reason to believe that the Turks are greatly addicted to
that detestable vice which nature starts at and which if there
were not too certain proof that such crimes have been
perpetrated, no innocent man could suppose possible.'[27] He
saw no 'certain proof', of course: he only listened to a great
deal of hearsay and inflamed chatter. The best he could
observe was a group of boys on board a ship whom he was
told were the captain's catamites; Ottomans similarly assumed
that the midshipmen on British naval vessels were their
captain's playthings. However, like Halet Efendi, he also
visited a brothel in the interests of research. He noted that:

It may seem unnecessary to observe that in these houses Turkish
women are never met with. The ladies here to be obtained are
Greeks, Jewesses or Armenian Christians, many of whom are
extremely beautiful and are well skilled in the necessary arts and
allurements of their calling. As it is the duty of travellers to leave
nothing unseen, our curiosity, and perhaps something more, has
sometimes enticed Burton [his travelling companion] and me to
these hospitable receptacles.[28]

However, these 'receptacles', as he described them, brought him no closer to the mysteries of the harem, since none of them were Muslim, although he had heard tell that many young Muslim men (rather like young Christian Irish noblemen) were wont to visit them.

The longest section of Charlemont's notes, bound in two large folio volumes, concerns 'Turkish women and marriage', two subjects about which he had virtually no direct knowledge at all. Nevertheless, he had no trouble in compiling a list of activities that went on behind the closed doors. He managed neatly to connect the supposed addiction to 'unnatural vice' with the overheated heterosexual atmosphere of the harem:

The variety in which the Turks indulge themselves *forcibly* [my emphasis] inclines them to transgress the bounds of nature in sensual pleasure . . . Refinement of manners, however extraordinary and paradoxical it may seem, has generally been productive of unnatural vices. Refinement leads to luxury, one principle of which is an unrestrained intercourse with women, and this naturally brings satiety and a consequent desire to search after novelty.[29]

To the modern reader, this sounds more like an autobiography of Lord Charlemont than an analysis of the Ottomans; but it illustrates the dilemma faced by an honest inquirer. He came East with expectations and found no answers. He liked the people he met, saying 'The Turks in general and indeed all Orientals, seem to possess a graceful Action which remark may be extended to the lower classes of the people. Grace indeed, as far as I could observe, seems to be a native of the East and to degenerate as she travels westward.'[30] He had been treated with 'such amazing and much more than Christian politeness among a people whom I had been taught to believe as little less than barbarous.'[31] His inner conflict became almost painful, and is honestly – if confusingly – rendered in his journal. Eventually he gave up trying to rationalize the irreconcilable and simply recorded disparity. So he noted that:

Our consuless at Cairo – for I am obliged to bring together all the little knowledge I have been able to collect upon this mysterious subject [the harem] was known to many Turkish women and often visited them. When . . . she told them of Christian liberty and of the freedom indulged to women in our countries, they seemed rather to look upon such customs with disgust and horror than with any degree of envious desire. They exclaimed against our ladies as unnaturally licentious and treated those liberties which we account innocent as criminal to the last degree. In a word, they cried out against our customs as our women do at the naked simplicity of the Indians or at the liberty of love which Otaheite [Tahiti] has lately disclosed to us.[32]

Contact did little to modify the stereotypes so deeply rooted in Western culture. The new fashion for the East, stimulated by the rediscovery of Egypt after Napoleon's invasion in 1798, simply reinforced the old impressions with the new. The Byronic mixture of lust and cruelty, the paintings of Delacroix and Géricault, set the tone for the post-1825 view of the Ottomans, setting aside the more rational tone of many of the eighteenth-century travellers. Charlemont did not find 'any tortures or cruel punishments of any kind are common among the Turks. Impalement, that shocking cruelty, which we are taught is daily practice, I never so much heard of. During the whole month that I was at Constantinople, I heard of but one execution.'[33] In fact, impalement was still practised, as Mayer's drawing eloquently demonstrates (plate 25), but not in the streets of the capital. But Charlemont's surprise that what he saw was not what he had been led to expect is significant. There was, of course, cruelty and brutality, but not on the scale that the West believed. But from the early years of the nineteenth century – especially after the horrors of the Greek War of Independence, in which only the suffering of the Christians was called into the account (see page 165) – the image of the Terrible and Lustful Turk was omnipresent.

'The Lustful Turk' was a quite common phrase used to describe the Ottomans, but it was also the title of a salacious novella, which was apparently first published in 1828.[34] It is an advance on many of the French volumes of the seventeenth century, still popular in the eighteenth.[35] The cruelties of the Turks are now more subtle than mere brutality; the equation between lust and violence, which was common in the writers of the Middle Ages, has been reinforced, but also transformed.[36] There is much violent taking of maidenheads, some chastisement, and endless copulations – inevitable in male-directed pornography – but the situations portrayed are more than merely conventional Oriental lust. Nor is the violence all one way. The Dey (Ruler) of Algiers, the Byronic anti-hero of the piece, has been engaged with a number of women including the English narrator, Emily Barlow. She describes how:

In this way we were frequently (all three of us) dissolved at the same time in a flood of bliss.

This continued for several months, when an awful catastrophe put an end to our enjoyments. The Dey had received a Greek girl from one of his captains. She passively submitted to his embraces and uttered no complaint until he commenced the attack on her second maidenhead: then did she seem inspired with a strength of Hercules. She suddenly grasped a knife, which she had concealed under a cushion, grasped his pinnacle of strength, and in less than thought drew a knife across it and severed it from his body – then plunged it into her own heart and expired immediately. [Aid was immediately summoned to stop him bleeding to death, and] with the fortitude that characterised greatness, he ordered his physician to remove him of those now useless appendages [earlier described as 'his pendant jewels'], his receptacles of the soul-stirring juice, remarking at the same time that life would be very hell if he retained the power after the desire was dead.[37]

After he had recovered, he sent for his companions in pleasure and 'disclosed to our view the lost members in spirits of wine in glass vases'. He then arranged for the women to return to their native countries, and showered them with gifts before their departure. Emily Barlow left him 'with a heavy heart'.

The Dey is part Shakespeare's Noble Moor, unmanned, part Byron's heroic Ottoman from *The Giaour*:

> With sabre shivr'd to the hilt,
> Yet dripping with the blood he spilt;
> Yet strained within the sever'd hand
> Which quivers round that faithless brand;
> His turban far behind him roll'd,
> And cleft in twain its firmest fold;
> His flowing robe by falchion torn,
> And crimson as those clouds of morn
> That, streak'd with dusky red, portend
> The day shall have a stormy end;
> A stain on every bush that bore
> A fragment of his palampore,
> His breast with wounds unnumber'd riven,
> His back to earth, his face to heaven,
> Fall'n Hassan lies – his unclos'd eye
> Yet lowering on his enemy,
> As if the hour that seal'd his fate
> Surviving left his quenchless hate;
> And o'er him bends that foe with brow
> As dark as his that bled below.[38]

The piece, in passing, also reverses the usual European stereotype of the eunuch. But it has a deeper meaning, constructed by the political situation of the day. The Greek girl takes revenge upon the body of her oppressor, for her country as well as herself. The Greek nation, like her, had lain supine beneath the Ottoman; but at last, after centuries, Greece had risen in an act of superhuman and savage revenge. Better to die triumphant than live abused. Emily Barlow's sympathies are plainly mixed. She does not appear to have a 'heavy heart' for the Greek girl, who, after all, was merely expected to perform in the same way as the other members of the harem, who had sacrificed their 'virgin sanctuary': she describes but does not sympathize with her desperate act. Nor would philhellenism have been universal among the readers of this tale.

In *The Lustful Turk* the old equation of Islam and sodomy is again played out, in graphic detail. By the 1870s the situation could also be reversed, so to speak. In *The Pearl*, supposedly 'A Journal of Facetiae and Voluptuous Reading', published monthly, the Turk now features as a victim, for 'an anonymous correspondent on board Admiral Seymour's ship at Ragusa has favoured the Editor with the following:'

> Who'll bugger the Turk?
> 'I' said Gladstone, 'as Chief of the Nation,
> And Premier of England, to gain reputation.
> I'll bugger the Turk
> And ne'er let him shirk,
> My p****'s Grand Demonstration[39]

This is a coarsely and graphically expressed metaphor for Gladstone's evident desire as to how the Turks should be treated. His hugely successful pamphlet on the 'Bulgarian atrocities', which sold 40,000 copies within a few days of its first publication in 1876, explicitly made the connection between Turkish lust and Turkish violence.

From the 1870s, whether as victim or ravisher, the Turk is always viewed in traditional terms. In *The Sultan's Reverie: an Extract from the Pleasures of Cruelty*[40] all the well-worn elements are there. It describes 'a sultan who, being middle-aged and worn out with the amorous exertions in the well-filled seraglio determines to seek some fresh excitement, everything seems so insipid and blasé to him'. He decides to take his pleasure from the previous sultan's mother, described as one 'who in the lifetime of his predecessor had intrigued in every possible manner to set aside his successor in favour of her own son contrary to the usual Osmanif custom'. The new sultan was told by his chief eunuch that 'she was suspected of indulging in every degree of voluptuousness with the ladies of her suite in private'. He decided to lie in wait for her the following morning, when:

Seating himself on the grass behind an Oleander thicket, he gave himself up to a private reverie of his chibouque [pipe]. 'Ah, to think I never thought of that before, the haughty beauty. Oh, Allah what a fine revenge for all she did against me. What a delicious time of day ... I have indulged in too much Frankish brandy overnight ... Ah Allah, why did the prophet forbid us the glorious wine? Spirits were not known then or he would have put a veto in to that also. Women, women, nothing but women for good believers ... Of course I am a true Musselman but it takes a big faith to believe all that, or about Isa either. Religion is a manufactured article in all countries, a monopoly not to be interfered with lightly, but no one will know the mystery until after death.

What is this long philosophical digression doing in a tale of unbridled lust? It is to set the tone, the Ottoman context, and it is accurate in most particulars [41] – at least to the travellers' tales of the day. Thereafter the sultan behaves in approved style, exactly as Charlemont outlined more than a century before. Only in this case a birching scene is added, and finally 'gathering several tufts of grass with the earth clinging to the roots [he] then proceeds to pelt her c***y with them until one fairly sticks to the entrance.' No reason is offered for this bizarre final humiliation, which caused no particular pain. Could it not be an attempt to associate the sultan's rape of his victim with dirt and filth – qualities which had come to be associated implicitly with the Ottomans in the later nineteenth century?

Earlier travellers had been impressed by the cleanliness of Ottoman cities, but from early in the nineteenth century –

Walsh was perhaps the first – there is a growing preoccupation with the filthiness of Ottoman life. An American writer, William Elroy Curtis, author of *The True Thomas Jefferson* and *The Yankees of the East*, expressed the new sense of revulsion: 'Their houses are positively filthy; too filthy as a rule for human beings to occupy; and the streets of Constantinople and every other Turkish town are indescribable in their nastiness. Their clothing is as dirty as their bodies are clean [a reference to the religious ablutions] and their food is often unfit for sanitary reasons.'[42]

The public standards of the West had changed, largely with the discovery that dirt could be equated with disease and the pestilence associated with squalor (cholera, typhoid) could afflict the middle and upper classes as much as it did the poor. But the standards of many quarters of the great European cities were no better than those of Constantinople, and there was nothing to choose between the rural filth of Andalusia, the Mezzogiorno or central Anatolia. Even Curtis's own nation had its 'hells' kitchens' recorded by photographers like Edward Stieglitz. The assertion of Ottoman filth had a moral as much as a sanitary connotation. Curtis went on to damn all things Turkish: 'The idea of wearing the veil is to make women as hideous as possible, and the Turk succeeds in that purpose, if in no other. Women who do not wear veils ... are not Mohammadans and may be treated with ordinary courtesy.'[43] In its context this may mean no more than the fact that he cannot raise his hat to a Turkish lady, but taken as a whole with the rest of his long book it is completely Turcophobic in tone. Curtis, like Gladstone, rejects the Ottomans as an 'anti-human species'. In this context their bestial behaviour, as in *The Sultan's Reverie*, is but a logical if distasteful consequence.

Even more opprobrium was piled on the Ottomans. In *The Lustful Turk* there is a long section that deals with the evil lusts of monks and nuns – part of the stock in trade of both pornographers and extreme Protestants alike. Steven Marcus

finds it an odd digression, but it seems to me to fit neatly with
the all-embracing condemnations of the Turk current at the
time. Luther had first linked the two together ('Turk and Pope
do not differ or vary in form of religion or ceremonies . . . An
alliance of the papists and the Turk . . . is the malice of
Satan'[44]) and the fiery anti-papist Archibald Mason, 'minister
of the Gospel' at Wishawtown, preached a sermon in 1827
that brought Luther up to date:

The fall of the Turkish kingdom will remove a principal defence
from the Anti-Christian Kingdom of Rome . . . The European
Peninsula, consisting of Spain and Portugal, is Antichrist's western
high tower, and the empire of Turkey its Eastern bulwark . . . The
heads and supporters, both of Islamism and Popery, are set in
opposition to the civil and religious privileges of mankind . . . the
Turkish firman and the Popish bull . . . breathe the same spirit and
speak the same language.[45]

The political opposition to the Ottomans was strong in
Protestant circles, and it was largely the Protestant missionaries
who provided the material which supported the wilder accusations against the Ottomans. Frequently the accusations degener-
ated into the realm of the absurd, based on the same kind of
hearsay that had coloured the image of the Lustful Turk.

The roots of prejudice are hard to trace, but it seems clear
that the Ottomans became a focus of fear and hatred, breaking
out in many forms, but with a remarkable consistency over
time. The myths often had nothing to do with the reality.
Eyewitnesses frequently claim to have seen events – like the
slave market in Constantinople in the 1870s[46] – that were
impossible. That they saw something is not in dispute, and
that they either misunderstood or were misinformed by others
about an alien culture is the most likely explanation. But their
confident assertions added to the historic burden of myth, so
heavy that no Ottoman could hope to overcome it.

Of Ottoman misapprehensions of the West it is more

difficult to comment. The attitudes of those who feared the West remained consistent, but Ottomans who looked to the West to transform the empire had their expectations dashed. They were mocked for aping Western manners, never wholly trusted or accepted, always seen as capable of regression, as either the Lustful Turk in their private relations or the Terrible Turk in their public life. They existed in a limbo between two worlds. As T. E. Lawrence wrote himself, 'Easily was a man made an infidel but hardly might he be converted to another faith ... madness would be near the man who sees things through the veils at once of two customs, two educations, two environments.'[47]

CHAPTER 8

'The Terrible Turk'

In the sixteenth century, Francis Bacon described the Turks as 'a Cruell People':[1]

Without morality, without letters, arts or sciences; a people that can scarce measure an acre of land or an hour of the day; base and sluttish in building, diet and the like; and in a word, a very reproach to human society . . . it is truly said concerning the Turk, where the Ottoman's horse sets his foot, people come up very thin.[2]

These assertions of 'cruelty' from Bacon and his contemporaries are special pleading: there was little to choose in terms of horror between an English execution for treason under Queen Elizabeth and King James and the most savage Turkish punishments, such as 'execution on the hooks' or 'impalement', so carefully recorded (and drawn) by European visitors to the Ottoman empire. Europeans suggested that the cruelty lay not so much in the punishment inflicted as in its arbitrariness. Adolphus Slade described the seemingly casual killing of 'Hamid':

His accusation was read to him enumerating with other charges, the unjust one of grinding the poor. So false an accusation, without the power of refuting it, must have added a pang to the bitterness of death; that is, if any, for he betrayed no fear, neither probably, with true Ottoman stoicism, would he have said one word, had not the captain pasha, at that moment come out of his cabin to look at his old friend, who, one little spark yet burning among the embers of hope, cried once 'Aman'. He might have spared his breath. The

231

pasha answered by a slight wave of the hand, the usual signal in such cases ... the guards led him below to the prison where two slaves attended ... The bowstring soon did its task, and in a few minutes the receipt, the head of Hamid (the countenance as calm as sleep), was brought up to be shown to the pasha, before being transmitted to the seraglio. It is startling to see a human head carried on a platter up a ladder, down which you have seen it descend, just before, sentient and well posed on a pair of shoulders.[3]

To Slade the most remarkable aspect of the incident was the offhand manner of the execution; for Hamid's former fellows, the other naval officers on the captain pasha's ship, who 'gave an involuntary shudder, as well they might: the reign of terror was begun', it was the uncertainty of where the bowstring would strike next.

Although the Ottoman reformers promised that arbitrary power would be abolished, and that all criminals would have the right of appeal (although poor Hamid does not appear to have benefited from Mahmud II's edict of redress), arbitrary power continued to lie at the heart of the Ottoman system. Those who were well inclined to the Ottomans, such as Robert Curzon, suggested that injustices stemmed from inferior officers of the government who were oppressors without the knowledge or acquiescence of their superiors. He also pointed out that arbitrary power was not exclusive to the Ottoman empire, that the USA was 'a land of liberty, where every free and independent citizen had the right to beat his own nigger'.[4] In many cases it was maladministration, not bad faith, that produced injustice; but underlying the Ottoman practice of government was a culture of fear. Abdul Hamid once confided that he often punished good and honest officials while favouring those who were corrupt and incompetent. He liked to cut down the tall poppies, as he did with Midhat Pasha, but in countless other smaller and less fatal ways he terrorized the whole body of the ruling class. They lived in fear, and they passed it on to those beneath them. The

Ottoman cold-bloodedness to which Slade alluded was a calm induced by terror.

Fear, carefully and precisely applied, was the normal condition of the Hamidian state, and it was not very different under his predecessors. But it was a clinically imposed atmosphere of terror, that gained its effect not from the cruelty of punishments but from their random application. Lord Charlemont observed that the bowstring and sword, used in private, were much more humane than the English scaffold, where the objective was the degradation of the criminals, leading them if possible to repentance. An Ottoman hanging was a much more casual affair than its English equivalent, while Ottomans thought the guillotine both extraordinary and barbarous. But the West regarded Ottomans as vicious brutes, and the occasions of public violence were ascribed to some deep and pernicious moral failing. The connection between the Ottomans' carnal lusts and their yearning for violence was made explicit. History was dragged into service: the cruelties on the battlefields of the fifteenth and sixteenth centuries, the obsolete practice of killing the brothers and male cousins of a new sultan (abandoned by the Ottomans within a few generations of its enactment as unnecessary and cruel), ancient and long-disused punishments – all were considered part of the Ottoman *present*, rather than the distant past. On three occasions in the nineteenth century the West was roused against the Turks for their atrocious violence towards Christians: first, for the many deaths in the Greek War of Independence; second, for the slaughter in Bulgaria and Bosnia in 1875–7; and, third, for the merciless campaign against the Armenians lasting from the 1890s into the First World War. Each of them roused a near-identical pattern of public fury in the Western nations.

In each case, it appeared that the Terrible Turk was behaving true to type. The 'unspeakable Turk' (Thomas Carlyle's phrase) savaged women and children and raped, murdered and pillaged, sparing neither young nor old. Nor was it, as the

Ottomans claimed, a fratricidal strife, Muslims against Christians, or hereditary enemies settling ancient scores: this must be an act of state, carried out deliberately by the Ottoman government. The naïve folk-drawings from the Greek war show Egyptian soldiers and janissaries killing (presumably) Greek women, while the Greeks (in their white kilts) are only shown attacking enemy soldiers. Yet we know that many thousands of Turkish women and children were killed, often with appalling savagery, in the Morea. In Western cartoons of the 'Bulgarian atrocities', the killings are often shown being carried out by Ottoman regular soldiers, (notably in a Punch cartoon – see page 241). In the case of the Armenian killings, Ottoman claims of long-standing hatreds between Kurds and Armenians were simply dismissed out of hand. In each case the ethnic murders were, it was asserted, uniquely and solely at the behest of the Ottoman government – part of some age-old attempt to trample on Christians in the East.

Why would the Ottomans do it? Because they were bloodthirsty savages. Gladstone's pamphlet on *The Bulgarian Horrors and the Question of the East* is one of the great denunciations in the history of rhetoric. His polemic, measured in its tone, denounced not only the atrocities themselves but the whole Turkish nation. He sketches

in the rudest outline, . . . what the Turkish race was, and what it is. It is not a question of Mahometism simply, but of Mahometism compounded with the peculiar character of a race . . . They were, from the first black day they entered Europe, the one great anti-human specimen of humanity. Wherever they went, a broad line of blood marked the track behind them, and as far as their dominion reached, civilisation vanished from view.[5]

Three centuries before, Bacon was saying much the same thing.

Gladstone cites an American source, a Mr Schuyler, who says, 'No Turkish women or children were killed in cold

blood. No Musselman women were violated. No purely Turkish village was attacked or burned. No Musselman house was
pillaged. No mosque was desecrated or destroyed.'[6] This, in
Gladstone's view is the 'report that turns the scale'[7] and
justifies his declaration concerning the 'elaborate and refined
cruelty – the only refinement of which Turkey boasts! – the
utter disregard of sex and age – the abominable and bestial
lust – and the utter and violent lawlessness which still stalks
over the land'.[8] Whether the Turkish government itself created
the 'abominable and bestial lust' etc. or whether it was the
product of the 'utter and violent lawlessness which still stalks
over the land' was not clearly stated. In essence, it was Turks,
by their very nature, who were responsible; it was a blood
guilt that tainted the whole Turkish race. Similarly, he asserts
that the killings come from the 'agents', 'at once violent and
corrupt, of a distant central Power ... which always has
physical force at its command to back outrage with the
sanction of authority, but has no moral force whatever, *no
power either of checking evil or of doing good* [my emphasis]'.[9]
The Ottomans are damned for being anti-human, damned for
allowing abominable lusts, and damned for having no power
to do anything to prevent murder on a huge scale. His famous
fulmination 'Let the Turks now carry their abuses away' rises
sonorously in tone, heaping denunciation upon denunciation.
And, he warns, unless the Ottomans are removed, bag and
baggage, 'all the foul and all the fierce passions ... may
spring up again, in another murderous harvest, from the soil
soaked and reeking with blood, and in the air tainted with
every imaginable deed or crime'.[10]

The events in Bulgaria and Bosnia were horrific, but they
were not without parallel in British experience. Twenty years
before, Britain had been the 'distant central Power' suppressing
a mutiny in India. In putting down the Indian Mutiny in
1857–8, a Colonel Neill and other British officers initiated a
campaign of racial terror, hanging almost any Indians on

whom they could lay their hands in an orgy of vengeance. (Worse still were the parties of civilian irregulars.) When the British reached Cawnpore and saw the results of the atrocities committed there, they became frenzied. Neill devised special forms of execution which, depending on whether he was a Hindu or a Muslim, would damn the victim eternally. He forced prisoners to lick up the dried blood from the floor of one small house where women and children had been killed. Stories were invented that women had been raped and mutilated, their white womanhood ravaged by 'black-faced curs', and children deliberately and slowly tortured.[11] The British instituted a policy of terror, aided by those, who, like the Sikhs, hated both the Hindus and the Muslims. One officer came across a party of Sikhs roasting a sepoy over a slow fire; he made no attempt to stop them. It was not an isolated incident. There was an official campaign to restore death by torture, hanging being too swift for those who had committed 'vile acts'. The most ceremonious form of dispatching mutineers was to strap them to the front of cannon, and then blow them in half, often so that their scattered remains would splatter the faces of their former comrades, lined up to observe the execution. This was British justice in the face of colonial mutiny. Other Western nations committed similar atrocities in their colonial possessions, if not on the same scale. Thus Gladstone's denunciation was not delivered to a nation with entirely clean hands.

What made the Ottomans seem so abominable in Bulgaria? Their peculiar crime lay in the combination of lust and violence. The British in India were led by officers, like General Henry Havelock, who claimed that they wrought a pure and divine vengeance on the mutineers. Justice, not pleasure, drove them forward. The British believed that the Turks, with their foul lusts, enjoyed killing, and enjoyed rape and torture even more. Sadism was believed to be a dominant Ottoman quality. In his famous account of being beaten and sexually abused by the Turks at Deraa, T. E. Lawrence subtly suggests physical unhealthiness, corpulence, slovenliness, dirt and sloth, as well as the grossly perverted desires which were, as suggested in Chapter 7, considered the regular practice of the Ottoman. The factual truth of Lawrence's experiences has been questioned,[12] but what is significant here is that his popular audience in 1935 would have accepted his assertion concerning the Turks without question: after all, everyone knew that that was what Ottomans 'did'. I have emphasized a number of key usages in the following passage, in which Lawrence is passing as a Circassian.

We passed to a *mud* room, outside which was an earth platform whereupon sat a *fleshy* Turkish officer, *one leg tucked underneath him* . . . He turned to me and said very slowly, 'You are a liar . . . do what is necessary until the Bey sends for him . . .' [The ordinary soldiers, Syrians, treat Lawrence well and seek to reassure him. Then he is summoned by the Bey.] They took me upstairs to the Bey's room; to his bedroom rather. He was another *bulky* man . . . and sat on to bed in a night gown, *trembling and sweating* as though with fever . . . he flung himself back on the bed and dragged me down with him in his arms. When I saw what he wanted I twisted round and up again, glad to find myself equal to him, at any rate in wrestling.

He began to fawn on me saying how white and fresh I was, how fine my hands and feet . . . how he would even pay me . . . if I would love him. I was obdurate, so he changed his tone and sharply ordered me to take off my drawers. When I hesitated, he snatched at me and I pushed him back. He clapped his hands for the sentry who hurried in and pinioned me. The Bey cursed me . . . and made the man holding me tear away my clothes bit by bit . . . finally he *lumbered* to his feet, with a glitter in his look and began to *paw* me over. I bore it for a little, till he got too *beastly*; and then jerked my knee into him . . . [Then the Bey hit him in the face with his slipper, and then] leaned forward and fixed his teeth in my neck and bit till the blood came. Then he kissed me. Afterwards he drew one of the men's bayonets. I thought he was going to kill me, and was sorry:

but he only pulled up a fold of flesh over my ribs, worked the point through, after considerable trouble, and gave the blade a half turn. This hurt, and I winced, while the blood wavered down my side and dribbled to the front of my side ... He looked pleased and *dabbled* it over my stomach with his finger tips.[13]

The other stages of Lawrence's symbolic Crucifixion followed. Several pages of an epic scourging are described in detail, and finally he escapes, through an unlocked door. This did not represent the reality of what actually happened to Lawrence: it is an allegory of the Lustful Turk toying with his victim. It builds its effects slowly and carefully, and for the reader, by this point in *The Seven Pillars of Wisdom* accustomed to the clean lithe limbs of Lawrence's Arabs, pure as the desert sands, the Turkish Bey is utterly repellent. Lawrence's passing as a Circassian is odd as well, for the Bey was, Lawrence thought, a Circassian himself: surely he would have noticed Lawrence's unlikely accent. However, Lawrence tells us that he was never suspected. The incident raises many questions, but, reduced to its essentials, Lawrence's 'experience' at Deraa provides that conjuncture of sex and violence considered the unique hallmark of the Ottoman.

Every age has its ogres – the alien 'other' – and the Ottomans filled the part for Christian Europe long after the military threat that gave the role some meaning had vanished: they simply became a threat of a different sort. There is a parallel case that highlights the unique role ascribed to the Ottomans by Western society. In the nineteenth century the Japanese followed the same trajectory: from being mysterious and dangerous outsiders, through a process of modernization, to become in the twentieth century once again 'savage and barbarous' and at the same time a butt for cruel humour. John Dover[14] tells how British officers in the 1920s assured their government that Japanese officers and their 'little yellow men' would never be able to fight because their eyesight was so poor. He charts the many obsessions which the West developed about the Japanese. They were looked down upon as animals, as figures of fun, as primitive savages or as vermin, but they were rarely thought of as sexually threatening: there was virtually no popular pornographic literature in the West about the Lusty Samurai. This is paradoxical, because the tradition of the 'pillow book' makes the Japanese much more apt than the Ottoman for such a stereotypical role. Of course, for Europe, Japan is far away and Turkey close at hand (although for the western United States the position is reversed).

Modern Turkey is encumbered with its origins, but in the West it still carries an additional burden of terror and loathing whose origins vanish into the far distant past. The image of the Turk, dissolving and constantly reforming, will never be free from its deep roots: in European fears of sex and violence looming out of the East.

WHAT IT MUST COME TO.

(Above) *The Minority Western View of the Ottoman Empire*

(Right) *The Dominant Western View of the Ottomans*

NEUTRALITY UNDER DIFFICULTIES.

DIZZY: "Bulgarian Atrocities! I can't find them in the 'Official Reports'!!!"

EVER READY TO OBLIGE!

Abdul Hamid: "DEAR ME! OUGHT I TO BE FRIGHTENED?"

(Above and Right) *The Indolent Ottoman*

THE TERRIBLE TURK AGAIN.

J.B.: Look here, I have had enough of your nonsense. I mean it this time.

"DEEDS—NOT WORDS!"

John Bull: "Look here—we've had enough of your palaver!
Are you going to let the girl go, or have we got to make you?"

The Lustful (and Craven) Turk

In the meantime the *Cretans* see to it that not much is left for the authorities to do.

The Terrible Turk

(Above and right) *Abdul Hamid, 'the Red Sultan'*
(red from the blood of his victims), was also lampooned as
a drunkard and lecher

CONCLUSION

Autres temps, autres mœurs

The theme of this book is that there is no closure: that the relationship between the Ottoman and Europe, between the Turk and the West, is constantly changing and reforming. But equally it can never escape from the embrace of fundamental misunderstanding.[1] Ezel Kural Shaw has made the point that 'we must thank the travellers for their information, within its own limits, but we must free ourselves from those limits to develop a comprehensive knowledge of the Ottoman system on its own terms.'[2] But there is a danger that this greater knowledge will not solve the problem of misunderstanding. An idea mooted by Edmund Burke was that the Turks were 'wholly Asiatic . . . what had these worse than savages to do with the powers of Europe?'[3] If there are still many in Europe who believe that to be true, there are many in Turkey who wish it were true. But the facts of geography, if nothing more, demand an interrelationship. So how can it be handled?

In 1839, David Urquhart published *The Spirit of the East, or Pictures of Eastern Travel*. In outward form it is a traditional 'traveller's tale', but it is informed by neither an excessive Turcophilia nor an excessive Turcophobia. Urquhart makes no pretence to imagine himself a Turk. He considers himself to be difficult and 'prickly', and he describes the Turks thus:

The Turks remind one of a porcupine: grate their feelings or their prejudices and everywhere a sharp and hostile point is presented to

248

your hand; know them and be known by them, and they are as smooth and pliable as down. Having experienced each of the effects I connect both with the same cause, *which was in myself and not in them* [my emphasis]. When I first quitted the outlines of Turkey, it was with hatred in my heart and contempt on my lips ... chance and perseverance taught me otherwise.[4]

Recently I asked the doyen of Turkish folk-tales, Dr Warren Walker, how he had been able to collect his extraordinary range of material. He told me that he and his collaborator had criss-crossed Turkey eleven times to collect tales, often going to small villages which an urban Turk today, like his Ottoman forebears, would have considered impossibly primitive and utterly devoid of interest. They would go to the *mukhtar* (village leader), who would welcome them, and over many cups of tea they would be asked to explain who they were and where they had come from. Then the *mukhtar* would pause, sigh, and ask them the same questions again. Perhaps a whole day would be spent in this process, and the next day the village religious leader, the *hoca*, would come and ask the same questions again. And then at some point the *mukhtar* would pause and say, 'You honour us with your presence. How can we help you?' Then the folk-tales would be told, and they would be wonderfully entertained and fed for days.

Usually the people were very poor, and the cost of entertainment was obviously great for the villagers. But hospitality was a duty and a privilege, so of course no money could be offered and even provisions would be refused. But Walker discovered that tea and sugar were often in short supply, so on each trip thereafter he would take supplies of both. He would never offer them to the villagers, however, but would ask if he might be allowed to give these presents to the village children. Yes, he was told, he might give presents to the children. The tea and sugar were not reserved for the children but were enjoyed by the whole village. All concerned had behaved with

honour and with understanding, and all had gained from the meeting. For the West, the result was a unique collection of remarkable folk-tales, some now published;[5] for the villagers, a friend whom they welcomed back on every subsequent visit.

Urquhart faced a similar problem. He noted how

when there is a difference of original impressions, there cannot be said to be a common language, because the ideas represented in the speech of one are not conveyed to the intelligence of the other; and in nothing is this absence of a common language felt more than in our estimate of the domestic state and feelings of the East.[6]

His answer was to accept the divide and to look across it with love and admiration when he felt moved to it (as by the relationship between Turks and their children) or with a reluctance to form a judgement when he did not. Perhaps, by that point, he was no longer a traveller but had, like Warren Walker, 'come home'.

Notes on the Illustrations

All the images in the plates are taken either from the Searight Collection in the Victoria and Albert Museum, London, or from the author's own collection. In these notes, Searight images are marked (S) and images from the author's collection are marked (W).

Of the many thousands of images in the Searight Collection, quite a number that I have chosen come from two artists: the 'Turkish Anonymous' and Amadeo, Count Preziosi. This is because it seemed to me that they both had the dispassionate eye that I was seeking. It is noteworthy that neither was a Westerner in the normal sense: the 'Turkish Anonymous' is thought to have been a Greek living in Constantinople, and Preziosi was a Maltese.

Cartoons often reveal unconscious attitudes to the Ottomans better than more formal works of art, and I am grateful to Professor Roy Douglas for supplying the cartoons from *Judy*, *Punch* and *Kladderadatsch* from his extensive collection.

The vignettes within the text are taken from Charles White's *Three Years in Constantinople, or Domestic Manners of the Turks in 1844* (1845).

Title-page

The device reproduced on the title-page is the *tuğra*, or seal, of Abdul Hamid II. (W)

Cover Picture

In J. F. H. Lewis's Romantic image of a Cairo bazaar, the tranquillity and easy calm of the Ottoman world are accurately reflected. Much of the composition and the detail existed more in Lewis's mind than in everyday reality, but he was both a scrupulous observer and a supreme artist, so this rich depiction assembles a benign view of a traditional, exotic and sensually charged world shortly before it disappeared under the pressure of Western values. (S)

Plates

1 *Women and Children Leaving a Bathhouse*, by Camille Rogier (1810–48)

An imaginary scene, though Rogier spent the years 1840–43 in Constantinople. Unlike many Western depictions of the bathhouse, this lacks the hothouse sensuality of Ingres' equally imaginary *Le Bain turc*. Here one of the women (perhaps because she is a mother, holding the child's hand) is chastely covered, and even her companions carry only a slight erotic charge. The details of the pattens worn in the bathhouse and the striped towels are authentic details, as in the straightforwardly narrative depiction of the men's bathhouse (see plate 14). (S)

2 *The Turkish Letter-Writer* (*Arzuhalci*), 1855, by Amadeo, Count Preziosi (1816–82)

The letter-writer was skilled at choosing not only the appropriate calligraphic style, but also the phraseology appropriate to the circumstance, rather as petitions to government officials in Italy had (and have) to be couched in a particular form. Letter-writers were also widely used to interpret the baroque complexities of official Ottoman texts to the ordinary citizen. (S)

3 *The Coffee-House*, 1854, by Amadeo, Count Preziosi
(1816–82)

This, one of the magical but accurate water-colours by
Preziosi, shows Constantinople as the crossroads of the empire.
His scene, set in a 'modern' building on the waterfront of the
Golden Horn, with the background of Stamboul, embraces
the many 'types' of the empire. On the left, a Greek sits cross-
legged, next to a dervish with his tall felt hat. By the door is a
Circassian, with his fur hat and cartridge pouches, next to two
more Greeks. Preziosi sought out the most exotic types, so
that, while each character is accurately depicted, the overall
reality of the coffee-house may have been embellished. (S)

4 *The Eating-House*, c.1810

Set in Pera, and overlooking the Golden Horn, this shows
with great accuracy a traditional Ottoman eating-house. This
and other images show how deserted were the city streets in
the heat of the day. The artist is 'unknown' but is believed to
have been a Greek who painted scenes in a mixture of Ottoman
and Western styles. This image, with many others, was bought
by Stratford Canning, 'the Great Elchi [ambassador]', the
most notable and successful of all the British diplomats to the
Sublime Porte. (S)

5 *Janissaries in the Second Court of the Yeni Saray*, c.1810

European visitors described the unseemly rush of the janissaries for their pay in the second court, but it was a time-
honoured formula – almost a military drill. Other, more
formal, evolutions were also carried out here, but more often
the janissaries practised their 'warlike skills', brandishing
their arms, at Et Meydan and on drill-grounds outside the
city. (S)

6 *The Chief Eunuch*

The chief eunuch (*kizlar ağasi*) headed the sultan's household. Always a black man, he was feared both for his powers of life and death within the harem and for the supposed tendency to extreme cruelty resulting from his altered state. Castration and 'negritude' epitomized the Western view of the 'dark side' of harem life, the counterpoint to the pampered bodies of the 'odalisques'. The last chief eunuch was hanged for his part in the counter-coup against the Young Turks in 1909. (S)

7 *The Aga of the Janissaries*

By his uniform this is certainly a senior janissary officer, and most likely the commander (aga) of the janissary regiments. But officers rarely held their command for very long – part of an often vain attempt to restrain the power of the already overmighty troops. The regiments all had slight variations to their uniforms, and most janissaries proudly bore the badge of their detachment tattooed on their body, evidence of their superior status as the chosen warriors of the sultan. (S)

8 *The Turkish Courier*, after Sir David Wilkie RA (1785–1841)

Wilkie's scene of the coffee-house is 'romanticized' in a way that Preziosi's was not. The main characters strike heroic poses. The relaxed but carefully poised Tartar messenger – whose fine embroidered 'winged' boots have perhaps a suggestion of Mercury, the messenger of the gods, about them – dominates the scene and has every eye fixed upon him in an eager expectation. The only characters who are not paying attention are the 'supernumeraries': the children and the black slave boy, who were probably added to the image at a later stage. Again, there is an amazing diversity of characters and types – Ottomans, Armenians, Jews, dervishes and merchants

– a *mélange* which was certainly observable everywhere in the capital. Wilkie was in Constantinople when the news of the Anglo-Turkish victory over the Egyptians in November 1840 arrived in the city; but he died on the voyage home, in 1841, so his paintings were prepared for the lithographic press by Joseph Nash. (S)

9 *Mehmed Ali*, 12 May 1835, by David Roberts RA (1796–1864)

Mehmed Ali, *vali* of Egypt, was the most effective modernizer of the Ottoman world, but in this image he is seen as a traditional languid, lolling figure, surrounded by his retinue. Compare him with the alert and upright Europeans at the right of the picture. Again, there is an element of truth in this depiction, but it presents a contrast that soon became a stereotype – the indolent Ottoman confronted by the thrusting European (see the cartoon of Abdul Hamid confronted by Emperor Franz Joseph and Tsar Nicholas I on page 242). (S)

10 *Interior of the Dome of the Rock, Jerusalem*, 1863, by C. F. H. Werner (1808–94)

A holy place for both Muslims and Jews: where the Prophet Muhammad ascended to heaven on his horse, and the site where Abraham offered Isaac up for sacrifice. (S)

11 *Turkish Pasha Receiving a Petition*, by William Craig

This engraving, published between 1810 and 1820, embodies almost every Western stereotype of the Ottomans. The indolent pasha is languidly sucking at his chibouk with the seductive female recipients of his lusts ranged behind him watching him in besotted admiration. His black slave, bringing coffee, is symbolically catering to his every whim. The pasha looks down contemptuously on the suppliant, cruelly crushing his neck beneath a slippered foot, with much more force than the tradition required, as his victim seeks to relieve the intolerable pressure with his hands. (S)

12 *View of Constantinople from the Hills behind Scutari, 1829*

To English ears, 'Scutari' would become synonymous with Florence Nightingale and her hospital during the Crimean War. To Ottomans, it meant a much venerated mosque on the shores of the Bosporus, and the great barracks built by Selim III. This view is taken from Charles Macfarlane's *Constantinople in 1828.*

13 *The Streets of Stamboul*

This provides an unusually realistic view of Stamboul. The relative emptiness of the streets off the main thoroughfares was partly dictated by the difficulties of getting around a city with muddy tracks that became a quagmire in winter. The streets were cleaned by scavenging dogs, who would pick up the scraps dropped by the kebab vendor. (S)

14 *The Men's Bathhouse, c. 1810*

Painted from life rather than the imagination, by the 'Turkish Anonymous' who produced the collection for Stratford Canning, it entirely lacks the air of sexuality which dominates most 'Orientalist' images and which is even present to an extent in Rogier's image of women leaving the bathhouse (plate 1). (S)

15 *Wrestling at the Yeni Saray*

The Turkish passion for wrestling was as powerful in the Ottoman empire as it is in modern Turkey. Here the sultan views from his kiosk while the wrestlers perform, with women separated from the male spectators. (S)

16 *Travelling in the Ottoman Empire*, *c.* 1800, by Luigi Mayer (*c.* 1750–1803)

Luigi Mayer, widely known as an artist of Egypt and the Holy Land, left this sketch of his journey in the Ottoman domains. The European-style coaches lurch across the ill-made roads, bracketed on either side by the impaled corpses of malefactors. By Mayer's day, impalement would more likely take place after death by hanging, rather like gibbeting in England, but no doubt the full horrors of Turkish cruelty were employed by some local officials, a law unto themselves. (S)

17 *Costume of the New Troops*, 1828, by J. Clarke

The symbolism of Ottoman costume has been remarked upon elsewhere. This image, from Charles Macfarlane's *Constantinople in 1828*, shows how careful Mahmud II was to design a uniform that was not 'European' in style. There were other, less obvious, allusions to the past: for his '*eskenji*' troops, the sultan selected the same colours as those of the ill-fated *Nizam i-Cedid* of Selim III. Here two officers flank a private soldier, who is armed with a short flintlock musket and bayonet; they still wear the traditional red or yellow sandals and boots of the Ottoman court. Soon after this engraving was made, these were replaced by brown or black boots, and the uniforms became more 'Western' in style. But even up to the end of the empire the Ottoman soldiers looked different from Western troops.

18, 19 *Ottoman Women*

This traditional dress of women changed more slowly than that of men, but once the harem adopted Western styles the transformation was the more profound. Here the 'Turkish Anonymous' contrasts the extravagant richness of a great Ottoman lady – an egret feather in her hair, her clothes made of silks emblazoned with jewels – with the rather simpler costume of a non-Muslim, still elaborate but less ornate, and including a little green cap. The delight in colours and textures, however, was common to all – a taste obscured when European fashion supplanted the more comfortable and practical traditional styles, and the old freedom of the flowing Eastern dress gave way to corsets and constraint. (S)

20 *Turkish Houses of the Bosphorus*, by J. C. Bentley

From Julia Pardoe's *Beauties of the Bosphorus*, Bentley shows the old wooden houses to which Ottomans escaped in high summer from the stifling heat of the city. During the nineteenth century, more and more leading Ottomans abandoned the city for the 'rural' life along the Bosporus. (S)

21 *The Mosque at Eyub*, by J. Carter

The mosque of Eyüp (or 'Eyub') was a sacred shrine outside the capital; here the sultan ceremonially girded himself with the sword of Omar at his accession, symbolizing his determination to be a warrior of Islam. To be buried in the great cemetery of Eyüp was the heart's desire of many Ottomans, while the novelist Pierre Loti, who had his house in Eyüp, also found his heart's desire there in the lovely Aziyadé. (S)

22 *The Sultan's Gardener* (Bostancı)

The Ottoman love of gardens and gardening elevated the status of the palace gardeners. Sultans used them as bodyguards, secret messengers and executioners, as well as for their more formal duties of tending the gardens and, above all, preparing for the annual tulip ceremonies. Here a head gardener stands resplendent in his heavy red felt head-dress and scarlet robes. (S)

34. *The Holy Places, 1878*

The Ottomans proved good guardians of the holy places in the nineteenth century, providing a stable environment, arbitrating dispassionately between the conflicting Christian sects, and accommodating the growing Jewish presence in Palestine.

35. A *Caravanserai at Beirut, 1860s*
The '*hans*', both of the capital and of the provincial cities, were the launching-point
of the innumerable caravans that criss-crossed the empire like the small ships that plied
a continuous trade along the coast.

36. (Opposite) *The Pasha's Child, his Wet Nurse and Eunuch, Mecca, 1885*
The slave trade was abolished by Abdul Meçid, but domestic slavery continued to
function in families throughout the empire.

37. The Byzantine Walls, 1860s
Time and the assaults of 1453 had eroded the old Byzantine fortifications. In the centuries that followed, much more of the rampart collapsed, although the sound work of the original builders meant that sections still survive in the state seen in this image.

38. (Opposite above) *The Old Genoese Tower of Galata, 1860s*
Below can be seen the 'picturesque' Ottoman tombstones, beloved by travellers.

39. (Opposite below) *The Golden Horn, late 1880s*
The already busy port became a centre of trade as the age of the steamship arrived. Here the harbour is at a transition, with converted sailing-ships dominating in the port. Twenty years later the surface of the water could barely be seen for all the maritime traffic.

40. (Above) *The* Sebil *Outside the Great Gate of the Yeni Saray, 1860s*
Compare this, carefully posed to show Eastern 'types', with the image of the Tophane
sebil (plate 26). The decaying state of the city is evident.

41. (Opposite above) *Women Dressed for the Street and the Home, 1886*
These women, photographed by the Dutch Orientalist Hurgronje, were long thought to
be prostitutes, for they posed before a European male. But this assumption is not certain,
because Hurgronje had access to Islamic homes through his Muslim wife.

42. (Opposite below) *The Pasha's Household, 1886*
The pasha and his son are surrounded by their household. Here, in miniature, is
the Ottoman tradition of the slave household, which went back to the time of
Suleiman and beyond.

43. *Dervish in a Trance*, c. 1900
The dervish has plunged a skewer
through his cheeks in his trance. Despite
the suppression of the Bektaşi dervishes
after the fall of the janissaries, dervishes
remained a powerful force in the empire
until its last days.

44. *Syrian Chieftain*
As with so many rebels against Abdul
Hamid, this chieftain was taken as a hostage
to the capital, to live out his life in genteel
constraint, losing in the process much of the
Romantic passion that the photographer
plainly saw in him.

45. *Albanian Mountaineers, 1878*
Albanians were noted for their loyalty and fearlessness, and Ottoman sultans relied on
them for their bodyguards, their finest soldiers and many of their most effective viziers.
The 'Arnaut' or Albanian became a synonym for the wild and fearsome mountaineer.

23 *The Grand Vizier*

The imposing figure of the vizier, with his white robe, heavy
furs and dignified mien, was appropriate for the most senior
official of the Ottoman hierarchy. Under a weak or
incompetent sultan, the grand vizier was the monarch in all
but name. Like the sultan, the senior viziers wore heavy furs
winter and summer alike, as emblems of their superior status.
(S)

24 *Interior of an Ottoman House, Cairo* by Frank Dillon RI
(1823–1909)

This interior of the Cairene house of a senior Ottoman official
bears all the marks of a wealthy Ottoman home before the
intrusion of Western styles. Its cool purity is very different
from the extraordinary mixture of Eastern and Western styles
found in the great houses of Constantinople, Cairo and
Alexandria later in the century, described by Emine Foat
Tugay. (S)

25 *Women and Children around a* Sebil *or Street Fountain,*
c. 1845, by Amadeo, Count Preziosi, (1816–82)

Ottomans lavished care and attention on their children, as can
be seen by the fine garments worn by the girl and boy in this
image. (S)

26 *The Fountain at Tophane*, 1829, by William Page (1794–
1872)

The water for the city was brought by aqueduct from great
reservoirs in the heights above Constantinople. Running water
was essential for the ritual ablutions required of all Muslims
before prayer, and the courtyard of each mosque was supplied
with places where the devout could prepare themselves.
Similarly, the elaborate fountain, or *sebil*, provided water for
the entire neighbourhood and became a place for meeting,

trade and gossip. Compare this with the photograph about forty years later, of the fountain outside the gate to the Yeni Saray (plate 40). In the background can be seen the Galata tower, at the heart of the 'European' city of Pera. The Tophane quarter was where the Ottoman artillery barracks and arsenal were located. (S)

27 *Street Scene in Pera, c.* 1810

The clean and orderly streets of Pera seen here are something of a fiction: the 'European' city (where all the embassies and Western business were located) was reputedly more disreputable than Stamboul, across the Golden Horn. Here a party of janissaries on fire-watch passes a European embassy, although it is impossible to decipher the coat of arms on the embassy wall. A token European appears in the otherwise near-deserted street. This was a convention of Western depictions (whether of Constantinople or the sites of classical antiquity). Sometimes these showed the artist's patron, but sometimes any European was added to give a 'human scale' to the picture – Ottomans or 'Arabs' were merely 'types' or local colour. (S)

28 *The Sultan in Procession Leaving the Great Gate of the Yeni Saray, c.* 1810

The ceremonial procession of the sultan from the palace to Friday prayers or to the war camp at Davut Paşa was a timeless feature. Depictions of sixteenth-century processions differ little from this observation of Mahmud II on his horse. The image shows the Ottoman passion for furs, fine patterned fabrics, and feathers, all used to denote rank or status. The sultan, surrounded by senior janissaries, proceeded at a slow walking pace, as the surrounding crowds bowed before him. The processions emphasized the sultan's separation but also his presence among his people; when Abdul Hamid immured himself within the towering walls of his Yıldız palace it was seen as an act of un-Ottoman renunciation of contact with his people. (S)

29 Janissaries with their Cooking-Pots

These are small cooking-vessels; the regiments possessed larger pots as well, from which the whole detachment would take their soup or stews, and it was these which were ceremoniously overturned to symbolize that the janissaries would no longer eat the sultan's rations and were in rebellion.(S)

30 The Entrance to the Golden Horn, 1852, by Amadeo, Count Preziosi (1816–82)

The Golden Horn and the Bosporus were the highways of Constantinople, linking the Asian and European shores, and Stamboul and Pera. As the sultans and the leading Ottomans built their palaces along the shores of the Bosporus, traffic became even busier: there were many collisions, made more likely by the powerful currents in the waterway. (S)

31 An Arab from Iraq, by Amadeo, Count Preziosi (1816–82)

Preziosi sought out exotic types at the point when they were becoming a rarity in the Ottoman capital. Many of those he depicted were recently arrived in the city, or travellers, like this Arab from Iraq. But, as always, his depiction is accurate, and may be compared with the photograph of the Syrian in plate 44. (S)

32 Massacre in a Balkan Village, 1876, by Orlando Norie (1832–1901)

The image of the 'Terrible Turk' was heightened by pictures such as this. Imaginary in its elaborate detail, based solely on highly coloured newspaper reports, it is in the tradition of the *Massacre at Chios* by Delacroix. However, Norie might equally have painted *Christian* Bulgarians killing *Muslim* villagers with a similar ferocity. (S)

33 *Kurdish Warrior from the Region of Lake Van, c.* 1843,
by Amadeo, Count Preziosi (1816–82)

The 'irregulars' who flocked to the sultan's standard were
responsible for much of the savagery that attached to the
name of Ottoman. The descendants of these Kurdish warriors
might well have been enrolled in Abdul Hamid's special militia
(*Hamidye*) or have been responsible for killing Armenians,
thereby adding fresh horrors to the bloody tally. (S)

*Photography came early to the Ottoman Empire, as pictures
from the Bible lands, harem scenes and general 'Oriental
exotica' found a ready market in the West. Both Ottoman and
Western photographers produced photographs that catered to
Western needs.*

34 *The Holy Places,* 1878

The Ottomans proved good guardians of the holy places in
the nineteenth century, providing a stable environment,
arbitrating dispassionately between the conflicting Christian
sects, and accommodating the growing Jewish presence in
Palestine. Tourism to the holy sites reached considerable
proportions with the development of visits organized by
Thomas Cook, the pioneer of the new 'grand tour' to Egypt
and the Bible lands. (W)

35 *A Caravanserai at Beirut,* 1860s

The '*hans*', both of the capital and of the provincial cities,
were the launching-point of the innumerable caravans that
criss-crossed the empire like the small ships that plied a
continuous trade along the coast. Beirut was a meeting-point
of the land and sea trades. The group gathered here vividly
depicts the great range of racial 'types' that made up the
empire. (W)

36 *The Pasha's Child, his Wet Nurse and Eunuch*, Mecca, 1885

The slave trade was abolished by Abdul Meçid, but domestic slavery continued to function in families throughout the empire. Slaves were more like slaves in the Roman empire than in the plantations of Jamaica or the American south: they would be valued members of the household. The child of a wet nurse would become the 'milk brother' of the pasha's child, and the special bond would continue throughout their lives. (W)

37 *The Byzantine Walls*, 1860s

Time and the assaults of 1453 had eroded the old Byzantine fortifications. In the centuries that followed, much more of the rampart collapsed, although the sound work of the original builders means that sections still survive in the state seen in this image. (W)

38 *The Old Genoese Tower of Galata*, 1860s

Below can be seen the 'picturesque' Ottoman tombstones, beloved by travellers. (W)

39 *The Golden Horn*, late 1880s

The already busy port became a centre of trade as the age of the steamship arrived. Here the harbour is at a transition, with converted sailing-ships dominating in the port. Twenty years later the surface of the water could barely be seen for all the maritime traffic. (W)

40 *The Sebil outside the Great Gate of the Yeni Saray*, 1860s

Compare this, carefully posed to show Eastern 'types', with the image of the Tophane *sebil* (plate 26). The decaying state of the city is evident. (W)

41 *Women Dressed for the Street and the Home*, 1886

These women, photographed by the Dutch Orientalist Hurgronje, were long thought to be prostitutes, for they posed before a European male. But this assumption is not certain, because Hurgronje had access to Islamic homes through his Muslim wife. (W)

42 *The Pasha's Household*, 1886

The pasha and his son are surrounded by their household. Here, in miniature, is the Ottoman tradition of the slave household, which went back to the time of Suleiman and beyond. The loyalty of servant to master, and vice versa, was that of a close family, and the tradition of clan ties was passed on from father to son, as symbolized here. (W)

43 *Dervish in a Trance*, c. 1900

The dervish has plunged a skewer through his cheeks in his trance. Despite the suppression of the Bektaşi dervishes after the fall of the janissaries, and a constant attack on the other sects, dervishes remained a powerful force in the empire until its last days. (W)

44 *Syrian Chieftain*

As with so many rebels against Abdul Hamid, this chieftain was taken as a hostage to the capital, to live out his life in genteel constraint, losing in the process much of the Romantic passion that the photographer plainly saw in him. This is as much a posed stereotypical portrait as the sketches by Wilkie or the water-colours of Preziosi. (W)

45 *Albanian Mountaineers*, 1878.

Albanians were noted for their loyalty and fearlessness, and Ottoman sultans relied on them for their bodyguards, their finest soldiers and many of their most effective viziers. The

'Arnaut' or Albanian became a synonym for the wild and fearsome mountaineer. (W)

Cartoons within the Text

Page 240 – The Minority Western View of the Ottoman Empire

John Bull separates Christian and Ottoman (*Judy*, 4 October 1876). Both wear tattered clothes, but the Christian has obviously come out of the conflict rather worse than the Turk. The Ottoman is a regular soldier carrying his 'Pacificator' portable gallows, while the Christian guerrilla is just as violent, with his 'tool chest' stuffed with weapons. But this image suggests 'a pox on both their houses' rather than prejudice against the Ottoman.

Page 241 – The Dominant Western View of the Ottomans

In this famous cartoon (*Punch*, 5 August 1876), Britannia exhorts the torpid British prime minister, Disraeli, to action. Meanwhile, in the background, Ottoman *regular soldiers* (not wild bashi-bazouks) burn, stab and skewer heads on their bayonets. Maidens are ravaged, and babies dashed to the ground. This is in the same spirit as Norie's '*Massacre*' (plate 32).

Pages 242–4 – The Indolent Ottoman *and* The Lustful (and Craven) Turk

Here in two separate images (*Punch*, 1903, with Emperor Franz Joseph and Tsar Nicholas I) and *Judy*, 1903 (with John Bull), Abdul Hamid is depicted in almost identical form: cross-legged on his divan, faced by the straight-backed, manly Europeans, his self-indulgent pipe close at hand. In an earlier *Punch* cartoon, 15 June 1895, (page 244) the cringing, flabby Turk confronts the stalwart Europeans.

Page 245 The Terrible Turk

Kladderadatsch, 30 August 1896, shows that the German attitude to the Ottoman was not so very different from that of the other European nations. Once again the Ottomans impale, stab and kill at will – this time in Crete. The cartoon mocks the Ottoman claim that this was a civil war.

Pages 246–7 – Abdul Hamid, 'the Red Sultan' . . .

Ottoman visual satire is rare, and was extremely dangerous for its perpetrators. But in this remarkable collection, by Ali Nouri, Abdul Hamid becomes, successively, Hamlet, bloody and indecisive; a mass-murderer tossing the bodies of his victims into the Bosporus; a lecher in a hooped bathing-costume, ogling naked women to the amused contempt of his eunuchs; and, finally – a special touch – with a bottle under his arm, a mere plaything in the hands of naked blonde woman mounted on his shoulders, enveloping him with her breasts and stomach and, worst of all, holding a glass of forbidden liquor in her hand. In the many other cartoons the sultan is damned politically, socially and as an apostate. The collection was reissued after the sultan's fall from power; earlier versions had circulated secretly.

Notes on the Text

Introduction

1 'The West' is a shorthand for the Christian nations of Europe. It embraces eastern and western Europe in a single undifferentiated form – Russia as well as Britain, France, Germany, Austria-Hungary, Italy, Spain etc. Of course each nation had its own attitudes and politics, and each political and social grouping within each nation was also differentiated. Thus the British Liberals were traditionally anti-Ottoman and the Conservatives pro-Ottoman. But the concept of 'the West' as a single mass remained a near-universal perception for the Ottomans until the end of the empire. 'Frank', the universal epithet applied to a Westerner, did not distinguish the French from the Germans or the British. In the same way that I use 'the West' in a crudely generic sense, I use 'the East' in the same undifferentiated fashion. It means the Orient of the Orientalists, in the mind. What the East/Orient meant can best be seen in the work of artists working with the subject-matter of the imagined Orient; see Philippe Jullien, *The Orientalists: European Painters of Eastern Scenes* (Oxford, 1977), for a good visual introduction. In fact the Ottoman empire sits uneasily between the variant post-colonial theories. In relation to Europe its position was unquestionably subordinate, as evidenced by Western writing on the Ottomans, but in relations with its own subject nationalities, and surrounding societies, to the south and east, its role was hegemonic. For a spirited introduction to these nuances, see Robert Young,

White Mythologies: Writing History and the West (London and New York, 1990), especially pp. 119–75.

2 For a clear analysis of the coercive power of language, see Robert Hodge and Gunther Kress, *Language as Ideology* (London and New York, 2nd edn, 1993). For the distinctive feminist approach, see Deborah Cameron, ed., *The Feminist Critique of Language* (London and New York, 1990).

3 Richard Ford, *The Handbook for Travellers in Spain* (London, 2 vols., 1845).

4 Edward Said, *Orientalism* (London, 1978)

5 Blackheath speech, cited in John Morley, *The Life of William Ewart Gladstone* (London, 2 vols., 1908), vol. 2, p. 121.

Chapter 1

1 Synax, 29 May 1453; cited in Alexander Van Millingen *Byzantine Churches: Their History and Architecture* (London, 1891), p. 165.

2 Cited in Steven Runciman, *The Fall of Constantinople, 1453* (Cambridge, 1965), p. 58.

3 Michael Kritovoulos, *History of Mehmed the Conqueror*, (tr., Princeton, NJ, 1954), p. 56.

4 Edward Gibbon, *The Decline and Fall of the Roman Empire* (London, 6 vols., 1910 edn), vol. 6, p. 447.

5 Kritovoulos, *History*, p. 72.

6 Ibid., p. 72.

7 Ibid., pp. 73–4.

8 Cited in Van Millingen, *Byzantine Churches*, p. 169.

Chapter 2

1 Robert Schwoebel, *The Shadow of the Crescent: the Renaissance Image of the Turk, 1453–1517* (Nieuwkoop, 1967),

p. and, for Agarathos, text translated in *Byzantion*, XXII (1952), pp. 379–87.

2 Schwoebel, *Shadow*, p. 12.

3 Fernand Braudel *The Mediterranean and the Mediterranean World in the Age of Philip II*, tr. Sîan Reynolds (London, 2 vols., 1973), vol. 2, p. 665.

4 John Lyly, *Euphues, The Anatomy of Wit*, (London, 1868 edn), p. 42.

5 See Seigneur Michael de Baudier de Languedoc, *The History of the Serrail and the Court of the Grand Seigneur* (London, 1635).

6 Cited in Bernard Lewis, *Istanbul and the Civilization of the Ottoman Empire* (Norman, Okla., 1963), p. 26–27.

7 Lewis, *Istanbul*, p. 27.

8 Michael Kritovoulos, *History of Mehmed the Conqueror*, (tr., Princeton, NJ, 1954), p. 140.

9 Kritovoulos, *History*, pp. 207–8.

10 Gerlach, cited in Barnette Miller, *Beyond the Sublime Porte: the Grand Seraglio of Constantinople* (New Haven, Conn., 1931), p. 152.

11 Bassano, 1545; see Miller, *Sublime Porte*.

12 Nicholas de Nicolay, *Quatre Premiers Livres*, 1561 version, p. 51; cited in Nicholas Penzer, *The Harem* (London, 1936), p. 83.

13 See J. P. de Tournefort, *Journey into the Levant*, (tr., London, 3 vols., 1741).

14 See Ottaviano Bon, '*Descrizione del seraglio ...*' in F. Contarini, *Relationi degli stati europei ... dagli ambiascatori veneti* (Rome, 1866), p. 61.

15 Halil Inalcik, *The Ottoman Empire* (London, 1973), p. 90, citing '*Illustrations de B. de Vigenère Bourbonnais sur l'histoire de Chalcocondyle athenien*', in *Histoire de la décadence de l'empire grec et l'établissement celvy turcs*, (Rouen, 1660), p. 19.

16 Miller, *Sublime Porte*, p. 54.

17 See Steven Runciman, *Byzantine Civilisation*, London, 1933, p. 203.

18 Miller, *Sublime Porte*, pp. 97–8.

19 See J. von Hammer-Purgstall, *Histoire de l'empire otto-man*, (tr., Paris, 1835).

20 F. Babinger, *Mehmed the Conqueror* (Princeton, NJ, 1978), p. 44.

21 Théophile Gautier, *Constantinople of Today* (tr., London, 1854), p. 301.

Chapter 3

1 See Sonia P. Anderson, *English Consul in Turkey: Paul Rycaut at Smyrna, 1667–78* (Oxford, 1989), and C. J. Heywood, 'Sir Paul Rycaut, a seventeenth-century observer of the Ottoman state: notes for a study', in Ezel Kural Shaw and C. J. Heywood, *English and Continental Views of the Ottoman Empire, 1500–1800* (Los Angeles, 1972).

2 See Ogier Ghislain de Busbeq, *Turkish Letters of Ogier Ghislain de Busbeq*, tr. and ed. E. Forster (Oxford, 1927).

3 'Relatione particolare . . . dell Conte Alberto Caprara anno 1682 e 1683'; cited in John Stoye, *The Siege of Vienna* (London, 1964), p. 52.

4 Kemal Zadeh Pasha, *Histoire de la campaigne de Mohács*, tr. and ed. A. J. B. Pavet de Courteille (Paris, 1859), p. 90.

5 See Zadeh Pasha, *Mohács*.

6 Cited in Christopher Duffy, *Siege Warfare: the Fortress in the Early Modern World, 1494–1660* (London, 1979), p. 196.

7 Cited in Duffy, *Siege Warfare*, p. 195.

8 Adam Zamoyski, *The Polish Way: a Thousand-Year History of the Poles and Their Culture* (London, 1987), p. 3.

9 The 'meaning' of Lepanto is impossible to decipher without an understanding of the complex fears of the

Spanish for 'the Moors' and their own internal *bêtes noires* (*sic*) the Moriscos, before their expulsion in the 1570s. Even in modern Spanish a phrase for danger is 'There are Moors on the coast' – '*Hay moros en la costa.*' There are distinctions in the way in which the terms '*Moro*' and '*Turco*' were used as terms of opprobrium, just as '*Arabe*' carries the same negative weight in French – the legacy of nineteenth-century colonial battles. The Spanish archives from the seventeenth century are full of references to this terror of collaboration between Moriscos and Turks. The account by Diego Hurtado de Mendoza of the war in Granada refers to '*Turcos*' – professional soldiers who have come to the aid of the Moriscos. See, among many others, the case of Diego Hernandez in 1569, for 'fleeing to Barbary' ('*sobre transfugía en Berbería*') (Archivo del Alhambra, Legajo A63, Pieza 6), and also the letter of M. de Chantonney, writing from the imperial court, 'Of the request for help to the Turk from the Moriscos of Spain' ('*sobre petición de socorro al Turco que hicieron los Moriscos de España*'), Prague, 15 February 1570, in *Colección de documentos inéditos para Historia de España*, vol. 103, pp. 450ff.

10 See Sir Robert Sutton, *The Dispatches of Sir Robert Sutton, Ambassador in Constantinople 1710–14*, ed. Akdes Nimet Kurat (London, 1953), pp. 58ff.

11 See Sutton, *Dispatches*, pp. 58ff.

12 De Tott remarked of Bonneval, 'I must observe that M. de Bonneval only failed in his project [of forming a European-style corps in Turkey] from ignorance of the character of the nation he had adopted, which led him to begin where he should have finished.' (Baron François de Tott, *Memoires du Baron de Tott sur les turcs et les tartares* (Paris, 2 vols., 1785), vol. 1, p. 197.)

13 Cited in Bernard Lewis, *The Muslim Discovery of Europe* (New York, 1982), p. 281, and in his *The Emergence of*

Modern Turkey (London and New York, 2nd edn, 1968), p. 108.

14 See James C. Davis, *Pursuit of Power: Venetian Ambassadors' Reports on Spain, Turkey and France in the Age of Philip II* (New York and London, 1970), pp. 126–55.

15 See Sutton, *Dispatches*, pp. 58ff.

16 See Sutton, *Dispatches*, pp. 58ff.

17 Flachet, cited in Alev Lytle Croutier, *Harem: the World Behind the Veil* (New York, 1989), p. 67.

18 Cited in Lewis, *Discovery*, pp. 234–5.

19 Mark Girouard, *The Victorian Country House* (New Haven, Conn., and London, 2nd edn, 1979), p. 28.

Chapter 4

1 Robert Walsh, *Narrative of a Residence at Constantinople* (London, 2 vols., 1836), vol. 1, pp. 351–2.

2 Ernst Laudon to Joseph II, 22 September 1788, cited in Christopher Duffy, *The Fortress in the Age of Frederick the Great and Vauban* (London and Boston, Mass., 1985), p. 244.

3 Adolphus Slade, *Record of Travels in Turkey, Greece etc. and of a Cruise in the Black Sea with the Captain Pasha in the Years 1828, 1829, 1830, 1831* (Philadelphia, 2 vols., 1833) vol. 1, p. 265.

4 Robert Walsh, *Narrative of a Journey from Constantinople to England* (London, 1828), p. 67.

5 Slade, *Record*, vol. 1, pp. 264–5.

6 Ibid., p. 364.

7 Baron François de Tott, *Memoires du Baron de Tott sur les turcs et les tartares*, (Paris, 2 vols., 1785), vol. 1, p. 215.

8 See Metin Kunt, 'Ethnic-regional solidarity in the seventeenth-century Ottoman establishment', *International Journal of Middle East Studies*, 5 (1974), 233–9.

9 I. M. D'Ohsson, *Tableau général de l'empire ottoman*, (Paris, 7 vols., 1788–1824), vol. 7, pp. 336–8. See also H. A. Reed, *The Destruction of the Janissaries by Mahmud II* (unpublished Ph.D. thesis, Princeton University, NJ, 1951), pp. 178–82.

10 See E. S. Creasy, *History of the Ottoman Turks, from the Beginning of their Empire to the Present Time* (London, 2 vols., 1856), vol. 2, pp. 340–1.

11 Preamble to the *Eskenji* ordinance, 1826; see Reed, *Destruction*.

12 On feathers in Ottoman society, see Zdzislaw Zygulski Jr, *Ottoman Art in the Service of the Empire* (New York and London, 1992), p. 113.

13 William McNeill, *The Pursuit of Power* (Oxford, 1983), pp. 123–4.

14 Ibid.

15 Jevad Pasha, cited in Reed, *Destruction*, p. 323.

16 On Selim's reforms, the reliable source is Stanford J. Shaw, *Between Old and New: The Ottoman Empire under Sultan Selim III* (Cambridge, Mass., 1971); see especially Part III.

17 W. A. Eton, *A Survey of the Turkish Empire* (London, 2nd edn, 1799), pp. 98–9.

18 See Reed, *Destruction*, *passim*, for the events of 1826. His texts are translated from the Ottoman chroniclers.

19 Charles Macfarlane, *Constantinople in 1828: a Residence of sixteen months in the Turkish Capital and Provinces etc.* (London, 2 vols., 1829), vol. 2, p. 101.

20 Creasy, *History*, vol. 2, II, pp. 366–7.

21 Ibid., pp. 392–3.

22 Ibid., p. 339.

23 Bernard Lewis, *The Muslim Discovery of Europe* (New York, 1982), p. 56; citing E. Ziya Karal, *Halet Efendinin Paris Büyük Elçiligi 1802–06* (Istanbul, 1940).

24 Macfarlane, *Constantinople*, vol. 2, p. 108.

25 William St Clair, *That Greece Might Still be Free* (London, 1972), pp. 9–12.

26 See Reed, *Destruction*.

27 Cited in Reed, *Destruction*, p. 195.

28 Stanley Lane Poole, *The Life of the Right Honourable Stratford Canning, Viscount Stratford de Redcliffe* (London, 2 vols., 1888), pp. 418–9.

29 Reed, *Destruction*, p. 263.

30 Lane Poole, *Life*, I, p. 421.

31 Ibid.

32 The Ottoman phrase is *Vakayı Hayriye*.

Chapter 5

1 The Islamic *hicri* calendar was used for most normal purposes. The Ottoman administration used the *mali* calendar, which worked on the basis of the financial year; *mali* dates were between one and three years in advance of the *hicri* dates during the nineteenth century. Most Christians used the Gregorian calendar, but some groups still remained faithful to the old-style Julian calendar, which ran about twelve to fifteen days behind the Gregorian. Clocks and watches showed mosque time as well as the normal European-style day.

2 Albert Smith, *A Month at Constantinople* (London, 1850), p. 42.

3 Julia Pardoe, *The Beauties of the Bosphorus* (London, 4 vols., 1838), vol. 1, p. 4.

4 Ibid., p. 3.

5 Robert Walsh, *Narrative of a Residence at Constantinople* (London, 2 vols., 1836), vol. 1, p. 238.

6 Ibid., p. 228.

7 Ibid., p. 25.

8 J. Foster, ed., *The Travels of John Sanderson in the Levant, 1584–1602* (London, 1931), pp. 70–1.

9 Godfrey Goodwin, *A History of Ottoman Architecture* (London, 1971), pp. 124–7.

10 John Murray, *Handbook for Travellers in Turkey* (London, 1878), pp. 6–7.

11 Annie Jane Harvey, *Turkish Harems and Circassian Homes* (London, 1871), pp. 55 6.

12 Walsh, *Residence*, vol. 1, pp. 266–7.

13 Théophile Gautier, *Constantinople of today*, (tr., London, 1854), p. 263.

14 Edwin Augustus Grosvenor, *Constantinople* (Boston, Mass., 2 vols., rev. edn, 1900), vol. 1, p. 93.

15 Nassau W. Senior, *A Journal Kept in Turkey and Greece in the Autumn of 1857 and the Beginning of 1858* (London, 1859), p. 52.

16 Smith, *A Month at Constantinople*, p. 50.

17 Ibid.

18 See Zeynap Çelik, *The Remaking of Istanbul: Portrait of an Ottoman City in the Nineteenth Century* (Seattle, Wash., and London, 1986).

19 Grosvenor, *Constantinople*, p. 103.

20 Mehmed Beyri Halit, *Istanbul* (Istanbul, 1951), pp. 85–6.

21 Charles White, *Three Years in Constantinople, or Domestic Manners of the Turks in 1844* (London, 3 vols., 1845), vol. 1, p. 72.

22 See J. H. Ubicini, *Letters on Turkey*, (tr., London, 2 vols., 1856) and Çelik, *Remaking of Istanbul*.

23 See Charles Issawi, *An Economic History of the Middle East and North Africa* (New York and London, 1982), p. 114, citing *UK Parliamentary Accounts and Papers, 1883, vol. 7: Constantinople*.

24 Stanford J. Shaw and Ezel Kural Shaw, *History of the Ottoman Empire and Modern Turkey* (Cambridge, 2 vols., 1977), vol. 2, p. 242.

25 See Issawi, *Economic History*, pp. 114–15.

26 See Robert Walsh, *Constantinople and the Scenery of the Seven Churches of Asia Minor* (London, n.d.).

27 Gautier, *Constantinople*, p. 301.

28 Ubicini, *Letters*, vol. 1, p. 284.

29 See Murray, *Handbook*, Introduction.

30 Ibid.

31 See White, *Three Years*, vol. 3, p. 322.

32 Ibid., pp. 289–90.

33 Julia Pardoe, *The City of the Sultans and Domestic Manners of the Turks in 1836* (London, 2 vols., 1837), vol. 1, p. 280.

34 Charles Eliot, *Turkey in Europe* (London, 1900), p. 9.

35 Halit, *Istanbul*, p. 94.

36 Roderic H. Davison, *Reform in the Ottoman Empire 1856–1876* (Princeton, NJ, 1963), p. 349.

37 20 November 1895; cited in Dennis Quataert, *Social Disintegration and Popular Resistance in the Ottoman Empire, 1881–1908: Reactions to European Economic Penetration* (New York, 1983).

38 See Eliot, *Turkey*, p. 15.

39 Halit, *Istanbul*, pp. 128–9.

40 Cited in Davison, *Reform*, p. 72.

41 Eliot, *Turkey*, p. 318.

42 1886 Ottoman census.

Chapter 6

1 Peter Mundy, *The Travels of Peter Mundy in Europe and Asia, 1608–1667* (Cambridge, 2 vols., 1907), vol. 1, p. 187; the description is that of Thomas Gainsford.

2 Roderic H. Davison, *Reform in the Ottoman Empire, 1856–1876* (Princeton, NJ, 1963), pp. 37–9.

3 Davison, *Reform*, p. 40, fn. 66, draws attention to this discrepancy and remarks, 'One wonders whether the Turkish and French texts were prepared with their respective domestic and foreign audiences in mind.' Certainly Reşid

would have appreciated the distinction, and could have drafted equally in either language.

4 Charles Macfarlane, *Turkey and its Destiny: the Results of Journeys Made in 1847 and 1848 to Examine into the State of that Country* (London, 2 vols., 1850), vol. 1, p. 43.

5 Cited in Bernard Lewis, *The Emergence of Modern Turkey* (London and New York, 2nd edn, 1968), p. 146.

6 Charles Macfarlane, *Constantinople in 1828: a Residence of Sixteen Months in the Turkish Capital and Provinces etc.* (London, 2 vols., 1829), vol. 1, p. 253.

7 See Avidgor Levy, 'The officer corps in Sultan Mahmud II's new Ottoman army, 1826–39', *International Journal of Middle East Studies*, 2 (1971), 22.

8 Ibid.

9 Ibid., p. 24.

10 Helmut von Moltke, *Briefe über Zustände und Begebenheiten . . . in Türkei aus den Jahren 1835 bis 1839* (Berlin, 1839), p. 418.

11 Macfarlane, *Constantinople*, vol. 3, p. 165.

12 Ibid., p. 318.

13 Ibid., p. 323.

14 Memorandum of the report of Alexander Pisani's interview with Ibrahim; cited in Davison, *Reform*, p. 31.

15 Luigi Fernandino Marsigli, *L'État militaire de l'empire ottoman*, (Amsterdam, 2 parts, 1732; facsimile edn., Graz, 1972), vol. 1, p. 64.

16 See Carter V. Findley, *Bureaucratic Reform in the Ottoman Empire: the Sublime Porte, 1789–1922* (Princeton, NJ, 1980), pp. 125–40.

17 Macfarlane, *Constantinople*, vol 2, pp. 127–8.

18 E. S. Creasy, *History of the Ottoman Turks, from the Beginning of their Empire to the Present Time* (London, 2 vols., 1856), vol 2, p. 412.

19 Moltke, *Briefe*, p. 456.

20 Davison, *Reform*, pp. 34–5, fn. 54. Davison cites Edmund

Hornby, *An Autobiography* (London, 1928), p. 90, but also mentions that Friedrich Hellwald, who was violently anti-Ottoman in his outlook, remarked that government office was bought and sold, in both the United States and the Ottoman Empire, and to roughly the same degree. Likewise, Lord Charlemont in the previous century had made a similar comparison (see Lord Charlemont, *The Travels of Lord Charlemont in Greece and Turkey, 1749* ed. W. R. Stanford and E. J. Finopoulos (London, 1984), p. 215).

21 Cited in Lewis, *Modern Turkey*, p. 72.

22 Macfarlane, *Turkey*, vol. 2, p. 146.

23 Durand de Fontemagne, *Un séjour à l'ambassade de France* (Paris, 1902), p. 45; cited in Davison, *Reform*.

24 Samuel Huntington, *Political Order in Changing Societies* (New Haven, Conn., 1968), pp. 154–6.

25 Mary Eliza Rogers, *Domestic Life in Palestine*, (London, 1862), p. 189.

26 Davison, *Reform*, p. 3.

27 W. E. Gladstone, *The Bulgarian Horrors and the Question of the East* (London, 1876), p. 15.

28 Hornby, *Autobiography*, p. 83.

29 Creasy, *History*, vol. 2, p. 478.

30 Davison, *Reform*, p. 112, fn. 90.

31 She had wanted to award him the Order of the Bath.

32 See MS Vertragsbuch, Steyr Daimler Puch AG, Steyr, Austria, for the resulting orders, and the private Werndl Museum for material supplied.

33 Henry Harris Jessup to Revd F. F. Ellinwood, 12 February 1874; cited in Davison, *Reform*, p. 277.

34 Jennifer Scarce, 'Turkish fashion in transition', *Costume: The Journal of the Costume History Society*, 14 (1980), 114–67, and her *Women's Costume in the Near and Middle East* (London and Sydney, 1987), pp. 68–131, for the effects throughout the Ottoman world.

35 For Midhat's career in Syria, see N. E. Saliba, 'The achieve-

ments of Midhat Pasha as governor of Syria, 1878–80',
International Journal of Middle East Studies, 9 (1978),
307–23.

36 Stanford J. Shaw and Ezel Kural Shaw, *History of the
Ottoman Empire and Modern Turkey*, (Cambridge, 2 vols.,
1977), vol. 2, pp. 221–6, and Roger Owen, *The Middle
East in the World Economy, 1800–1914* (London and New
York, 1981), pp. 101–5.

37 The Ottomans were not alone in their financial troubles.
Of the Public Debt Commission nations, Austria defaulted
on her debts five times in the century, while the
Netherlands defaulted on seven occasions.

38 For a full treatment of this whole subject, see W.
Ochsenwald, *The Hijaz Railroad* (Charlottesville, NC,
1980) and Saleh Muhammad Al-Amr, *The Hijaz under
Ottoman Rule, 1869–1914: Ottoman Vali, the Sharif of
Mecca, and the Growth of British Rule* (Riyadh, 1978),
passim.

39 see Al-Amr, *The Hijaz*, pp. 125–31.

40 Records of the Western Turkey Mission, 6 September
1876; cited in Davison, *Reform*, p. 355.

41 For all this, see Findley, *Bureaucratic Reform*, pp. 226–39.

42 See Shaw and Shaw, *History*, vol. 2, pp. 174–8.

43 Cited in Davison, *Reform*, p. 403.

44 The excesses of his political police owed more to the
ambitions of their leader than to any policy of the sultan.

45 Aïché Osmanoğlu, *Avec mon père le sultan Abdulhamid
de son palais à sa prison* (Paris, 1991), p. 74.

46 See Carl Brockelmann, ed., *History of the Islamic Peoples*
(London, 1980), p. 379.

47 See Roderic H. Davison, *Essays in Ottoman and Turkish
History, 1774–1923: the Impact of the West* (Austin, Tex.,
and London, 1991): 'The advent of the electric telegraph in
the Ottoman empire', pp. 133–65.

48 See Stanford J. Shaw, 'The population of Istanbul in the

nineteenth century', *International Journal of Middle East Studies*, 10 (1979), 265, for the use Abdul Hamid made of the census:

the modern Ottoman census as resumed in 1880 was a result of the personal interest of Sultan Abdulhamid II, based on a personal registration system; each individual counted was given a census ticket which served also as a birth certificate and identity card ... it had to be produced in all dealings with the government. Changes brought about by birth, marriage, divorce, *change of domicile* [my italics] and the like had to be registered with the local authorities.

This document had to be produced to the authorities before buying, selling or inheriting property, before being entered in an occupation or profession, for obtaining travel documents, and for conducting all official business. Failure to produce the document on demand was punished by a jail sentence ranging from twenty-four hours to one month. See E. Karpat, 'Ottoman population records and the census of 1881/2', *International Journal of Middle East Studies*, 9 (1978), 237–74.

49 Charles Eliot, *Turkey in Europe* (London, 1900), pp. 158–9.

50 Robert Curzon, *Armenia: a Year at Erzeroom and on the Frontiers of Russia, Turkey and Persia* (London, 1854), p. 20.

51 The archive is now located in the Research Centre for Islamic History, Art and Culture, located (appropriately enough) in the Yıldız palace. Another (different) set of photographs was sent to Washington, DC, and may be seen in the Library of Congress. See the Introduction by Professor Ekmeleddin Ihsanoğlu in his *Istanbul: a Glimpse into the Past* (Istanbul, 1987).

52 See William V. Herbert, *The Defence of Plevna, 1877, Written by One Who Took Part in It* (London, 1895).

53 For all this, see the *Mitteilungen des Technische*

Administratifs Militä Committee and the private reports located in the Kriegsarchiv, Vienna.

54 See Gwynne Dyer, 'Turkish "Falsifiers" and Armenian "Deceivers": historiography and the Armenian massacres', *Middle East Studies*, 12 (1976), 99–107.

55 See Roy Douglas, 'Britain and the Armenian Question, 1894–7', *The Historical Journal* 19:1 (1976), 113–33.

56 Seymour's diary; cited in Alan Palmer, *The Banner of Battle: the Story of the Crimean War* (London, 1987), pp. 14–15.

57 Report of Lorenzo Bernardo to the doge and senate of Venice, translated in James C. Davis, *Pursuit of Power: Venetian Ambassadors' Reports on Spain, Turkey and France in the Age of Philip II, 1560–1600* (New York and London, 1970), p. 166.

58 Bernard Lewis, 'Ottoman observers of Ottoman decline', *Islamic Studies*, 1 (1962), 71–87.

59 See David Fromkin, *A Peace to End All Peace: the Fall of the Ottoman Empire and the Creation of the Modern Middle East* (New York, 1989).

60 See Lord Kinross, *Atatürk: the Rebirth of a Nation* (London, 1964).

Chapter 7

1 See Lord Kinross, *Atatürk: the Rebirth of a Nation* (London, 1964).

2 After the freeing of women, there was less said about the life of the harem.

3 For the link between lust and tyranny, see Alain Grosrichard, *Structure du sérail, la fiction du despotisme asiatique dans l'Occident classique* (Paris, 1979).

4 Marquis de Sade, *The One Hundred and Twenty Days of Sodom* (London, 1989), p. 238.

5 Cited in Bernard Lewis, *The Muslim Discovery of Europe* (New York, 1982), p. 291.

6 Ibid., p. 288.

7 See Patricia Anderson, *The Printed Image and the Transformation of Popular Culture, 1790–1860* (Oxford, 1991).

8 W. F. Moneypenny and G. H. Buckle, *The Life of Benjamin Disraeli, Earl of Beaconsfield* (London, 6 vols., 1910–20), vol. 1, p. 175.

9 See Billie Melman, *Women's Orients: English Women and the Middle East* (Basingstoke, 1992), for the travellers in the nineteenth century.

10 Alexander Pope, *Moral Essays: Epistle to a Lady*, lines 199–203, in *The Poems of Alexander Pope* (London, 1963), p. 567.

11 See Alain Corbin, *The Foul and the Fragrant: Odor and the French Social Imagination* (Cambridge, Mass., 1986), p. 154.

12 Lady Mary Wortley Montagu, *The Complete Letters of Lady Mary Wortley Montagu: vol. 1, 1708–1720*, ed. Robert Halsband (Oxford, 1965), pp. 307–8.

13 Ibid., pp. 313–15.

14 Ibid., pp. 327–8.

15 Ibid.

16 Ibid., p. 329.

17 Ibid.

18 The fifty-two 'letters' are a literary device, based on a journal which she kept and which was afterwards destroyed by her daughter. But they were also based on *actual* letters sent at the time, and the differences in tone based on the gender of her correspondents are evident in the one actual letter and the various drafts or rough copies that survive. Plainly the actual letters were as sharp and vivid as their simulacra. Conti handed her letters to friends in Paris, and was said to opine that he had 'never seen such precision with so much liveliness' from any other correspondent. See Montagu, *Letters*, pp. xiv–xvii.

19 Montagu, *Letters*, pp. 380.

20 Ibid., pp. 380–1.

21 Ibid., p. 381.

22 Ibid.

23 See Norman Daniel, *Islam and the West: the Making of an Image* (Edinburgh, 1980), pp. 145 and 135–61 *passim*.

24 Ibid., p. 143.

25 Ibid.

26 Cited in Lewis, *Discovery*, pp. 290–1.

27 Lord Charlemont, *The Travels of Lord Charlemont in Greece and Turkey, 1749*, ed. W. R. Stanford and E. J. Finopoulos (London, 1984), p. 202. These remained as an unpublished MS until this first printing.

28 Ibid., p. 206.

29 Ibid., p. 202.

30 Ibid., p. 168.

31 Ibid., pp. 170–1.

32 Ibid., p. 203.

33 Ibid., p. 214.

34 For the history of *The Lustful Turk*, see Steven Marcus, *The Other Victorians: a Study of Sexuality and Pornography in Mid-Nineteenth-Century England* (London, 1964), pp. 197–216. The text I have used is a reissue dated 1985.

35 See Clarence Dana Rouillard, *The Turk in French History, Thought and Literature, 1520–1660* (Paris, 1941).

36 Daniel, *Islam and the West*: 'Sexuality and violence were the characteristic marks of Islam: *fornicationes et furta* and *terror mundanus et voluptis carnalis.*' pp. 145ff.

37 Anon, *The Lustful Turk, or Scenes in the Harem of an Eastern Potentate, Faithfully and Vividly Depicted in a series of letters from a young and beautiful English lady to her Cousin in England – The full particulars of her ravishment and of her complete abandonment to all the salacious Tastes of the Turks described with the zest and simplicity*

which always gives guarantee for its authenticity, (1828, repr. London, 1985), p. 140. On the 'semantic derogation' of women, see Muriel R. Schulz, 'The semantic derogation of women', in B. Thorne and N. Henley, eds., *Language and Sex: Difference and Dominance* (Rowley, Mass., 1975), reprinted in Deborah Cameron, ed., *The Feminist Critique of Language: a Reader* (London and New York, 1990). The other material in both Cameron and Thorne and Henley is also relevant.

38 Lord Byron, *The Giaour*, lines 655–74, in *Lord Byron: The Complete Poetical Works*, ed. Jerome J. McGann (Oxford, 7 vols., 1980–93), vol. 3, p. 60. See also the contemporary book illustration to these lines from the first edition, reprinted on the facing page. Byron's own ambivalent attitude to the Ottomans was summed up in his 'Advertisement' to *The Giaour*, where he remarked on the desolation of the Morea, 'during which the cruelty exercised on all sides was unparalleled even in the annals of the faithful [that is, the Turks]' (ibid., p. 40). Malcolm Kelsall's remark, 'We know that things "Turkish" were a common enlightenment signifier for all types of tyranny and superstition' details the context of Byron's approach. See pp. 317–18 of Malcolm Kelsall, 'The slave woman in the harem', *Studies in Romanticism*, 31:3 (fall 1992), 315–31.

39 'A Propos of the Naval Demonstration', *The Pearl*, 13 (1878), 463.

40 *The Pearl*, 18 (1878), 617–25.

41 This accuracy in detail can be found in other pornographic accounts. *Rose d'Amour* (n.d., repr. New York, 1985), a similar anonymous American pornographic novelette of the time, has as its centrepiece a visit to Constantinople, where the protagonist staffs his harem. Unlike many visitors to the city who claimed to have seen the slave market, which was in fact closed under Abdul Meçid, he accurately

describes the process of private treaty by which Circassian slaves could still be acquired:

I then engaged an interpreter and paying a visit to one of the slave merchants, engaged him as an agent to find out and procure me a lot of the handsomest females to be found in the market. And knowing that the poor class of the inhabitants were in the daily habit of selling their daughters, such as were handsome enough to grace the harems of rich and lustful Turks I directed him to . . . search out all the families among the poor quarters who had beautiful girls and who would be apt to exchange them for gold.

42 William Elroy Curtis, *The Turk and his Lost Provinces* (Chicago, 1903), p. 45.
43 Ibid, p. 109.
44 Daniel, *Islam and the West*, pp. 285 and 383.
45 Archibald Mason, *Remarks on the Sixth Vial and the Fall of the Turkish Empire* (Glasgow, 1827), p. 9.
46 See note 41.
47 T. E. Lawrence, *The Seven Pillars of Wisdom: a Triumph* (London, 1935), p. 32.

Chapter 8

1 Francis Bacon, 'Of Goodnesse and Goodnesse of Nature', in *The Essays or Counsels, Civill and Morall*, ed. Michael Kiernan (Oxford, 1985), p. 39.
2 Francis Bacon, 'An Advertisment touching an Holy Warre written in the year 1622', in *The Works of Francis Bacon, Baron of Verulam, Viscount St Albans and Lord High Chancellor of England*, coll. and ed. James Spedding, Robert Leslie Ellis and Douglas Denon Heath (London, 16 vols., 1861), vol. 7, p. 22.
3 See Adolphus Slade, *Record of Travels in Turkey, Greece, etc. and of a Cruise in the Black Sea with the Captain*

Pasha in the Years 1828, 1829, 1830, 1831 (Philadelphia, 2 vols., 1833), vol. 1, p. 265.

4 Robert Curzon, *Armenia: a Year at Erzeroom and on the Frontiers of Russia, Turkey and Persia* (London, 1854), p. 93.

5 W. E. Gladstone, *The Bulgarian Horrors and the Question of the East* (London, 1876), pp. 12–13.

6 Ibid., p. 28.

7 Ibid., p. 33.

8 Ibid.,

9 Ibid., p. 61.

10 Ibid., p. 62. On the positive/negative connotations of language use, see Robert Hodge and Gunther Kress, *Language as Ideology* (London and New York, 2nd edn, 1993), especially pp. 77–82 and 193–201.

11 Christopher Hibbert, *The Great Mutiny* (London, 1978), pp. 201–14.

12 See Lawrence James, *The Golden Warrior: the Life and Legend of Lawrence of Arabia* (London, 1990), pp. 209–21.

13 T. E. Lawrence, *The Seven Pillars of Wisdom: a Triumph* (London, 1935), pp. 442–7.

14 See John Dover, *War Without Mercy: Race and Power in the Pacific War* (New York, 1986).

Conclusion

1 This distortion extended into every sphere. Gran has observed:

Modernization theory, be it orientalist or Marxist, gives relevant information about the rise of periphery capitalism, but it places too much explanatory emphasis on the acts of a few Europeans and reformers, failing to see a larger internal dynamic. A great conflict, invisible in modernization theory, was resolved in favour of a male, waged-labour economy, to the detriment of women who were not waged, of nomads, who were forcibly sedentarized, and the peasants who lost the advantage of the older, local self-sufficiency ... to attribute change to the West when so much involved local events, seems a great over-simplification.

See P. Gran, 'Political economy as a paradigm for the study of Islamic history', *International Journal of Middle East Studies*, 11 (1980), 511–26.

2 Ezel Kural Shaw, 'The double veil: travelers' views of the Ottoman empire, sixteenth through eighteenth centuries', in Ezel Kural Shaw and C. J. Heywood, *English and Continental Views of the Ottoman Empire, 1500–1800* (Los Angeles, 1972), p. 26.

3 Cited in V. G. Kiernan, *The Lords of Human Kind: European Attitudes to the Outside World in the Imperial Age* (London, 1969), p. 110.

4 D. Urquhart, *The Spirit of the East, or Pictures of Eastern Travel*, (London, 2 vols. in 1, 1839), pp. 379–80.

5 These are Warren S. Walker and Ahmet E. Uysal, *Tales Alive in Turkey* (Lubbock, Tex., 1990) and *More Tales Alive in Turkey* (Lubbock, Tex., 1992). The collection is housed in the Center for Oral Turkish Narrative in the Library of the University of Texas Tech, Lubbock, Texas, and is invaluable for material obtainable from no other source.

6 Urquhart, *Spirit*, vol. 1, p. 354.

Bibliography

Abou-el-Haj, Rifaat Ali, *Formation of the Modern State: the Ottoman Empire: Sixteenth to Eighteenth Centuries* (Albany, NY, 1991)

Ahmad, Feroz, *The Young Turks: the Committee of Union and Progress in Turkish Politics, 1908–14* (Oxford, 1969)

Al-Amr, Saleh Muhammad, *The Hijaz under Ottoman Rule, 1869–1914: Ottoman Vali, the Sharif of Mecca, and the Growth of British Rule* (Riyadh, 1978)

Alderson, Anthony D., *The Structure of the Ottoman Dynasty* (Oxford, 1956)

Allen, W. E. D., *Problems of Turkish Power in the Sixteenth Century* (London, 1963)

Allen, W. E. D., and Muratoff, P., *Caucasian Battlefields: a History of the Wars on the Turco-Caucasian Border, 1828–1921* (Cambridge, 1953)

Anderson, M. S., *The Eastern Question, 1774–1923: a Study in International Relations* (New York and London, 1966)

Anderson, Patricia, *The Printed Image and the Transformation of Popular Culture, 1790–1860* (Oxford, 1991)

Anderson, Sonia P., *English Consul in Turkey: Paul Rycaut at Smyrna, 1667–78* (Oxford, 1989)

Andreossy, Comte Antoine François, *Constantinople et le Bosphore de Thrace,* (Paris, 3rd edn, 1841)

Anecdotes sur l'histoire secrette de la maison ottomane (Amsterdam, 1722)

Angelomatis-Tsougarakis, Helen, *The Eve of the Greek*

Revival: British Travellers' Perceptions of Early Nineteenth Century Greece (London and New York, 1990)

'A Propos of the Naval Demonstration', *The Pearl*, 13 (1878), 463

Archivo del Alhambra, Legajo A63

Askeri Müze ve Kültur Sistesi Komutanligi, *Ottoman Military Organisation and Uniforms, 1876–1908* (Ankara, 1986)

Atil, Esin, *The Age of Suleyman the Magnificent* (New York, 1987)

Aubignosc, L. P. B. D', *La Turquie nouvelle . . .* (Paris, 2 vols., 1839)

Autobiography of a Constantinople Story-teller (London, 1877)

Babinger, F., *Mehmed the Conqueror* (Princeton, NJ, 1978)

Bachet, Erich, ed., *La Turquie se dévoile 1908–1938: de l'empire ottoman à la republique d'Atatürk* (Paris, 1980)

Bacon, Francis, *The Essayes or Counsels, Civill and Morall*, ed. Michael Kiernan (Oxford, 1985)

Bacon, Francis, *The Works of Francis Bacon, Baron of Verulam, Viscount St Albans and Lord High Chancellor of England*, coll. and ed. James Spedding, Robert Leslie Ellis and Douglas Denon Heath (London, 16 vols., 1861)

Balkan War Drama, The, by 'A Special Correspondent' (London, 1913)

Barber, Karl K., *Ottoman Rule in Damascus, 1708–1758* (Princeton, NJ, and Guildford, 1980)

Baudier de Languedoc, Seigneur Michael de, *The History of the Serrail and the Court of the Grand Seigneur* (London, 1635)

Berton, J. M., *Les Turcs dans la balance politique de l'Europe au dix-neuvième siècle* (Paris, 1822)

Blaisdell, D. C., *European Financial Control in the Ottoman Empire* (New York, 1929)

Bodleian Library, *Life in Istanbul 1588: Scenes from a Traveller's Picture Book* (Oxford, 1977)

Bon, Ottaviano, '*Descrizione del seraglio . . .*', in F. Contarini, *Relazioni degli stati europei . . . dagli ambiasciatori veneti*, ser. 5, vol. 1, par. 1 (Rome, 1866)

Boppe, Auguste, *Les Peintures du Bosphore au XVIII siècle*, revised and illustrated by Catherine Boppe (Paris, 1989)

Boue, Ami, *La Turquie d'Europe* (Paris, 4 vols., 1840)

Bouvard, Michel, *Photo legendes: essai sur l'art photographique* (Lyon, 1991)

Bradford, Ernle, *The Great Siege: Malta 1565* (London, 1961)

Braudel, Fernand, *Civilization and Capitalism: Fifteenth to Eighteenth Century*, tr. Sîan Reynolds (London, 3 vols., 1985)

Braudel, Fernand, *The Mediterranean and the Mediterranean World in the Age of Philip II*, tr. Sîan Reynolds (London, 2 vols., 1973)

Brockelmann, Carl, ed., *History of the Islamic Peoples* (London, 1980)

Burnaby, F., *Through Asia Minor on Horseback* (London, 1898)

Busbeq, Ogier Ghislain de, *Turkish Letters of Ogier Ghislain de Busbeq*, tr. and ed. E. Forster (Oxford, 1927)

Cameron, Deborah, ed., *The Feminist Critique of Language* (London and New York, 1990)

Carlyle, Thomas, *Shall Turkey Live or Die?* (London, 1854)

Caussin de Perceval, A. P., *Précis de la destruction de la corps des janissaries par le Sultan Mahmoud en 1826* (Paris, 1833)

Çelik, Zeynap, *The Remaking of Istanbul: Portrait of an Ottoman City in the Nineteenth Century.* (Seattle, Wash., and London, 1986)

Charlemont, Lord, *The Travels of Lord Charlemont in Greece and Turkey, 1749*, ed. W. R. Stanford and E. J. Finopoulos (London, 1984)

Chew, Samuel C., *The Crescent and the Rose: Islam and England During the Renaissance* (New York, 1937)

Chishull, Edmund, *Travels in Turkey and Back to England* (London, 1747)

Clark, E. C., 'The Ottoman industrial revolution' *International Journal of Middle East Studies*, 5 (1974), 65–76

Collas, B. C., *La Turquie en 1864* (Paris, 1864)

Collas, B. C., *La Turquie en 1861* (Paris, 1861)

Cooke, M. A., and Parry, V. J., eds., *A History of the Ottoman Empire to 1730* (Cambridge, 1976)

Corbin, Alain, *The Foul and the Fragrant: Odor and the French Social Imagination* (Cambridge, Mass., 1986)

Creasy, E. S., *History of the Ottoman Turks, from the Beginning of their Empire to the Present Time* (London, 2 vols., 1856)

Croutier, Alev Lytle, *Harem: The World Behind the Veil* (New York, 1989)

Cuinet, Vital, *La Turquie d'Asie: géographie administrative statistique descriptive et raisonée* (Paris, 4 vols., 1890)

Curtis, William Elroy, *The Turk and his Lost Provinces* (Chicago, 1903)

Curzon, Robert, *Armenia: a Year at Erzeroom and on the Frontiers of Russia, Turkey and Persia* (London, 1854)

Daniel, Norman, *Islam and the West: the Making of an Image* (Edinburgh, 1980)

Davey, R., *The Sultan and his Subjects* (New York, 2 vols., 1897)

Davis, Fanny, *The Ottoman Lady: a Social History from 1718 to 1918* (Westport, Conn., 1986)

Davis, James C., *Pursuit of Power: Venetian Ambassadors' Reports on Spain, Turkey and France in the Age of Philip II* (New York and London, 1970)

Davison, Roderic H., *Essays in Ottoman and Turkish History, 1774–1923: the Impact of the West* (Austin, Tex., and London, 1991)

Davison, Roderic H., *Reform in the Ottoman Empire, 1856–1876* (Princeton, NJ, 1963)

Devereux, Robert, *The First Ottoman Constitutional Period: a Study of the Midhat Constitution and Parliament* (Baltimore, Md., 1963)

Douglas, Roy, 'Britain and the Armenian Question, 1894–7', *The Historical Journal*, 19:1 (1976) 113–33

Dover, John, *War Without Mercy: Race and Power in the Pacific War* (New York, 1986)

Duffy, Christopher, *The Fortress in the Age of Frederick the Great and Vauban* (London and Boston, Mass., 1985)

Duffy, Christopher, *Siege Warfare: the Fortress in the Early Modern World, 1494–1660* (London, 1979)

Dwight, H. G., *Constantinople Old and New* (New York, 1915)

Dwight, H. G., *Turkish Life in Wartime* (New York, 1881)

Dyer, Gwynne, 'Turkish "Falsifiers" and Armenian "Deceivers": historiography and the Armenian massacres', *Middle East Studies*, 12 (1976), 99–107

Eliot, Charles, ('Odysseus'), *Turkey in Europe* (London, 1900)

Engelhardt, E., *La Turquie et le Tanzimat . . . ou l'histoire des reformes depuis 1826* (Paris, 1882)

Eton, W. A., *A Survey of the Turkish Empire* (London, 2nd edn, 1799)

Eyries, J. B. B., *La Turquie ou costumes mœurs et usages des turcs* (Paris, n.d.)

Farley, J. L., *The Decline of Turkey, Financially, Politically* (London, 1875)

Fesch, Paul, *Constantinople aux derniers jours d'Abdul Hamid* (Paris, 1907)

Findley, Carter V., *Bureaucratic Reform in the Ottoman Empire: the Sublime Porte 1789–1922* (Princeton, NJ, 1980)

Fine Art Society, *Travellers Beyond the Grand Tour* (London, 1980)

Flandrin, Jean-Louis, *Un temps pour embrasser: aux origines de la moralle sexuelle, VIe–XIe siècle* (Paris, 1983)

Focief, O., *La Justice turque et les reformes à Macedoine: perles de la justice turque* (Paris, 1907)

Fontemagne, Durand de, *Un séjour à l'ambassade de France* (Paris, 1902)

Ford, Richard, *The Handbook for Travellers in Spain* (London, 2 vols., 1845)

Foster, J., ed., *The Travels of John Sanderson in the Levant, 1584–1602* (London, 1931)

Fromkin, David, *A Peace to End All Peace: the Fall of the Ottoman Empire and the Creation of the Modern Middle East* (New York, 1989)

Garnett, Lucy, *The Women of Turkey and their Folklore* (London, 2 vols., 1890)

Gaulis, Georges, *La Ruine d'un empire: Abd-ul-Hamid, ses amis et ses peuples* (Paris, 1913)

Gautier, Théophile, *Constantinople of Today* (tr., London, 1854)

Geary, Grattan, *Through Asiatic Turkey: Narrative of a Journey from Bombay to the Bosphorus* (London, 2 vols., 1878)

Gibbon, Edward, *The Decline and Fall of the Roman Empire* (London, 6 vols., 1910 edn)

Girouard, Mark, *The Victorian Country House* (New Haven, Conn., and London, 2nd edn, 1979)

Gladstone, W. E., *The Bulgarian Horrors and the Question of the East* (London, 1876)

Göcek, Fatma Müge, *East Encounters West: France and the Ottoman Empire in the Eighteenth Century* (New York and Oxford, 1987)

Gollner, Carl, *Turcica: Die Europäischen Turkendrucke des XVI Jahrhunderts* (Bucharest and Baden-Baden, 2 vols., 1968)

Goodwin, Godfrey, *A History of Ottoman Architecture* (London, 1971)

Gran, P., 'Political economy as a paradigm for the study of

Islamic history' *International Journal of Middle East Studies*, 11 (1980), 511–26

Grey, Hon. Mrs William, *Journal of a visit to Egypt, Constantinople . . . in the Suite of the Prince and Princess of Wales* (London, 1869)

Grosrichard, Alain, *Structure du sérail: la fiction du despotisme asiatique dans l'Occident classique* (Paris, 1979)

Grosvenor, Edwin Augustus, *Constantinople* (Boston, Mass., 2 vols., rev. edn, 1900)

Habesci, E., *The Present State of the Ottoman Empire etc.* (London, 1784)

Haddad, William W., and Ochsenwald, William L., eds., *Nationalism in a Non-National State: the Dissolution of the Ottoman Empire* (Columbus, Ohio, 1977)

Halit, Mehmed Beyri, *Istanbul* (Istanbul, 1951)

Hamlin, Cyrus, *Among the Turks* (New York, 1878)

Hamlin, Cyrus, *My Life and Times* (Boston, Mass., 1893)

Hammer-Purgstall, J. von, *Histoire de l'empire ottoman* (tr., Paris, 1835)

Harris, David, *Britain and the Bulgarian Horrors of 1876* (Chicago, 1939)

Harvey, Annie Jane, *Turkish Harems and Circassian Homes* (London, 1871)

Heath, Ian, *Armies of the Middle Ages, Vol. 2: the Ottoman Empire, Eastern Europe and the Near East, 1300–1500* (London, 1985)

Heper, Metin, *The State Tradition in Turkey* (London, 1985)

Herbert, William V., *The Defence of Plevna, 1877, Written by One Who Took Part in It* (London, 1895)

Hess, Andrew, *The Forgotten Frontier: a History of the Sixteenth-Century Ibero-African Frontier* (Chicago, 1978)

Hess, Andrew, 'The Battle of Lepanto and its place in Mediterranean history' *Past and Present*, 57, November 1972, 53–73

Hess, Andrew, 'The evolution of the Ottoman seaborne empire

in the light of oceanic discoveries, 1453–1525', *American Historical Review*, LXXV (December 1970), 1889–1919

Hess, Andrew, 'The Moriscos: an Ottoman fifth column in sixteenth-century Spain', *American Historical Review*, LXXIV (October 1968), 1–25

Heyd, Uriel, 'The Ottoman *Ulema* and westernisation in the time of Selim III and Mahmud II', *Scripta Hierosolymitana*, IX (1961), 63–96

Heywood, C. J., 'Sir Paul Rycaut, a seventeenth-century observer of the Ottoman state: notes for a study', in *English and Continental Views of the Ottoman Empire, 1500–1800* (Los Angeles, 1972)

Hibbert, Christopher, *The Great Mutiny* (London, 1978)

Hodge, Robert, and Kress, Gunther, *Language as Ideology* (London and New York, 2nd edn, 1993)

Hornby, Edward, *An Autobiography* (London, 1928)

Hourani, Albert, *A History of the Arab Peoples* (Cambridge, Mass., 1991)

Hubbard, G. E., *The Day of the Crescent: Glimpses of Old Turkey* (Cambridge, 1920)

Huntington, Samuel, *Political Order in Changing Societies* (New Haven, Conn., 1968)

Ihsanoğlu, Ekmeleddin, *Istanbul: a Glimpse into the Past* (Istanbul, 1987)

Inalcik, Halil, *The Ottoman Empire* (London, 1973)

Inalcik, Halil, *The Ottoman Empire: Conquest, Organisation and Economy – Reprinted Essays* (London, 1978); includes 'Ottoman methods of conquest' and 'Military and fiscal transformation of the Ottoman empire'

Issawi, Charles, *An Economic History of the Middle East and North Africa* (New York and London, 1982)

Itzkovitzs, Norman, 'Eighteenth-century Ottoman realities', *Studia Islamica*, Fas. XVI (1962), 73–94

Itzkovitzs, Norman, *Ottoman Empire and Islamic Tradition* (Chicago, 1980)

Itskovitzs, Norman, and Mote, Max, *Mubadde: an Ottoman–Russian Exchange of Ambassadors* (Chicago, 1984)

James, Lawrence, *The Golden Warrior: the Life and Legend of Lawrence of Arabia* (London, 1990)

Juchereau de St Denys, *Histoire de l'empire ottoman depuis 1792 jusqu'en 1844* (Paris, 4 vols., 1844)

Juler, Caroline, *Les Orientalistes de l'école italienne* (Paris, 1987)

Jullien, Philippe, *The Orientalists: European Painters of Eastern Scenes* (Oxford, 1977)

Kabbani, Rana, *Europe's Myths of Orient: Devise and Rule* (Basingstoke, 1986)

Karpat, E., 'Ottoman population records and the census of 1881/2', *International Journal of Middle East Studies*, 9 (1978), 237–74

Kellner-Heinkele, Barbara, and Rohwedder, Dorothea, eds., *Türkische Kunst und Kultur aus Osmanischer Zeit* (Recklinghausen, 2 vols., 1985)

Kelsall, Malcolm, 'The slave woman in the harem', *Studies in Romanticism*, 31:3 (fall 1992), 315–31

Kent, Marian, ed., *The Great Powers and the End of the Ottoman Empire* (London, 1984)

Kiernan, V. G., *The Lords of Human Kind: European Attitudes to the Outside World in the Imperial Age* (London, 1969)

Kinross, Lord, *Atatürk: the Rebirth of a Nation* (London, 1964)

Kinross, Lord, *The Ottoman Centuries: The Rise and Fall of the Turkish Empire* (New York, 1977)

Kreutal, Richard E., ed., *Kara Mustafa vor Wien: Das Turkische Tagebüch der Belägerung Wiens 1683, verfasst von Zeremonienmeister des Hohen Pforte* (Graz, 1960)

Krikorian, Mesrob K., *Armenians in the Service of the Ottoman Empire, 1860–1908* (London and Boston, Mass., 1977)

Kritovoulos, Michael, *History of Mehmed the Conqueror* (tr., Princeton, NJ, 1954)

Kunt, Metin, 'Ethnic regional solidarity in the seventeenth-century Ottoman establishment', *International Journal of Middle East Studies*, 5 (1974), 233–9

Kushner, David, *The Rise of Turkish Nationalism, 1876–1908* (London, 1977)

Landau, Jacob M., *Abdul-Hamid's Palestine: Rare Century-Old Photographs from the Collection of the Ottoman Sultan now Published for the First Time* (London, 1976)

Landau, Jacob M., *Pan-Turkism in Turkey* (London, 1981)

Lane Poole, Stanley, *The Life of the Right Honourable Stratford Canning, Viscount Stratford de Redcliffe* (London, 2 vols., 1888)

Lane Poole, Stanley, ed., *The People of Turkey* (London, 2 vols., 1878)

Langer, William L., *European Alliances and Entanglements* (New York, 1931)

Larpent, George, *Turkey: its History and Progress* (London, 2 vols., 1854)

Lawrence, T. E., *The Seven Pillars of Wisdom: a Triumph* (London, 1935)

Levy, Avidgor, 'The officer corps in Sultan Mahmud II's new Ottoman army, 1826–39', *International Journal of Middle East Studies*, 2 (1971), 21–39

Lewis, Bernard, *The Emergence of Modern Turkey* (London and New York, 2nd edn, 1968)

Lewis, Bernard, *Istanbul and the Civilization of the Ottoman Empire* (Norman, Okla., 1963)

Lewis, Bernard, *The Jews of Islam* (London, 1984)

Lewis, Bernard, *The Muslim Discovery of Europe* (New York, 1982)

Lewis, Bernard, 'Ottoman observers of Ottoman decline', *Islamic Studies*, 1 (1962), 71–87

Lewis, Bernard, 'Some reflections on the decline of the Ottoman empire', *Studia Islamica*, Fas. IX (1958), 111–27

Lewis, Raphaela, *Everyday Life in Ottoman Turkey* (London and New York, 1971)

Llewellyn, Briony, *The Orient Observed: Images of the Middle East from the Searight Collection* (London, 1989)

Llewellyn, Briony, and Newton, Charles, *The People and Places of Constantinople: Watercolours by Amadeo Count Preziosi, 1816–1882* (London, 1985)

Loti, Pierre, *Aziyadé*, tr. Marjorie Laurie (London, 1927)

Lott, Emmeline, *The Governess in Egypt: Harem Life in Egypt and Constantinople* (London, 2 vols., 1865)

Lustful Turk, or Scenes in the Harem of an Eastern Potentate, Faithfully and Vividly Depicted in a series of letters from a young and beautiful English lady to her Cousin in England – The full particulars of her ravishment and of her complete abandonment to all the salacious Tastes of the Turks described with the zest and simplicity which always gives guarantee for its authenticity, The (London, 1985 edn)

Lyly, John, *Euphues, The Anatomy of Wit* (London, 1868 edn)

McCullagh, F., *The Fall of Abd ul Hamid* (London, 1910)

Macfarlane, Charles, *Constantinople in 1828: a Residence of Sixteen Months in the Turkish Capital and Provinces with an Account of the Present State of the Naval and Military Power and of the Resources of the Ottoman Empire* (London, 2 vols., 1829)

Macfarlane, Charles, *Turkey and its Destiny: The Results of Journeys Made in 1847 and 1848 to Examine into the State of that Country* (London, 2 vols., 1850)

Macgill, Thomas, *Travels in Turkey, Italy and Russia During the Years 1803, 1804, 1805, and 1806, with an Account of Some of the Greek Islands* (London, 2 vols., 1808)

McNeill, William, *Europe's Steppe Frontier, 1500–1800* (Chicago, 1964)

McNeill, William, *The Pursuit of Power* (Oxford, 1983)

Mantran, Robert, ed., *Histoire de l'empire ottoman* (Paris, 1989)

Mantran, Robert, *La Vie quotidienne à Istanbul au siècle de Soliman le Magnifique* (Paris, 1990)

Marcus, Steven, *The Other Victorians: a Study of Sexuality and Pornography in Mid-Nineteenth-Century England* (London, 1964)

Marsigli, Luigi Ferdinandino, *L'État militaire de l'empire ottoman* (Amsterdam, 2 parts, 1732; facsimile edn Graz, 1972)

Marx, Robert F., *The Battle of Lepanto, 1571* (Cleveland and New York, 1966)

Mas, Albert, *Les Turcs dans la littérature espagnole du Siècle d'Or* (Paris, 2 vols., 1967)

Mason, Archibald, *Remarks on the Sixth Vial and the Fall of the Turkish Empire* (Glasgow, 1827)

Melman, Billie, *Women's Orients: English Women and the Middle East* (Basingstoke, 1992)

Melville Jones, J. R., tr. and ed., *The Siege of Constantinople, 1453: Seven Contemporary Accounts* (Amsterdam, 1972)

Midhat, Ali Haydar, *The Life of Midhat Pasha* (London, 1903)

Military Costume of Turkey, The (London, n.d.)

Miller, Barnette, *Beyond the Sublime Porte: the Grand Seraglio of Constantinople* (New Haven, Conn., 1931)

Miller, William, *The Ottoman Empire and its Successors, 1801–1927* (London, 1966)

Millingen, Frederick, (Osman Bey), *Les Femmes en Turquie* (Paris, 1878)

Millingen, Frederick, (Osman Bey), *La Turquie sous la regne de Abdul Aziz* (Paris, 1869)

Moltke, Helmut von, *Briefe über Zustände und Begenbenheiten . . . in Türkei aus den Jahren 1835 bis 1839* (Berlin, 1839)

Moneypenny, W. F., and Buckle, G. H., *The Life of Benjamin Disraeli, Earl of Beaconsfield* (London, 6 vols., 1910–20)

Montagu, Lady Mary Wortley, *The Complete Letters of Lady Mary Wortley Montagu: vol. 1, 1708–1720*, ed. Robert Halsband (Oxford, 1965)

Morley, John, *The Life of William Ewart Gladstone* (London, 2 vols., 1908)

Mundy, Peter, *The Travels of Peter Mundy in Europe and Asia, 1608–1667* (Cambridge, 2 vols., 1907)

Murphy, Dervla, *Embassy to Constantinople: the Travels of Lady Mary Wortley Montagu* (London, 1988)

Murray, John, *Handbook for Travellers in Turkey* (London, 1878 and 1893 edns)

Museum voor Volkenkunde, *Images of the Orient: Photography and Tourism, 1860–1900* (Amsterdam, 1986)

Nassibian, Akaby, *Britain and the Armenian Question, 1915–1923* (London and New York, 1984)

Necipoğlu, G., *Architecture, Ceremonial and Power: the Topkapi Palace in the Fifteenth and Sixteenth Centuries* (Boston, Mass., 1991)

Newton, Charles, 'Stratford Canning's pictures of Turkey' in *V & A Album No. 3* (London, 1984), pp. 76–83

Nouri, Ali, *Abdul Hamid in Karikatur: Intimes aus Yildiz Kiosk in Wort und Bild* (Constantinople, 1910)

Ochsenwald, W., *The Hijaz Railroad* (Charlottesville, NC, 1980)

Ohsson, I. M. D', *Tableau général de l'empire ottoman* (Paris, 7 vols., 1788–1824)

Osman Aga, *Leben und Abenteur des Dolmetschers Osman Aga: eine Türkische Autobiographie aus der Zeit der Grossen Krieg gegen Osterreich* (tr., Bonn, 1954)

Osmanoğlu, Aïché, *Avec mon père le sultan Abdulhamid de son palais à sa prison* (Paris, 1991)

Owen, Roger, *The Middle East in the World Economy, 1800–1914* (London and New York, 1981)

Pallis, Alexander, *In the Days of the Janissaries* (London, 1951)

Palmer, Alan, *The Banner of Battle: the Story of the Crimean War* (London, 1987)

Palmer, Alan, *The Decline and Fall of the Ottoman Empire* (London, 1992)

Pardoe, Julia, *The Beauties of the Bosphorus* (London, 4 vols., 1838)

Pardoe, Julia, *The City of the Sultans and Domestic Manners of the Turks in 1836* (London, 2 vols., 1837)

Parry, V. J., 'The Ottomans and the conquest of the Balkans' (unpublished paper delivered to the Past and Present conference, 1971)

Pears, Sir Edwin, *Forty Years in Constantinople* (London, 1916)

Penzer, Nicolas, *The Harem* (London, 1936)

Pereira, Michael, *Istanbul: Aspects of a City* (London, 1968)

Picturesque Representations of the Dress and Manner of the Turks (London, 1827)

Pierce, Joe E., *Life in a Turkish Village* (New York, 1964)

Polk, William R., and Chambers, Richard L., eds., *The Beginnings of Modernization in the Middle East: The Nineteenth Century* (Chicago, 1968)

Pope, Alexander, *The Poems of Alexander Pope* (London, 1963)

Progress of Turkey by Eyewitnesses, The (London, n.d.)

Quataert, Dennis, *Social Disintegration and Popular Resistance in the Ottoman Empire, 1881–1908: Reactions to European Economic Penetration* (New York, 1983)

Reed, H. A., *The Destruction of the Janissaries by Mahmud II* (unpublished Ph.D. thesis, Princeton University, NJ, 1951)

Regla, Paul de, *La Turquie officielle: Constantinople, son gouvernement, ses habitants, son présent et avenir* (Geneva, 1891)

Regla, Paul de, *Les secrets de Yildiz* (Paris, 1897)

Rogers, J. M., ed., *The Topkapi Saray Museum – Textiles* (Boston, Mass., 1986)

Rogers, J. M., and Ward, R. M., *Suleyman the Magnifcent* (London, 1988)

Rogers, Mary Eliza, *Domestic Life in Palestine* (London, 1862)

Rose d'Amour (New York, 1978 edn)

Rouillard, Clarence Dana, *The Turk in French History, Thought and Literature, 1520–1660* (Paris, 1941)

Runciman, Steven, *Byzantine Civilisation* (London, 1933)

Runciman, Steven, *The Fall of Constantinople, 1453* (Cambridge, 1965)

Rustow, D. A., 'The army and the founding of the Turkish Republic', *World Politics*, XI (1949), 513–52

Ryan, Sir Andrew, *The Last of the Dragomans* (London, 1951)

Sade, Marquis de, *The One Hundred and Twenty days of Sodom* (London, 1989)

Said, Edward W., *Orientalism* (London, 1978)

St Clair, William, *That Greece Might Still be Free* (London, 1972)

Saliba, N. E., 'The achievements of Midhat Pasha as governor of the province of Syria, 1878–80', *International Journal of Middle East Studies* 9 (1978), 307–23

Scarce, Jennifer M., 'Turkish fashion in transition', *Costume: The Journal of the Costume History Society*, 14 (1980), 114–67

Scarce, Jennifer M., *Women's Costume in the Near and Middle East* (London, 1987)

Schama, Simon, *Two Rothschilds and the Land of Israel* (London, 1977)

Schlumberger, Gustave, *La prise et le sac de Constantinople par les Turcs en 1453* (Paris, 1926)

Schulz, Muriel R., 'The semantic derogation of women', in B. Thorne and N. Henley, eds., *Language and Sex: Difference and Dominance* (Rowley, Mass., 1975)

Schwoebel, Robert, *The Shadow of the Crescent: the Renaissance Image of the Turk, 1453–1517* (Nieuwkoop, 1967)

Searight, Sarah, *The British in the Middle East* (London, 1969)

Senior, Nassau W., *A Journal Kept in Turkey and Greece in the Autumn of 1857 and the Beginning of 1858* (London, 1859)

Setton, Kenneth M., *Venice, Austria and the Turks in the Seventeenth Century* (Philadelphia, 1991)

Setton, Kenneth M., *Western Hostility to Islam and Prophecies of Turkish Doom* (Philadelphia, 1992)

Shannon, Richard, *Gladstone and the Bulgarian Agitation, 1876* (London, 1963)

Shaw, Ezel Kural, 'The double veil: travelers' views of the Ottoman empire, sixteenth through eighteenth Centuries' in Ezel Kural Shaw and C.J. Heywood, *English and Continental Views of the Ottoman Empire, 1500–1800* (Los Angeles, 1972)

Shaw, Stanford J., *Between Old and New: the Ottoman Empire under Sultan Selim III, 1789–1807* (Cambridge, Mass., 1971)

Shaw, Stanford J., 'The population of Istanbul in the nineteenth century', *International Journal of Middle East Studies* 10 (1979), 265

Shaw, Stanford J., and Shaw, Ezel Kural, *History of the Ottoman Empire and Modern Turkey* (Cambridge, 2 vols., 1977)

Shay, Mary Lucille, *The Ottoman Empire from 1720–1734 as Revealed by the Dispatches of the Venetian Baili* (Urbana, Ill., 1944)

Sieverich, Gieron, and Budde, Heinrich, eds., *Europa und der Orient, 800–1900* (Berlin, 1989)

Slade, Adolphus, *Record of Travels in Turkey, Greece, etc. and of a Cruise in the Black Sea with the Captain Pasha in the Years 1828, 1829, 1830, 1831* (Philadelphia, 2 vols., 1833)

Smets, M., *Wien in und aus der Türken Bedrängnis, 1529–1683* (Vienna, 1893)

Smith, Albert, *A Month at Constantinople* (London, 1850)

Smith, C., *The Embassy of Sir William White at Constantinople, 1886–91* (London, 1957)

Smyth, Warington W., *A Year with the Turks, or Sketches of Travel in the European and Asiatic Dominions of the Sultan* (New York, 1854)

Some Notes on Turkey (London, 1867)

Spry, William, *Life on the Bosphorus: Doings in the City of the Sultan . . . Turkey Past and Present* (London, 1885)

Stoneman, Richard, *Across the Hellespont: a Literary Guide to Turkey* (London, 1987)

Stoye, John, *The Siege of Vienna* (London, 1964)

Sugar, Peter F., *South-Eastern Europe under Ottoman Rule* (Washington, DC, 1977)

'Sultan's Reverie: an Extract from the Pleasures of Cruelty', *The Pearl* 18 (1878), 617–25

Sumner, B. H., *Peter the Great and the Ottomans* (Oxford, 1949)

Sutton, Sir Robert, *The Dispatches of Sir Robert Sutton, Ambassador in Constantinople 1710–14*, ed. Akdes Nimet Kurat, (London, 1953)

Sykes, Mark, *Dar ul Islam* (London, 1904)

Thorne, B., and Henley, N., eds., *Language and Sex: Difference and Dominance* (Rowley, Mass., 1975)

Thornton, Lynne, *The Orientalists: Painters–Travellers, 1825–1908* (Paris, 1983)

Thornton, Lynne, *Women as Portrayed in Orientalist Painting* (Paris, 1983)

Thornton, Thomas, *The Present State of Turkey, or a Description . . . of the Ottoman Empire* (London, 2 vols., 1809)

Toledano, Ehud, *The Ottoman Slave Trade and its Suppression, 1840–1890* (Princeton, NJ, 1982)

Tott, Baron François de, *Memoires du Baron de Tott sur les Turcs et les Tartares* (Paris, 2 vols., 1785)

Tournefort, J. P. de, *Journey into the Levant* (tr., London, 3 vols., 1741)

Toynbee, Arnold J., and Kirkwood, Kenneth P., *Turkey* (London, 1926)

Tugay, Emine Foat, *Three Centuries: Family Chronicles of Turkey and Egypt* (London and New York, 1963)

Turkey in 1860 (London, 1861)

Turkey and Christendom: an Historical Sketch (London, 1853)

Turkey and Great Britain (London, 1849)

Turkish National Commission, for UNESCO, *Atatürk* (Ankara, 1981)

Turks' Vision of the Fall of Constantinople, The (London, 1877)

Ubicini, J. H., *Letters on Turkey* (tr., London, 2 vols., 1856)

Uras, Esat, *The Armenians in History and the Armenian Question* (Istanbul, 1988)

Urquhart, David, *The Spirit of the East, or Pictures of Eastern Travel* (London, 2 vols. in 1, 1839)

Vambéry, A., *Das Türkenvolk* (Leipzig, 1885)

Vambéry, A., *La Turquie d'aujourd'hui et d'avant quarante ans* (Paris, 1898)

Van Millingen, Alexander, *Byzantine Churches: their History and Architecture* (London, 1891)

Van Millingen, Alexander, *Byzantine Constantinople: the Walls of the City and Adjoining Historic Sites* (London, 1899)

Vaughan, Dorothy, *Europe and the Turk: a Pattern of Alliances, 1350–1700* (Liverpool, 1954)

Vigarello, George, *Le Propre et le sale: l'hygiène du corps depuis le Moyen Age* (Paris, 1985)

Vucinich, Wayne S., *The Ottoman Empire, its Record and Legacy* (Huntington, NY, 1979)

Walker, Warren S., and Uysal, Ahmet E., *More Tales Alive in Turkey* (Lubbock, Tex., 1992)

Walker, Warren S., and Uysal, Ahmet E., *Tales Alive in Turkey* (Lubbock, Tex., 1990)

Wallach, Jehuda C., *Anatomie eine Militärhilfe: die Preussich-Deutschen Militärmissionen in der Türkei* (Düsseldorf, 1976)

Walsh, Robert, *Constantinople and the Scenery of the Seven Churches of Asia Minor* (London, n.d.)

Walsh, Robert, *Narrative of a Journey from Constantinople to England* (London, 1828)

Walsh, Robert, *Narrative of a Residence at Constantinople* (London, 2 vols., 1836)

Ward, Robert E., and Ruston, Dankwaert A., eds., *Political Modernization in Japan and Turkey* (Princeton, NJ, 1964)

Washburn, G., *Fifty Years in Constantinople* (New York, 1909)

What is to be done with Turkey? (London, 1850)

White, W. W., *The Process of Change in the Ottoman Empire* (Chicago, 1937)

White, Charles, *Three Years in Constantinople, or Domestic Manners of the Turks in 1844* (London, 3 vols., 1845)

Young, Robert, *White Mythologies: Writing History and the West* (London and New York, 1990)

Zadeh Pasha, Kemal, *Histoire de la campaigne de Mohács*, tr. and ed. A. J. B. Pavet de Courteille (Paris, 1859)

Zamoyski, Adam, *The Polish Way: a Thousand-Year History of the Poles and Their Culture* (London, 1987)

Zygulski, Zdzislaw, Jr, *Ottoman Art in the Service of the Empire* (New York and London, 1992)

Index

Figures in italics refer to cartoons within the text.